Mollie Katzen's

VEGETABLE
HEAVEN

Mollie Katzen's
VEGETABLE
HEAVEN

written and illustrated by

Mollie Katzen

HYPERION

New York

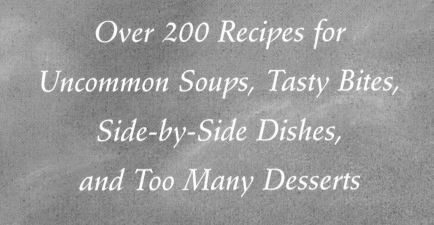

Over 200 Recipes for
Uncommon Soups, Tasty Bites,
Side-by-Side Dishes,
and Too Many Desserts

To Sam
on your thirteenth birthday,
with neverending love

Library of Congress Cataloging-In-Publication Data

Katzen, Mollie

Mollie Katzen's vegetable heaven — 1st ed.

p.   cm.

Includes index.

ISBN 0-7868-6268-8

1. Cookery (Vegetables) I. Title

TX801.K378 1997

641.6'5—dc21   97—22147

CIP

Cover art and all interior illustrations by Mollie Katzen

Cover and book design by Fifth Street Design, Berkeley CA with Mollie Katzen

FIRST EDITION

10 9 8 7 6 5 4 3 2 1

CONTENTS

ACKNOWLEDGMENTS

This book has had so many guardian angels, it practically named itself. First and foremost in this category is Tina Salter, Kitchen Goddess. Tina has been at my side throughout the unfolding of both this book and its companion public television series, generously and consistently offering her creativity, expertise, support, sense of humor, and friendship. She is a blessing, and I hope I get to work with her forever.

Christi Swett was at the helm of many, many recipe tests and the cooking show kitchen as well. I thank her for her cheerfulness, patience, and phenomenal skill. Bernice Chuck Fong assisted with many tests as well—and in the back kitchen of the show—bringing along her broad knowledge of food, her refined taste, and her helpfully frank opinions.

Jackie Wan has copyedited every book I've ever written, and I thank her for always moving me toward clarity. I depend on Jackie for much, and she always comes through.

Brent Beck and Jerry Meek, of Fifth Street Design in Berkeley, have been incredible partners-in-layout. We spent many hours together collaborating on the look of this book, striving for a user-friendly format that could fit all the important information *and* the artwork, and still retain quiet, readable pages. I hope we have achieved this, and I am grateful to them for their talent and patience.

Torri Randall has been a blessing. With her fantastic energy and brilliant sensibility, she pulled together many aspects of production and promotion, not just on the book, but on the television series as well. I owe much, also, to Ken Swezey, who oversaw all the legal (some with Karen Frieman—thanks, Karen!) and many of the business aspects of both the book and the show. He's been an absolute pleasure to work with, as has been Rick Kot, the world's most delightful editor. Thanks also to Rick's assistant, Michael Liss. I have many more people to thank at Hyperion, including Bob Miller, Brian DeFiore, Mollie Doyle, Victor Weaver, Lesley Krauss, Lisa Kitei, Claudyne Bedell, and others. Carol Perfumo: thanks to you too!

My husband, Carl Shames, is a treasured collaborator and sounding board for ideas that begin with the food and go far beyond. I thank him for always reminding me of the *context*. And attempting the impossible, I'd like to express my appreciation for my wonderful children, Sam and Eve, who inspire me on a daily basis, and who (mostly) generously tolerate my often-busy work schedule with grace and humor. And, as always, I thank my parents, Betty and Leon Katzen, for their unwavering support.

Thanks to Frances Bowles, indexer extraordinaire, to Tony Molatore for his meticulous work in photographing my artwork, and to Audrey Johnson for her expert proofreading. Deborah Feingold, photographer, and Sandra Cook, food stylist, did a wonderful job on the back cover photo. We had a lot of fun doing that shoot. And I especially want to thank Cheryl Leighton, not only for helping to keep my household running while I was working on both the show and the book, but also for assisting with some recipe tests and research as well.

In addition, thank you to Nabia Altieri for her constant support, and to Molly Hamaker and Syreeta Shepherd for providing help with this project as well.

★ ★ ★ ★ ★

Putting together a public television cooking series and a companion book at the same time sometimes feels like a high-wire juggling act. Throughout this whole adventure I have had the great fortune to work with Peggy Lee Scott, a multitalented, powerhouse producer, and a kind and generous friend. She has been a great source of moral and professional support. Thank you, Peggy!

Peggy Klaus, of Klaus and Associates, has been another godsend. Joe Strebler has been my cooking and baking *sensei*, as well as a cook and the chief baker behind the scenes on the show.

I had a wonderful crew and production staff helping me create *Mollie Katzen's Cooking Show: Vegetable Heaven* for public television. In addition to those mentioned above, Caroline Hockaday, associate producer, and Brian Murphy, director, have shared their gifts and energies beyond my wildest dreams. The same is true for Lorraine Battle, the brilliant prop stylist,

Kathleen Kennedy, the inspired food stylist, and Linda Giannecchini, assistant director. I also owe much gratitude to Debra Coleman, Joyce Quan, Robert Erdiakoff, Ron Haake and Scene 2, Jean Tuckerman, Danny Zemenek, Greg Overton, Mike Ratusz, Marcial Lopez, Bridget Baer, Joe Breen, Chris Millikan, Heidi Jane Rahlmann, Marta Wohl, Ed Rudolph, David Summerlin, Bob Johns, Mike Morgan, Steve Thomas, Laura Ammons, Mike Procopio, Lori Evans, Richard Starkey, Carol Odman, Michele Jaillett, Karen Wang, Paula Weber, Maelle De Schutter, Leslie Davis, Basma Faris, Tim Metzger, Alison Snow, Joe Rinaldi, Darrell Flowers, Mark Otewalt, Dick Favaro, and Steve Siegelman. Thank you to Rich Hartwig, Don Thompson, and Ed Cosci at KTVU Studios in Oakland, to Regina Eisenberg at KQED in San Francisco, and to Frankie Whitman of WCR (Women Chefs and Restaurateurs).

Special thanks to AkPharma (makers of Beano and Prelief), and to Near East, both of whom generously contributed underwriting to *Mollie Katzen's Cooking Show: Vegetable Heaven*. Extra appreciation to Alan Kligerman, Patti Smith, Janet Greenlee, Fleishman Hillard, and Pam Rhodes.

My gratitude goes out to Chantal Cookware Corp., KitchenAid, Whole Foods Markets, and Melissa's Produce/Specialty Foods, for providing their great products to use on the show. I also want to thank Wüsthof-Trident, Inc., Zyliss U.S.A. Corp., Rubbermaid, Oscartielle, U.S.A., Le Creuset, The Mary Engelbreit Company, All-Clad, Boda-Nova, Inc., Cost Plus, Inc., Cyclamen Studio/Berkeley, Daisy Hill, Better than Bouillon, Cascadian Farms, and Mori Nu / Morinaga Nutritional Foods.

INTRODUCTION

Vegetable Heaven. This is the place and mood I imagine—and try to create—whenever I cook. Here there are all kinds of vegetables, bursting with flavor and prepared in sumptuous, yet uncomplicated, ways. And there are fruit, grains, beans and legumes, nuts, state-of-the-art seasonings and herbs—gifts from the earth that are so vivid, I am as moved to paint their portraits and write odes to their brilliance, as I am to just hunker down and eat them.

Vegetable Heaven is a cuisine reflecting the evolution of my own cooking over the past twenty-five years. It embraces sparkling openers and salads, colorful soups made from ordinary and unusual ingredients, spectacular pastas, pilafs, and stews, exquisite little "bites," pizzas, vegetables roasted to perfection—or seared and glazed in a hot wok, savory baked things to eat for brunch or supper, and more desserts than you'll have time even to dream about. It's a fresh approach to vegetarian cooking, seeking to enhance, rather than overpower, the natural taste of the ingredients. Inspired by vegetables, fruit, and herbs at the peak of their season, this food is opulent, yet clean and simple; logical, yet whimsical. Based upon taste, but also rich in visual beauty, this is the cooking I love. I am delighted to share it with you, through recipes, menus, commentary, and pictures, and to show you just how easy and accessible this can be.

I haven't always known how to cook this way—my own education has been a gradual process. The first family meal I ever cooked by myself (ten years old and so proud) was a broiled flank steak, a package of frozen French-cut green beans, and Minute Rice. (The modern American concept of "vegetable" during this era was of some vague green stuff, frozen or canned, served in small portions on the side of the plate, and "seasoned"— always—with butter.) My main culinary focus at that time was chocolate desserts. But as I got older and became acquainted with fresh vegetables, I literally fell in love with the variety, the colors, the textures! For years to come, driven to the kitchen by utter passion, I wanted to prepare nothing else—except, of course, chocolate desserts. So my voyage into vegetarian cooking has been fueled by an infatuation that has lasted to this day.

Smitten with fresh fruits and vegetables—and the world of garden-based eating in general—I started creating vegetarian recipes in my late teens. In those days, the prevailing definition of a meal—especially a dinner—dictated that a substantial portion of some main dish, traditionally meat, be positioned squarely in the center of the plate. Other foods, called "side dishes" and generally considered to be of lesser appeal and importance, would be grouped in small amounts around the central hunk of whatever. Believing that a meal must have a single substantial focal point and that it must be filling, I used this model during my "early" vegetarian period. I created many cozy main-dish soups and casseroles (generally laden with eggs and/or dairy products for protein) that, even if they didn't exactly knock your socks off, would fill you up, and make you feel good. When I wrote my first cookbook (the *Moosewood Cookbook*, published nationally in 1977), I actually had in mind the mothers of my vegetarian friends, thinking these worried moms would appreciate some guidance when cooking for their kids. I hoped the richness of the recipes would reassure them that their children would survive without meat.

At this time, I also began learning about the cooking styles of India, China, Southeast Asia, Latin America, The Mediterranean, North Africa, Eastern, and Western Europe. These various cuisines, with their great and long traditions of cooking straight from the orchard, garden, and field, demonstrated for many of us young vegetarian cooks the value of using fresh produce, and also opened our eyes to fantastic uses for herbs, spices, garlic, grains, vegetables, and legumes. Over time, dishes like tabouli, spanakopita, cabbage borscht, quiche, vegetable curry, and pasta with pesto became familiar in many parts of this country, and one could even find such items on menus in ordinary restaurants. As the world became smaller, our repertoire grew.

Since then, I would say my cooking has evolved in three major ways:

★ Over the years, I have been cooking lighter meals for myself and my family, with no particular main dish, but rather with a series of two or three smaller dishes that go well together. I have found that I like this kind of cooking and eating better than the old model. A meal can be more interesting when there is no "center-of-the-plate" accompanied by "side" dishes, but a team of what I like to call "side-by-side" dishes. Because these dishes tend to be quite simple, this kind of meal can actually be prepared with relatively little effort.

Mollie Katzen's VEGETABLE HEAVEN

★ When I first began writing cookbooks, I thought long lists of ingredients and complicated procedures were the measure of culinary talent. I now call this The Kitchen Sink School, with its unspoken motto "The more fuss, the more impressive." In the years since, my attitude has undergone an about-face. I now consider it the ultimate challenge—and the true sign of sophistication—to use as *few* ingredients as possible when creating a dish. I bring to a recipe test a list of ingredients I anticipate using. But as I proceed with the experiment, I'll stop when the dish tastes delicious, even if I'm only halfway down that list. The recipe is complete for me at this point. This only means it will be easier for you (and for me, too) to prepare this dish, not only in terms of ingredients, but in terms of that increasingly precious commodity, time.

★ I have learned about *taste*. In my earlier cooking, I was relatively timid about seasoning. I didn't know very much about how to use garlic, or about the various kinds of oils, vinegars, chiles, mushrooms, herbs, and spice combinations that are now part of my everyday repertoire. Also, I was not well versed in certain techniques (roasting, caramelizing, infusing, deglazing, etc.) for bringing out the natural qualities of the ingredients. Now I make the food taste rich through *flavor*, rather than masking it with sauces, butter, cheese, or cream.

Fortunately for us all, flavor itself is much more accessible than ever. How has this come about? Sometime during the 1980s, unusual ingredients and unconventional combinations became an obsession for many young chefs. Some got a little carried away with exoticness for its own sake, and occasionally the quest for the Cutting Edge veered off into the Just Plain Weird. (A friend of a friend from New York returned from a much-hyped California restaurant complaining about her meal there, Pasta with Salami and Peaches. When asked why she had ordered it, she explained that it had been the simplest dish on the menu.) Specialty produce was considered quite precious and was treated as such, with "baby" varieties of everything served in tiny portions for high prices in upscale restaurants. Frequently I would come out of a "nouvelle" restaurant still hungry and not quite sure what I had just eaten.

But self-conscious and excessive though this era might have been, it left a very good legacy. The culinary faddishness of the 1980s did unleash a contagious spirit of bold seasoning, creative experimentation, and delightfully mixed metaphors—yielding greater than ever appreciation for nature's bounty. All that enthusiasm for high-quality, fresh, exotic produce and grocery items led to a greater demand for many wonderful ingredients that were practically unheard of two decades earlier. The proliferation of greengrocers and local farmers' markets throughout the United States, and the constantly improving produce departments in larger grocery stores have lifted the standards for superb fresh fruits, vegetables, and herbs straight through the roof. Opportunities for making beautiful, creative-yet-simple, healthful meals year-round have never been greater.

★ ★ ★ ★ ★

Chatting with a Nashville taxi driver, I reveal that I am a cookbook author, in town to make a television show. Intrigued, he inquires, "What kind of cookbooks do you write?" "Vegetarian," I reply. With a sigh of disappointment, he declares, "Sorry, that's not my thing. I need my meat at least once a day." I do a quick mental calculation. "Well, then, my recipes are for your other two meals. You want them to be delicious too, right?" He warms up to this idea. "Hey, yeah!" he responds, handing me his card. "Could you maybe send one of your cookbooks to my wife?" "Sure," I say, and when I get home I do just that. Seven weeks later, I receive a lovely, amazed note from his wife, reporting that her husband, the cab driver, just loves my soup recipes and even ate a vegetable pie.

These days, many people from all backgrounds and with greatly varying circumstances are interested in eating meatless meals on a regular basis. From the mail I get responding to my vegetarian cookbooks, I find that most of my readers don't identify themselves as strict vegetarians. Forget the labels. Most people just want to eat good food, some with meat, some without. These recipes are for when you want to eat good food without.

★ ★ ★ ★ ★

Mollie Katzen's VEGETABLE HEAVEN

Food is such a personal matter. For many of us, it is not a simple subject, but one often fraught with worry, confusion, and conflict. Yet, anxiety-ridden though we might be over it, we all have a great capacity for just plain *loving* food as well. We can find tremendous relaxation and enjoyment in both the preparation and the partaking of delicious meals, but we often lose touch with this gift. *Vegetable Heaven* is an invitation to tap into the beauty and pleasure of food—a reminder that we deserve good things, and that we have it within ourselves to *create* these good things that we deserve.

I have written this book hoping greatly that you will make good use of it, even though you are probably busy and may find it difficult to fit cooking into your routine. In these recipes, I have tried to keep time, cost, and labor to a minimum without compromising the quality and novelty of the results. I know that many of us are seeking simple pleasures, attempting to live well within our means and the constraints of our daily lives. Perhaps the whole realm of food—thinking about it, shopping for it, preparing it, *enjoying it*—can dovetail with this quest, becoming less a source of self-doubt and conflict, and more a wellspring of creativity, health, and happiness. If *Vegetable Heaven* brings you even one step closer to this goal, I will feel gratified indeed.

SOME INGREDIENT NOTES
IN A NUTSHELL

Roasted Garlic Paste

I use this ingredient in so many of my recipes, I am giving you a method here, at the front of the book, to encourage you to make Roasted Garlic Paste all the time. Keep it around, not just for using in the recipes, but also for spreading on bread, plain pasta, baked potatoes . . . anything. If you drizzle the top surface of the paste with a little olive oil, and keep it in an airtight container in the refrigerator, this stuff will keep at least a week. One 3-ounce garlic bulb yields about a tablespoon of Roasted Garlic Paste.

Preheat the oven to 375°F. Line a small baking pan with foil. Trim the tips of the garlic, then stand the bulbs upright on the foil. Roast for about 30 minutes, or until the bulb feels soft when gently pressed. (Larger bulbs will take longer to roast.) When cool enough to handle, simply break the bulb into individual cloves, and squeeze out the roasted garlic pulp into a small bowl. (This part will be a little messy, but worth the slight inconvenience.)

NOTE: You can also roast individual cloves of garlic. Use large ones and don't peel them first. Lightly oil the baking pan, and scatter the cloves on the oiled surface. Roast for only 10 minutes. Cool, and then squeeze out the pulp as in the instructions above.

Vegetable Bouillon

With a few exceptions, my soup recipes work perfectly with water and don't require any special broth or stock. Occasionally, though, I like to use a good vegetable bouillon, not only for soup, but also to cook grains or to add volume and/or flavor to a sauce. Of course, you can make an excellent mild vegetable stock simply by boiling a selection of mild-flavored vegetables in salted water. But I know of few people—if any—who actually bother to do this on any regular basis.

It used to be that the only instant vegetable broths came in the form of bouillon cubes, which contained a lot of salt and very little else. Recently, a few soup companies began producing canned vegetable broth, which I am not wild about. But now there are some very good brands of vegetable bouillon paste available in many grocery stores. They come in several flavors (including vegetable and mushroom), and are quite potent, so a single jar, if stored in the refrigerator, can last you half a year. My favorite brands are *Better Than Bouillon* and *The Organic Gourmet*. Use only 1 teaspoon per cup of hot water for regular strength, and $1\frac{1}{2}$ to 2 teaspoons per cup of water for strong bouillon. (For a superb flavor treat, add a tablespoon of bouillon paste to the water the next time you cook a batch of rice.)

Peeling and Seeding Tomatoes

Many of these recipes call for peeled, seeded tomatoes. Here are some simple instructions, if you have never done this before:

Heat a saucepan of water to the boiling point, then turn the heat down to a simmer. Core the tomatoes, then lower them gently into the simmering water for a slow count of 10 to 20, depending on their ripeness (i.e., less time if they are riper). Remove them from the water, and pull off the skins. Cut them open around the middle, and squeeze out and discard the seeds. What you'll have left is pure, smooth tomato pulp.

A Note about "Vegetable Oil"

Occasionally a recipe will simply call for "vegetable oil." In these cases, I recommend a cold-pressed, light-colored sesame oil (not the intensely-flavored Chinese sesame oil, which is a different ingredient altogether). You can also use cold-pressed canola oil. Buy these products in natural food stores.

TABLE OF CONVERSIONS

Dry Ingredients

Cornmeal, fine, 1 cup = 5 ounces = 155 grams

Herbs, dried = ⅓ to ½ the amount of fresh herbs

Flour, white unbleached, 1 cup = 4 ounces = 120 grams

Grains, dried (rice, bulgur, millet, barley, etc.),
   1 cup = 5 ounces = 155 grams

Sugar, brown, 1 cup (packed) = 5½ ounces = 170 grams

Sugar, granulated, 1 cup = 8 ounces = 240 grams

Bulk Ingredients

Beans (dried), ½ cup = 3 ounces = 90 grams

Cheese, 1 pound = 4 to 5 cups (packed) grated

Nut butter, 1 cup = 8 ounces = 240 grams

Nuts, chopped, ⅓ cup = 2 ounces = 60 grams

Onion, 1 small to medium = 1 cup, chopped

Raisins and dried fruit, ⅓ cup = 2 ounces = 60 grams

Seeds (sesame, pumpkin, sunflower), ¾ cup = 4 ounces = 120 grams

Liquids

1 tablespoon = ½ fluid ounce = 16 ml

1 cup = 8 ounces = 250 ml (16 tablespoons)

Oven Temperatures

300°F = 150°C

350°F = 175°C

375°F = 190°C

400°F = 205°C

OPENERS, CLEANSERS, AND SPARKLERS

Appetizers and Salads

Tables should be like pictures to the
    sight,
Some dishes cast in shade,
    some spread in light,
Some at a distance brighten,
    some near hand,
Where ease may all their
    delicace command;
Some should be mov'd when broken;
    others last
Through the whole treat;
    incentive to the taste.

          —William King

*I*t used to be that salads were synonymous with lettuce. Appetizers were more ambiguous, usually served warm or hot, and always on a small plate, to be pierced with toothpicks or grasped with the fingers and "popped" into the mouth. (Come to think of it, the popping itself might have provided the defining moment.)

    Nowadays, appetizers and salads seem almost impossible to define. When dining out, I frequently order several appetizers as my entire dinner, and end up utterly contented. Cooling palate cleansers—and even salads—can even be served for dessert, to everyone's surprise and refreshed satisfaction. So who knows? Try the following recipes as openers, but also try grouping them together to make complete, light meals.

OPENERS, CLEANSERS, AND SPARKLERS
Appetizers and Salads

AVOCADO-PEAR SORBET
RHIANNON'S STRANGE
AND WONDERFUL EXPERIMENT

*Sometimes the most adult ideas come from a child, as in this sophisticated
creation, which was dreamed up in part by nine-year-old Rhiannon Salter.
While making a cold avocado soup with her mother, Rhiannon got the idea of
adding pears, and this delightful combination was born. It was hot that day,
and someone suggested freezing the soup in an ice cream machine to see
what would happen. The result was this unusual, refreshing sorbet. Serve it
as an appetizer, a palate cleanser, or an impressively subtle dessert.*

Grate enough zest from the lemons to measure 1 packed teaspoon.
Then squeeze the juice from the lemons and set aside.

Peel, core, and mince the pear, and transfer it to a small bowl.
Drizzle with a little of the lemon juice to keep the pear from turning brown. If the pear is not perfectly sweet and ripe, add up to 2
teaspoons of sugar as needed, to taste. Set aside.

Place ¼ cup of the lemon juice in the food processor. Add the avocados, the teaspoon of lemon zest, pear nectar, and salt. Purée until
very smooth. (If you have some lemon juice left over, I'm sure
you'll easily find another use for it.)

Transfer the mixture to an ice cream machine, and freeze according to the manufacturer's instructions. Stir in the pears just before
it is finished. Store the sorbet, tightly covered, in the freezer. If you
are going to serve it within a few hours, you can leave it in the
freezer until serving time. However, if you are going to freeze the
sorbet for longer and it gets quite solid, let it soften in the refrigerator for about an hour before you plan to serve it.

Yield: 1½ quarts
Preparation time: About 40 minutes, depending on the ice
   cream machine (10 minutes of work)

3 lemons

1 medium-sized fresh pear,
   as ripe as possible

1 to 2 teaspoons sugar
   (optional)

3 medium-sized ripe avocados,
   peeled, pitted, and diced

3 cups pear nectar
   (2 11½-ounce cans)

A pinch of salt

....

*Be sure the avocados and pear are
as ripe as possible. Use any kind of
pear except Bosc, which is too crunchy
to work well in this smooth dish.*

*Although this sorbet can keep a
long time in the freezer, it tastes best
freshly made.*

For a menu suggestion, see page 211.

WATERMELON SPARKLER

WITH JICAMA, GINGER, AND LIME

4 cups bite-sized watermelon chunks (seeds removed)

1 cup diced jicama

3 tablespoons fresh lime juice

2 to 3 tablespoons minced crystallized ginger

OPTIONAL GARNISHES:

Twists of lime peel

Lime wedges

....

Watermelon Sparkler can be an appetizer or a salad, a between-course palate cleanser (especially after a spicy dish), or even a dessert.

The easiest way to mince crystallized ginger is with scissors.

This recipe keeps very well for several days if covered tightly and refrigerated.

For a menu suggestion, see page 213.

Something wonderful happens when you combine sweet, juicy chunks of watermelon with crunchy pieces of jicama, and then douse the whole concoction with lime juice. (I got the idea during a trip to Mexico, where serving jicama with fresh fruit is common, and sprinkling lime juice on just about any food is second nature.) Crystallized ginger adds heat and intensity to the watermelon, and spikes the lime juice quite nicely. Try this as an opening course for a summer brunch.

Combine the watermelon, jicama, lime juice, and minced ginger in a medium-sized bowl and mix well.

Cover tightly, and chill until cold.

Serve topped with a twist or two of lime peel, and with a lime wedge on the side, if desired.

Yield: 4 to 6 small servings
Preparation time: 10 minutes, plus time to chill

Mollie Katzen's VEGETABLE HEAVEN

SAVORY GRANITA DUET

Usually a granita (an upscale shaved ice) is made from something sweet and served as dessert. In these refreshing variations, the granita has become a savory dish to be served as an appetizer, a salad course, or a world-class palate cleanser. This sparkling duet looks like a bowlful of tiny frozen jewels. And needless to say, it is light, light, light.

Cucumber-Mint Granita

Peel and seed the cucumbers, and chop them into 1-inch pieces. Place them in a blender or a food processor with the mint and chives, and purée until smooth.

Transfer to a medium-small bowl, and season with the vinegar, salt, and pepper.

Place the bowl in the freezer, and stir (or poke at it) with a fork every half hour or so for the first 3 hours. Then leave it to freeze overnight, or for a minimum of 6 more hours.

Before serving, drag a fork through the frozen mixture to make ice crystals. This shouldn't be too difficult.

Serve immediately in a small glass bowl, side-by-side with Tomato-Basil Granita. Pass a cruet of seasoned rice vinegar to sprinkle on top.

Tomato-Basil Granita

Cut the tomatoes in half; squeeze out and discard the seeds. Coarsely grate the tomatoes with a hand-held grater. When you're done, all you'll have left in your hand will be the skin. Discard it, and place the grated pulp in a food processor or blender, along with the basil and garlic. Purée until smooth.

Transfer the mixture to a medium-sized bowl, and season with vinegar, salt, and pepper. Freeze as in the preceding recipe.

Drag a fork through the frozen mixture to make ice crystals, and serve immediately in a small glass bowl, next to the Cucumber-Mint Granita. Pass a cruet of red wine vinegar to sprinkle on top.

Yield: 4 to 6 small servings
Preparation time: 10 minutes of work, plus a minimum of 9 hours
   to freeze

Cucumber-Mint Granita

2 medium-sized cucumbers
   (about 10 ounces each)

3 tablespoons minced fresh mint

3 tablespoons minced fresh chives

2 tablespoons seasoned rice
   vinegar (plus extra for sprinkling
   on top)

A pinch of salt

1/8 teaspoon ground black pepper

Tomato-Basil Granita

6 medium-sized ripe tomatoes
   (about 2 1/2 pounds)

10 leaves of fresh basil, minced

1/2 teaspoon minced garlic

1 tablespoon red wine vinegar
   (plus extra for sprinkling on top)

1/4 teaspoon salt

1/8 teaspoon ground black pepper

....

Ideally these two granitas should be made at the same time and served together. But of course you can make and serve them separately as well.

Seasoned rice vinegar is lightly sweetened and salted. If you substitute plain rice vinegar, add 1 teaspoon sugar and increase the salt to taste.

For a menu suggestion, see page 213.

COUSCOUS-QUINOA TABOULI

1 cup uncooked quinoa

1¼ cups water

1 cup uncooked instant couscous

¾ cup boiling water

2 teaspoons cumin seeds

1 teaspoon coriander seeds

2 cups minced fresh parsley

1 cup minced fresh mint

3 to 4 scallions, finely minced

1 cup minced red onion

1 or 2 small (6-inch) cucumbers, peeled, seeded, and diced

1 heaping teaspoon minced garlic

½ teaspoon cinnamon

1 teaspoon salt (possibly more to taste)

Freshly ground black pepper

6 to 8 tablespoons fresh lemon juice

Up to 3 tablespoons extra virgin olive oil

OPTIONAL GARNISHES:

Tiny cherry tomatoes

A few toasted walnuts, minced

Toasted pita bread

Get everything else ready while the grains cook. You can mince the parsley, mint, and scallions together in the food processor.

Tightly covered and refrigerated, this keeps for up to 5 days. It goes well on a bed of greens, with Persian Eggplant Appetizer (page 9), or in a more elaborate scheme (see page 213).

Try this new variation on the traditional Mediterranean herb-and-grain salad. It's different and delicious—and a great way to slip some of that ultra-nutritious wonder-grain, quinoa, into your diet.

Place the quinoa in a strainer and rinse under cold running water. Transfer to a small saucepan, add 1¼ cups water, and bring to a boil. Cover, turn the heat way down, and simmer for 20 minutes. Remove from heat, and fluff with a fork to let heat escape. Set aside. (Continue to fluff the quinoa from time to time as you prepare the other ingredients, so the grains stay dry and separate.)

Place the couscous in a medium-large bowl, and add the boiling water. Cover with a plate and let stand for 10 minutes. Remove the plate, and fluff with a fork as you did with the quinoa. Then add the quinoa to the couscous, and fluff thoroughly.

Meanwhile, lightly toast the seeds in a small ungreased skillet over medium-low heat until they are fragrant. Hover and stir often, so they don't burn. Transfer to an electric spice grinder or a mortar and pestle. Grind to a powder, add this to the cooked grains, and stir with a fork until well combined. Set the bowl aside until the grains have cooled to room temperature.

When the grains have cooled, use a fork to stir in all the remaining ingredients except the optional garnishes. Cover tightly and chill for at least 2 hours before serving.

Serve cold, topped with cherry tomatoes and/or minced walnuts, and with some toasted pita bread on the side, if desired.

Yield: 6 to 8 servings, depending on what goes with it
Preparation time: 30 minutes, plus time to cool and then to chill (15 minutes of work)

SIMPLEST TOMATO SALAD

I have very few iron-clad cooking rules, but here's one I think few people would argue with: Vine-ripened tomatoes in season should be tampered with as little as possible. After all, who are we mortals to think we can improve upon perfection itself?

That said, here is a minimalist recipe for enhancing the tomatoes' natural brilliance. It calls for dressing them with a small amount of warmed, scallion-infused olive oil, then finishing the dish with a little salt and pepper. Rather than overshadowing the tomatoes, this treatment augments them beautifully.

3 tablespoons olive oil

4 scallions, minced

2 pounds firm tomatoes, perfectly ripe

$\frac{1}{2}$ teaspoon salt (or to taste)

Freshly ground black pepper

Heat the olive oil in a small skillet over medium heat. Add the scallions, and sauté for about 5 to 8 minutes, or until the scallions are completely wilted. Set aside to cool for about 5 minutes.

Meanwhile, slice the tomatoes in half; squeeze out and discard the seeds. Cut the tomatoes into bite-sized chunks, and place them in a medium-sized glass or ceramic bowl.

Pour the scallions and oil (still warm) over the tomatoes, and sprinkle on a little salt and a fair amount of black pepper. Stir gently and serve right away at room temperature, or cover tightly and chill.

Yield: 4 to 6 servings
Preparation time: 10 minutes

※ *Simplest Tomato Salad tastes best if eaten shortly after it is assembled. I like it at room temperature.*

※ *For a menu suggestion, see page 212.*

ROASTED EGGPLANT SALAD
WITH MUSTARD VINAIGRETTE

A little olive oil for the baking tray

4 small eggplants—any type—
(about ¼ pound apiece), halved
lengthwise

Mustard Vinaigrette (page 173)

Salt and pepper

About ½ pound small cherry
tomatoes, halved

Frizzled Leeks (page 59), optional

....

*If you can't find small eggplants,
substitute a 1-pound globe eggplant,
and cut it into ½-inch slices.*

*You can prepare all the ingredients up to several days ahead. (The
vinaigrette can be made weeks—or
even a month—ahead.) Assemble
shortly before serving.*

*If you have any left over, try cutting the eggplant into small pieces,
and serving it on top of Crostini
(page 55).*

For a menu suggestion, see page 212.

*Freshly roasted eggplant soaks up the delicious vinaigrette. Frizzled Leeks
add the perfect finishing touch.*

Preheat the oven to 375°F. Line a baking tray with foil, and brush it
lightly with olive oil. Place the eggplants facedown on the tray and
roast until tender (about 30 to 40 minutes). Remove the tray from
the oven, turn the eggplants over, and spoon a little vinaigrette over
the open surfaces. Set aside to cool to room temperature. (You can
chill the eggplants, if you choose to serve this dish cold.)

To serve, arrange the eggplants on individual plates (2 halves per
serving), and sprinkle lightly with salt and pepper. Divide the tomatoes among the plates, and drizzle on a little more Mustard
Vinaigrette. Top with a sprinkling of Frizzled Leeks, if desired.

Yield: 4 servings
Preparation time: 30 to 40 minutes, plus time to cool (10 minutes
of work)

Mollie Katzen's VEGETABLE HEAVEN

PERSIAN EGGPLANT APPETIZER

A perfect light lunch or appetizer with just a piece of crackerbread or toasted pita, this tasty eggplant salad can also be expanded into a major presentation, garnished lavishly in the Persian style. Here's how: Place the eggplant in the middle of a large platter lined with salad greens. Decorate the platter with sprigs of fresh herbs (mint, chives, basil, scallions, oregano, and/or dill), a few mounds of yogurt, a scattering of radishes and cucumbers, and little clusters of kidney beans, almonds, and raisins. And, in the unlikely event that you happen to have some exquisite dried rose petals lying around, sprinkle them over the top, for a romantic touch.

Preheat the oven to 375°F. Line a baking tray with foil and brush it lightly with olive oil.

Cut the eggplants in half lengthwise. Put them facedown on the tray, and place the pepper next to them. Roast the eggplants and pepper together for about 45 minutes, or until the eggplants are soft and the pepper's skin has puckered and pulled away from the flesh. (You can turn the pepper several times during the roasting process to help the skin blister more evenly.) Remove from the oven, and cool until all the vegetables are comfortable to handle.

Scoop the eggplant pulp from its skin, and transfer it to a medium-sized bowl. Add the garlic, parsley, turmeric, salt, and lime juice, and mash everything together until fairly smooth.

Peel, seed, and mince the bell pepper and stir it in. Cover the bowl tightly and chill. Serve cold, topped with a sprinkling of toasted cumin seeds, a drizzle of olive oil, and wedges of lime tucked into the side. (See the introductory notes above for a more elaborate serving plan.)

Yield: 4 cups
Preparation time: About 1½ hours (15 minutes of work)

A little olive oil for the baking tray

2 large eggplants (about 1½ pounds apiece)

1 medium-sized yellow bell pepper

1 or 2 medium cloves garlic, minced

A handful of fresh parsley, minced

1 teaspoon turmeric

¾ teaspoon salt (or to taste)

¼ cup fresh lime juice

1 teaspoon toasted cumin seeds

A drizzle of olive oil

Wedges of lime

If it's eggplant season (late summer/early fall) and the eggplants are shiny and tight, use them directly without salting them first. But if they're out of season, the eggplants might be bitter. So salt them lightly after cutting them open, and let them stand for about 30 minutes. Rinse and dry thoroughly before proceeding. This will remove the bitter juices. (If you follow this process, reduce the salt in the recipe.)

A menu suggestion for a full Persian feast is on page 213.

GREMOLATA-RICOTTA EGG SALAD

½ cup very finely minced parsley

2 tablespoons grated lemon zest

1 tablespoon plus 1 teaspoon minced garlic

6 hard-boiled eggs, chopped

½ teaspoon salt (or to taste)

⅔ cup ricotta cheese

OPTIONAL:

Crackers, Crostini (page 55), or bagel chips

Cucumber slices

Black pepper

Minced black olives

• •

Let the egg salad sit for a few hours, tightly covered, in the refrigerator. The lemon flavor will become more pronounced.

Before the soup at special family meals, my mother used to serve small individual plates of what she called "chopped egg and onion." So as a child, I came to regard egg salad as more of an appetizer than a sandwich filling—something deserving a special focus.

This "modern" egg salad has two new twists: Its richness comes from ricotta cheese rather than from oil or mayonnaise, and it is arrestingly seasoned with gremolata, a mixture of finely minced parsley, lemon zest, and garlic.

Combine the parsley, lemon zest, and garlic in a small bowl. (This is the gremolata.)

Place the eggs in a second, larger bowl, and add half the gremolata, the salt, and ricotta, and mix well. Cover tightly and refrigerate until just before serving.

To serve, spread thickly on crackers, crostini, bagel chips, or cucumber slices—or just onto a piece of crusty bread, and sprinkle with extra gremolata. You can also add some black pepper and a touch of minced olives, if you desire.

Yield: 2 cups
Preparation time: 10 minutes after the eggs are boiled

VIETNAMESE SALAD ROLLS

Vietnamese cooks will often place softened rice paper wrappers on the table at the beginning of a meal, so diners can wrap their own individually-selected combination of grilled meat, vegetables, and fresh herbs—whatever is available. Dipping sauce is provided to spoon onto each bite. In this delicious version, a salad, all tossed and lightly dressed, is wrapped in the rice paper. Dipping sauce is optional—and wonderful, but not necessary.

Fill a pie pan with lukewarm water. Have ready a roll of paper towels and a dinner plate. Place a rice paper wrapper in the water for about 2 seconds, then transfer it to the dinner plate. Lightly moisten a paper towel, and lay this on top. Repeat with all the remaining rice paper wrappers, one at a time, making a neat pile of dampened wrappers and towels. When you get to the end of this process, cover the top wrapper with a wet paper towel, and set aside. (The damp towels will keep the rice papers from sticking irreparably to themselves—and to each other.)

In a medium-large bowl, combine the romaine, bean sprouts, carrot, cilantro, mint, tofu, and peanuts. Add about ¼ cup Peanut-Chile Dressing, and toss gently.

Carefully remove the top rice paper wrapper from the pile, and place it flat on a clean, dry work surface. If the wrapper is square, lay it down as a diamond, with a point coming toward you. Place a small amount of the salad (about 3 tablespoons for each square wrapper; about ⅓ cup per round wrapper) on the half of the wrapper that is closest to you, and roll it up tightly, folding in the sides. Transfer the finished roll to a plate, and repeat this process with the remaining wrappers and salad.

When you have made all the rolls, cover the plate tightly with plastic wrap, and store in the refrigerator or at room temperature until serving time. These will keep up to a day.

To serve, cut each roll diagonally in half, and pass extra dressing and/or a small bowl of Sweet and Sour Dipping Sauce, as desired.

Yield: 12 large rolls; 24 small rolls
Preparation time: 30 minutes

12 round (8- to 9-inch-diameter) or 24 square (6-inch) rice paper wrappers

6 to 8 leaves romaine, cut into very thin strips (a "chiffonade")

1 cup mung bean sprouts (about 3 ounces)

1 large carrot, julienned or shredded

⅓ cup cilantro leaves

⅓ cup mint leaves

1 cup firm tofu, cut into thin strips (about 6 ounces)

¼ cup minced peanuts

Peanut-Chile Dressing (page 174)

Sweet and Sour Dipping Sauce (page 170), optional

★ *You can purchase dried rice paper wrappers at most Asian grocery stores.*

★ *If you don't have the exact ingredients on hand, you can improvise a little. Just about any salad, if it is cut small enough, will work.*

★ *Use plain, firm tofu or one of the baked, seasoned varieties.*

★ *For a menu suggestion, see page 213.*

JAMAICAN SALSA SALAD

It looks like a colorful, chunky guacamole at first glance, but you'll know it's something far more interesting and exotic as soon as it hits your mouth.

½ cup minced red onion

6 tablespoons fresh lime juice

1 to 2 small serrano chiles (2½ inches long), seeded and very finely minced

4 small, ripe avocados, peeled and diced (save the pits)

1 ripe mango, cut into small dice

1½ cups minced fresh pineapple

1½ cups minced jicama

2 teaspoons minced garlic

½ to ¾ teaspoon salt

3 tablespoons minced fresh cilantro

3 tablespoons minced fresh mint

½ teaspoon ground cumin

Put up about a quart of water to boil. Meanwhile, place the onion in a strainer or colander over a large bowl or in the sink. Pour the boiling water over the onion and let it stand while you prepare the other ingredients. (This slightly cooks the onion, softening its sharp edge.)

Combine the lime juice and minced chiles in a medium-sized bowl. Add the avocados, mango, pineapple, jicama, garlic, salt, herbs, and cumin, along with the onion. Mix everything together gently but thoroughly.

Place the avocado pits in the salad. (This helps the avocados retain their gorgeous color.) Cover tightly, and chill for about 2 hours. Remove the pits before serving.

Yield: 6 cups
Preparation time: 20 to 25 minutes, plus time to chill

Serve this as you would either a salsa or a salad. Scoop it up with chips before a summer meal, or use it as a terrific sandwich filling.

Jamaican Salsa Salad is also a perfect addition to a dinner of plain beans and rice. (Or a dinner of fancy beans and rice. See page 212.)

This tastes best soon after it is made. It doesn't keep very well beyond the first day.

If you don't have access to fresh chiles, substitute red pepper flakes to taste.

KUNG PAO LETTUCE CUPS

Kung Pao usually refers to a Northern Chinese chicken dish made with diced vegetables, hot chiles, and peanuts. In this crunchy salad, the peanuts and diced vegetables are still present, but the chicken has turned into tofu. No cooking is necessary—just chop everything, toss it together, fill the lettuce cups, and sprinkle on the toppings. This makes a great light summer lunch entrée.

NOTE: The filling can be combined several days in advance, then stored in a tightly covered container in the refrigerator. Fill the lettuce cups shortly before serving.

In a medium-sized bowl, combine the carrots, celery, water chestnuts, scallions, cilantro, tofu, chile paste, and seasoned rice vinegar. Mix well, and add salt, pepper, and red pepper flakes to taste, if desired.

Arrange the lettuce leaves like small bowls on a serving platter or on individual plates, and divide the salad evenly among the lettuce cups.

Top with a scattering of green peas and peanuts, and, if they're available, some sliced snow peas. You can make this a little more lavish, if you choose, by passing a bowl of Green Onion Wonton Strips and a small shaker bottle of chile oil.

Yield: About 6 servings
Preparation time: 20 minutes

6 medium-sized carrots, in small dice

3 celery stalks, in small dice

1 5-ounce can water chestnuts, rinsed, drained, and diced (about ¾ cup diced)

4 scallions, finely minced

A handful of cilantro, minced

¾ pound firm tofu, cut in small cubes

1 teaspoon chile paste

½ cup seasoned rice vinegar (possibly more, to taste)

Salt, pepper, and red pepper flakes to taste

6 leaves of butter (Boston) lettuce, cleaned, dried, and chilled

1 cup frozen peas, defrosted

⅔ cup lightly toasted peanuts

OPTIONAL GARNISHES:

A handful of snow peas, trimmed and cut in diagonal strips

Green Onion Wonton Strips (page 54)

Chile oil

....

You can use plain firm tofu or one of the baked, seasoned varieties available in natural foods stores.

Be sure to use <u>seasoned</u> *rice vinegar (check the label). It has a sweet/salty flavor that is essential to the success of this dish.*

For a menu suggestion, see page 212.

CARIBBEAN COMPOSED SALAD

1 small bunch ruby chard or kale, cut into very thin strips and steamed

1 cup diced cooked sweet potatoes

1 cup diced cooked beets

1 cup minced jicama

3 small ruby grapefruits, sectioned

1 cup minced fresh pineapple

1 cup julienned cucumber (peeled and seeded)

1 cup julienned kiwifruit

Finely minced chives (optional)

Squeezable wedges of lime

Orange Vinaigrette (page 173)

....

You need to prepare all of the components well in advance, except for the kiwifruit. The cooked vegetables should be at room temperature or cold. (Prepare the kiwifruit just before serving, so it doesn't turn to mush.)

The ingredients are flexible. You can use this recipe as a template, and then get creative.

For a menu suggestion, see page 211.

The food of the French Caribbean is a delightful combination of classic French and native Creole cuisines. I hatched the idea for this gorgeous composed salad while vacationing in Guadeloupe. The French-trained chef who prepared our lunch presented a menu from which we could select three or four small fruit or vegetable preparations as an appetizer. I looked around the table after our food came, and pictured all the various dishes arranged together on one big platter, dressed with a fruity vinaigrette. I came home and tried it—and voilà: it was wonderful, and so unusual!

Arrange all the vegetables and fruit on a large platter (or on individual serving plates) in small adjacent clusters. The idea is to make a lovely large plate with a small pile of each ingredient sitting in its own little spot. Sprinkle the edges of the platter with minced chives, if desired.

Serve with a dish of lime wedges and pass a cruet of Orange Vinaigrette for individual drizzlings.

Yield: 4 to 6 servings, depending greatly on the context (easily multiplied)
Preparation time: 1 hour

VEGETARIAN SALADE NIÇOISE

WITH FRIED CAPERS AND HORSERADISH AIOLI

Salade Niçoise is probably the original composed salad. A French classic, its components are usually tuna, anchovies, olives, tomatoes, hard-boiled eggs, green beans, potatoes, and capers, dressed in a basic vinaigrette. This vegetarian version expands on the vegetables, and is served with Horseradish Aioli, which is a creamy sauce laced with garlic and horseradish.

NOTE: For deeper flavor, you can roast the beets, potatoes, and beans (see page 97). You can also include other vegetables that are at the peak of their season—whatever looks good to you.

Thoroughly rinse and drain the capers, and dry them on paper towels. Heat the olive oil in a small skillet over medium heat. When it is hot enough to bounce a drop of water on contact, add the capers, and fry them until crisp (about 3 to 5 minutes). Remove the capers with a slotted spoon, and transfer to a paper towel to drain for a minute or two.

Meanwhile make a bed of lettuce leaves on a big platter or on individual plates. Add the beets, potatoes, beans, eggs, tomatoes, carrots, peas, olives, and cucumber in small clusters on top of the lettuce. Tuck small bunches of fresh herbs here and there among the eggs and vegetables. Add whatever optional garnishes appeal to you, and sprinkle on the fried capers.

Serve right away, with small bowls of Horseradish Aioli for dipping.

Yield: 4 to 6 servings
Preparation time: 20 to 30 minutes

A 4-ounce jar of capers

3 tablespoons olive oil

I small head soft lettuce (red leaf or oak leaf), cleaned, dried, and chilled

I dozen small beets, cooked until tender, peeled, and cut in half

½ to ¾ pound tiny potatoes, cooked until tender

½ pound fresh green or wax beans (as slender as possible), cooked until just tender

4 to 6 hard-boiled eggs, quartered

½ pound tiny cherry tomatoes

I medium carrot, shredded or julienned

I to 2 cups frozen peas, defrosted

½ cup Niçoise olives

I medium cucumber, peeled, seeded, and julienned

Small sprigs of fresh herbs (dill, basil, chives, chervil, parsley)

Horseradish Aioli (page 168)

Freshly ground black pepper

OPTIONAL GARNISHES:

Frizzled Leeks (page 59)

Pickled Red Onions (page 63)

Cherry Tomato Chewies (page 60)

Mushroom Pickles (page 61)

For a menu suggestion, see page 211.

PANZANELLA

Loosely translated from a Tuscan dialect, panzanella *means "little swamp." Descriptive as it is of this delicious bread-and-tomato salad, the name doesn't quite do it justice. If you use the right type of bread and the freshest, ripest tomatoes, the texture will be fantastic: crunchy, chewy, and juicy all at the same time. This is a great dish for a potluck picnic or a late summer party.*

The best bread to use is a country-style loaf with a light, airy interior—full of holes— and a thick, chewy crust. Ideally, the bread should be sturdy enough to soak up plenty of the delicious fresh tomato juices and vinaigrette without becoming too soggy. (Avoid soft breads that contain honey or sugar— they will disintegrate upon contact with the moisture.)

½ pound crusty country-style bread

⅓ cup minced red onion (or 3 to 4 scallions, chopped)

4 cups chopped ripe tomatoes, (about 2 pounds)

1 medium-sized cucumber, peeled, seeded, and chopped

½ cup (packed) torn basil leaves

⅓ cup chopped flat-leaf parsley

1 cup pitted, chopped olives (optional)

1 cup ricotta salata or feta cheese, crumbled

2 teaspoons minced garlic

4 to 6 tablespoons extra virgin olive oil (to taste)

3 to 4 tablespoons wine vinegar (to taste)

A big pinch of salt (omit if using feta cheese)

Freshly ground black pepper

Preheat the oven to 400°F. Cut the bread into 1-inch slices and place them directly on a rack in the center of the oven to toast for about 20 minutes, or until lightly browned. Remove from oven, and set aside to cool.

Combine all the remaining ingredients in a large bowl.

Tear the toasted bread into bite-sized pieces, and distribute half of them over the bottom of a large oval gratin pan or a 9 x 13-inch baking pan. Pour half the tomato-vegetable-vinaigrette mixture over the bread, then add a second layer of bread. Spread the remaining salad over the top, and cover tightly with plastic wrap.

Chill for at least an hour, to let the bread soak up the flavors and juices. Serve on small plates, or if it is very juicy, spoon it into bowls.

Yield: 6 to 8 servings
Preparation time: 20 minutes, plus 1 hour to sit

Make this when tomatoes and cucumbers are at their peak.

Ricotta salata is a dry, crumbly cheese similar to feta, but less salty. If you can't find it, use feta, and omit the salt.

For a menu suggestion, see page 211.

Mollie Katzen's VEGETABLE HEAVEN

BREADED SAUTÉED YOGURT CHEESE
ON SALAD GREENS

With a single ingredient, and equipment no more high-tech than a strainer, a coffee filter, and a bowl, you can make the most exquisite and rich-tasting nonfat cheese in your very own kitchen. And it will only take about 4 minutes of effort.

It's very easy to form yogurt cheese into little patties, dredge them in bread crumbs and sauté them in a hot pan. Serve the hot cheese—crunchy on the outside and divinely creamy on the inside— on a cool bed of salad greens for a sensational appetizer or lunch entrée.

Do this at least 24 hours ahead: Place a large coffee filter in a strainer over a bowl. Pour the yogurt into the filter, then leave it for up to 24 hours, at room temperature—or in the refrigerator, if your kitchen is very warm. Much of the liquid will drain out, and you should end up with about 1 cup of yogurt cheese.

To make each patty, place about 2 tablespoons of cheese on a piece of plastic wrap. Cover with another piece of plastic wrap, and gently pat it into a circle 2 inches in diameter and ¾ inch thick. (You can also skip the plastic wrap, and just use your hands. Dampen them first, so the cheese won't stick.)

Spread the bread crumbs on a sheet of waxed paper, and dredge the patties on both sides until they are thoroughly coated.

Place a heavy nonstick skillet over medium-high heat, and brush it lightly with oil. When the skillet is very hot, add the cheese patties and sauté for about 2 minutes on each side, or until golden brown. (You'll need to do this in several batches.)

Arrange the salad greens on individual small plates, and drizzle with a little vinaigrette. Place a sautéed cheese patty or two in the center of each salad, and grind some black pepper over the top. Garnish as desired and serve right away.

Yield: 16 small patties—enough to serve 6 to 8
Preparation time: 24 hours to make the cheese (2 minutes of work); 15 minutes of work after the cheese is ready.

2 cups nonfat yogurt

¾ cup fine bread crumbs

1 to 2 tablespoons olive oil

¾ to 1 pound mixed salad greens, cleaned, dried, and chilled

Mustard Vinaigrette (page 173)

Freshly ground black pepper

OPTIONAL GARNISHES:

Olives

Radishes

Tiny cherry tomatoes

Pickled Red Onions (page 63)

....

Make the yogurt cheese and the vinaigrette well ahead. You can also bread the cheese in advance, and store it, tightly wrapped, in the refrigerator. Sauté the cheese and assemble the salad at the last minute. (The cheese tastes best within about 10 minutes of being sautéed.)

Use the liquid that is left over after the yogurt drains in place of milk or water in baking bread or cakes.

Yogurt cheese can be used as a nonfat replacement for cream cheese in just about any recipe, even in unbaked cheesecakes. It's also a good spread for sandwiches and bagels.

For a menu suggestion, see page 213.

FRISÉE AND MUSHROOM SALAD
WITH WARM GARLIC VINAIGRETTE

You won't find a more stunning little salad—it's clean, crisp, and boldly flavored. The warm dressing soaks into the mushrooms and slightly wilts the frisée. Crunchy bread crumbs enhance the texture, and lend a rustic touch.

Frisée is a spunky tasting curly endive, often found in salad mixes ("mesclun"). To get an entire head of this delicious salad green, look in farmers' markets or in a high-quality produce store. Buy the youngest, freshest frisée you can find, with small and tender leaves.

Clean and thoroughly dry the leaf lettuce and frisée. Tear the lettuce into bite-sized pieces and put them in a medium-large bowl. Chop the frisée fairly small, and layer this on top of the lettuce.

Clean or peel the domestic mushrooms, and cut off the stems. Slice the mushrooms thinly, and spread them over the frisée. Sprinkle the enoki mushrooms over the top, if desired.

Heat the olive oil in a small skillet over medium heat. After about a minute, add the garlic, and cook it in the oil for about 10 seconds, or until it is aromatic. Be careful not to let the garlic brown. Remove from heat, and stir in the thyme, vinegar, and salt. Take a little taste (careful not to burn your tongue) to see if it needs a pinch of sugar to cut any sharpness. Pour this dressing over the salad, and let it sit without stirring it. (This will cause the mushrooms and the frisée to wilt slightly.)

Return the skillet to medium heat and add the bread crumbs. (They will conveniently soak up any dressing that is left in the pan.) Cook, stirring frequently, until they turn crunchy and golden, about 8 minutes.

Sprinkle the bread crumbs on top of the salad, and grind in some fresh black pepper. Toss thoroughly and serve right away.

Yield: 4 large or 6 small servings
Preparation time: About 20 minutes

- ½ head red leaf or oak leaf lettuce (5 to 6 ounces)
- 1 small head frisée (6 ounces)
- 10 medium-sized fresh domestic mushrooms (¼ pound)
- A small handful of enoki mushrooms (about 1 ounce), optional
- 3 tablespoons olive oil
- 1½ teaspoons minced garlic
- A pinch of thyme
- 1 tablespoon sherry vinegar or champagne vinegar
- ¼ teaspoon salt (possibly more)
- A pinch of sugar (optional)
- ½ cup coarse bread crumbs
- Freshly ground black pepper

Enoki mushrooms are an elegant miniature variety with a tiny head, and a long, threadlike stem. Look for them at a sophisticated greengrocer or in a Japanese food store.

The best bread crumbs for this salad are the ones you crumble with your own two hands from a loaf of your favorite bread. My personal choice for this salad is bakery whole wheat.

The undressed salad can be assembled in the bowl ahead of time and refrigerated. Dress shortly before serving.

For a menu suggestion, see page 213.

GREEN SALAD
WITH BLUE CHEESE, WALNUTS, AND FIGS

Fresh figs are sublime, but dried figs are quite delicious as well. You can successfully make this rich-tasting salad with either kind any time of year.

Place the greens in a large bowl. Drizzle in the oil, sprinkle in the salt, and toss until well coated.

Add the figs, blue cheese, and walnuts, and toss gently but thoroughly. Grind in some black pepper.

Serve immediately, and pass a dish of lemon wedges for squeezing over the top of each serving.

Yield: 4 to 6 servings
Preparation time: 10 minutes

½ pound fresh salad greens, cleaned, dried, and chilled

3 to 4 tablespoons walnut oil

A scant ¼ teaspoon salt

4 ripe fresh figs (or 4 to 6 dried figs), sliced

¼ cup crumbled blue cheese

¼ cup minced walnuts, lightly toasted

Freshly ground black pepper

2 lemons, cut into squeezable wedges

···

✷ *Some walnut oils are far more flavorful than others. I find the imported French brands to have the deepest, toastiest flavor. Experiment around to find a good walnut oil, and keep it refrigerated so you can use it over time. (A little bit goes a long way.)*

✷ *If you don't have walnut oil on hand, go ahead and make this salad with extra virgin olive oil. It will still taste fine.*

✷ *For a menu suggestion, see page 212.*

REVERSED SALAD IN ONE BOWL

2 tablespoons extra virgin olive oil

½ teaspoon minced garlic

¼ teaspoon prepared mustard

1 teaspoon red wine or sherry vinegar

A pinch of dried marjoram or oregano (optional)

8 ounces soft leaf lettuce, cleaned, dried, and chilled

Salt to taste

Freshly ground black pepper to taste

OPTIONAL ADDITIONS:

Tiny cherry tomatoes

Slices of cooked beet and/or potato

Shredded or julienned carrots

Alfalfa or radish sprouts

Leftover cooked grains

Anything else that appeals to you

. . . .

For a change of pace, serve Reversed Salad between two pieces of bread or in a whole-grain sandwich bun with a few slices of emmenthaler cheese. It makes a great lunch.

In the unlikely event that you need one, there is a menu suggestion on page 212.

Make the dressing first—right in the salad bowl. Then gradually add the lettuce and optional accoutrements, and toss from the bottom up. It's not only efficient, it's a great method for distributing the dressing quickly and evenly, with no puddles left in the bottom of the bowl when you're done. This might just become your standard green salad; if you vary the "optional additions," I guarantee it will remain interesting.

Place the olive oil, garlic, mustard, vinegar, and marjoram or oregano in a medium-large bowl, and stir until well blended.

Tear about a third of the lettuce leaves into bite-sized pieces, add them to the dressing, and toss with long-handled salad servers until the leaves are coated. Tear and toss in the remaining lettuce in two more batches, including whatever additions you might choose to add along the way. Keep tossing until everything is evenly coated.

Sprinkle lightly with salt and a little more heavily with pepper, and toss one more time. Serve right away.

Yield: About 4 servings (easily doubled if you have a bigger bowl)
Preparation time: 10 minutes or less

Mollie Katzen's VEGETABLE HEAVEN

ONION-WILTED SPINACH SALAD

WITH CUMIN, AVOCADO, AND APPLE

Fresh spinach becomes meltingly tender when it is combined with warmed ingredients, causing it to wilt slightly.

Onion-Wilted Spinach Salad tastes best immediately after it has been assembled, when the onion is still warm, the spinach and avocado are at room temperature, and the apple slices are very cold. Hint: Keep the apple slices refrigerated until the very last minute.

Cut the apple into thin slices onto a plate, and drizzle with about 2 teaspoons of the lemon juice. Cover the plate tightly with plastic wrap, and refrigerate.

Pour the remaining lemon juice onto a second plate. Peel and slice the avocado, then place the slices in the lemon juice, and turn them over until they are well coated. Set aside.

Heat the olive oil in a medium-sized skillet. When it is very hot, add the onion rings, and cook over high heat for 2 to 3 minutes. Sprinkle in the cumin seeds, and cook for just a minute longer.

Add the hot onion and cumin to the spinach, and toss until thoroughly mixed. The spinach will begin to wilt upon contact. To speed this process along—and to be sure you include every last drop of the flavorful oil— you can add some of the spinach directly to the pan and swish it around a little, then return it to the bowl. Sprinkle in the salt as you toss.

Gently mix in the avocado, including all the lemon juice, and the apple. Grind in a generous amount of black pepper, and serve right away.

Yield: 4 to 6 servings (depending on the context)
Preparation time: 20 minutes

---

1 medium-sized tart green apple

3 tablespoons fresh lemon juice

1 small, perfectly ripe avocado

3 tablespoons olive oil

2 cups thickly-sliced onion rings (any type of onion is fine)

1½ teaspoons cumin seeds

½ pound cleaned, stemmed spinach—in a large bowl

½ teaspoon salt

Freshly ground black pepper

....

You can prepare the apple up to an hour ahead of time.

The best spinach leaves to use for this salad are the smallest, and, of course, the freshest.

For a menu suggestion, see page 211.

ARUGULA SALAD
WITH ORANGE VINAIGRETTE

Arugula is very peppery and intensely flavored, so it works best when combined with softer, sweeter salad greens, like butter lettuce. The Orange Vinaigrette is quite tart, and gives this delicious salad a provocative edge.

1 medium-sized head butter (Boston) lettuce, cleaned, dried, and chilled

1 to 2 bunches arugula, coarsely chopped (about 3 cups)

10 radishes, thinly sliced

3 tablespoons minced chives (or 1 scallion, finely minced)

Orange Vinaigrette (page 173)

Freshly ground black pepper

Niçoise olives (optional)

··

Make sure all the salad vegetables are clean, dry, and cold, and add the dressing right before serving.

For a menu suggestion, see page 211.

Break the lettuce leaves into bite-sized pieces and place them in a medium-large bowl. Add the arugula, radishes, and chives, and toss until well combined.

Pour in about ¼ cup of the dressing, grind in some black pepper, and toss well from the bottom, so that everything gets evenly coated. Drizzle in small amounts of additional dressing, as needed, tossing until the salad is as dressed as you like it.

Serve immediately, garnished with Niçoise olives, if desired.

Yield: 4 to 5 servings
Preparation time: 10 minutes

YUPPIE PLATTER

The ingredients might seem a bit upscale and—how shall I say it?—very fin de siècle. *But just think: you can turn your own home into a trendy bistro with one quick trip to your state-of-the-art grocery store and only about 15 minutes of light work. This easy little appetizer/salad/lunch entrée is something you're going to want to make over and over.*

Heat a little olive oil in a sauté pan. Turn up the heat and add the radicchio. Stir-fry in the hot pan for just a minute or two, then add the watercress. Keep cooking over strong heat for just another minute, then transfer the mixture to a small platter. Sprinkle lightly with salt, and keep the platter nearby.

Using a teaspoon or your fingers, place a few nuggets of goat cheese inside each leaf of Belgian endive. Heat a little more oil in the same pan, and carefully add the filled endive leaves, facing up. "Grill" over medium heat for about 5 minutes, or until the endive leaves have wilted slightly, and the goat cheese is exquisitely softened.

Carefully remove the leaves from the pan, one by one, and arrange them in an understated design on top of the raddichio and watercress.

Heat the pan again, and add the vinegar. Swirl to deglaze the pan, then cook over medium heat for about 2 minutes. (Try not to breathe the fumes—they are potent!) Remove from heat and taste the vinegar. If it's exceedingly tart, sprinkle in a little sugar to soften its edge.

Drizzle the vinegar over the top of everything, and grind on some black pepper. Sprinkle with a few chopped, toasted walnuts, if desired, and serve warm.

Yield: 2 generous or 4 appetizer-sized servings (easily doubled)
Preparation time: 15 minutes

---

1 to 2 tablespoons olive oil

2 cups chopped radicchio
 (about 4½ ounces)

1 cup (packed) chopped watercress
 (a 4-ounce bunch)

A pinch of salt

12 leaves Belgian endive (about 2
 4-ounce heads)

¼ cup crumbled goat cheese

2 tablespoons balsamic vinegar

A pinch of sugar (optional)

Freshly ground black pepper

⅓ cup chopped walnuts, lightly
 toasted (optional)

....

As you remove the leaves from the head of Belgian endive, the core becomes exposed. Only the leaves actually go into this dish, but the core makes a great snack while you're working away.

Some varieties of balsamic vinegar are more acidic than others. The sugar in the recipe is optional, just in case the vinegar you are using tastes too sharp.

Serve Yuppie Platter with some good crusty bread as a first course or a light lunch.

For a menu suggestion, see page 213.

ORANGE, BEET, AND FENNEL SALAD

I think you will love this salad, even if you don't love beets or fennel. It's irresistibly colorful and refreshing. It's also oil-free.

10 medium beets, about 2 inches in diameter

6 oranges

¼ cup raspberry vinegar

½ teaspoon salt

1 to 2 teaspoons minced garlic

1 small fennel bulb, thinly sliced (about 2 cups)

Finely minced fennel tops, for garnish

....

The oranges and beets can be prepared up to 2 days ahead. In fact, it's preferable to do the oranges ahead, so they can give off a lot of juice.

I like to put in the full amount of garlic. It gives this very cool salad a nice touch of heat.

For a menu suggestion, see page 212.

Preheat the oven to 375°F, and line a baking dish with foil. Trim the leaves from the beets, place them in the dish, and cover with foil. Bake until they are soft enough to be pierced easily with a fork (about 1 hour). Set aside to cool.

Meanwhile, use a medium-sized serrated knife to cut the peel from the oranges, then section the oranges into a medium-sized bowl to catch all the juice. (Just cut with a sawing motion along the membranes to release the sections.) Squeeze the remaining juice into the bowl, and discard the membranes.

When the beets are cool enough to handle, use a small, sharp paring knife to peel them. Cut them first in half, and then into thin half-moon-shaped slices.

Transfer the beets to the bowlful of oranges, and add the vinegar, salt, and garlic. Stir gently until well combined.

Add the sliced fennel and stir again. Cover tightly and chill until serving time. The whole salad will turn an amazing color.

Serve topped with a light sprinkling of the minced fennel tops.

Yield: 6 or more servings
Preparation time: 1 hour, plus time to chill (15 minutes of work)

Mollie Katzen's VEGETABLE HEAVEN

UNCOMMON EVERYDAY SOUPS

There is nothing like soup. It is by its nature eccentric; no two are ever alike, unless of course you get soup from cans.

—Laurie Colwin, *Home Cooking*

A good soup attracts chairs.

—**African proverb**

*W*hether it is served hot or cold, thin or thick, chunky or smooth, soup is the universal comfort food, the primordial vehicle of nourishment. Curative properties are ascribed to soup in every known culture, and I wouldn't be surprised if, in many cases, the cure is for emotional hunger as well as for physical need.

It might seem like a big project to keep homemade soup on hand as a staple in your household, but once you get into the habit, it will feel absolutely ordinary and essential. Try setting aside some time on a regular basis to make a soup-of-the-week. Almost all of the following recipes keep and reheat beautifully.

NOTE: Most of these soups are made with water instead of stock, and the few that call for a stock or bouillon are accessible and straightforward. So I hope you won't be intimidated.

UNCOMMON EVERYDAY SOUPS

CHILLED HONEYDEW SOUP
WITH MINT AND LIME

Easy as can be—and a great choice for beginners—but this amazing soup will only be as amazing as the honeydew itself. So shop carefully for your melon, and be sure to pick one that has a creamy color on the outside and a strong fragrance even before you cut it open. Those are the two telltale signs of perfect ripeness.

Place everything except the optional blueberries in a food processor or blender and purée until smooth. You will probably need to do this in several batches.

Transfer to a container with a tight-fitting lid, and chill until very cold.

Serve in bowls or in glasses with a few whole blueberries plunked in, if desired.

Yield: 5 to 6 servings (easily multiplied, if you have another perfectly ripe honeydew)
Preparation time: 10 minutes, plus time to chill

1 medium-sized (4½-pound) honeydew melon, perfectly ripe, cut into chunks (about 6 to 8 cups)

¼ cup fresh lime juice

2 tablespoons minced fresh mint

A few blueberries for garnish (optional)

⭐ *Serve this on a warm day for any meal—even breakfast (my favorite)—or, you can get downright serious and make it into a granita, which is sort of an adult snow cone. Simply transfer the soup to a shallow dish, and freeze it for several hours, stirring every 30 minutes or so to prevent it from becoming completely solid. Just before serving, chop it up with a fork, so it turns into ice crystals. Serve as an appetizer, a between-course palate cleanser, or even a light dessert.*

⭐ *For a menu suggestion, see page 212.*

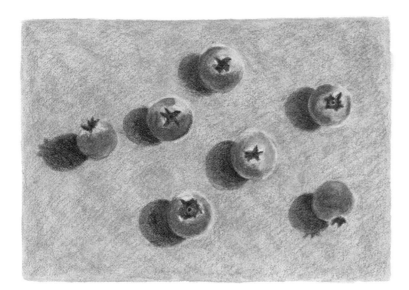

RICH MUSHROOM BROTH

3 ounces dried shiitake mushrooms

3 cups boiling water

1 pound fresh domestic mushrooms, cleaned

1½ teaspoons salt

About 8 scallions, cleaned and cut
in half

6 medium cloves garlic, peeled and
left whole

2 or 3 sprigs fresh thyme

A few torn parsley leaves for the
top (optional)

A few drops of dry sherry or vermouth (optional)

Frizzled Leeks (page 59), optional

....

★ This recipe calls for a combination of fresh domestic and dried shiitake mushrooms. However, if you
have access to fresh shiitakes, you
can use them instead of the dried
ones. Substitute 8 medium-sized fresh
shiitakes. Chop them together with
the fresh domestic mushrooms and
increase the cooking water to 6 cups.

★ If you want to make use of the
strained out mushrooms, put them in
sandwich spreads, vegetable pies,
quiches, omelette fillings, rice, stir-
fries, mashed potatoes, casseroles, or
anything else your creative, frugal
mind can think of.

Sometimes it's refreshing to serve something pure, uncluttered, and deeply, quietly delicious. This richly flavored broth is just such a thing. You can serve it absolutely plain, or with a few mushrooms or Frizzled Leeks floating on the surface. You can also use this broth for cooking grains (it makes fabulous rice) or as a stock for other soups. It freezes perfectly.

Rinse the dried shiitake mushrooms, and place them in a medium-sized bowl. Add 3 cups boiling water, and let soak for at least 20 minutes. Strain the mushrooms over a second bowl, pressing out and reserving all the liquid.

Pull off and discard the shiitake stems, then place the shiitake and fresh mushrooms together in a food processor and pulse until they are cut up into small pieces. (If you don't have a food processor, just chop everything very small.)

Put all the mushrooms in a soup pot or a Dutch oven with the reserved mushroom-soaking water, 4 additional cups of water, and the salt, scallions, garlic, and thyme. Bring to a boil, then lower heat to a simmer. Cover and cook gently for about 40 minutes.

Line a strainer with two layers of clean cheesecloth, and strain the soup into another pot (or a storage container with a lid, if you don't plan to serve it right away). You can put some of the mushrooms back in the broth, or reserve them for another use.

Serve the broth hot, possibly with a few mushrooms and/or a few drops of dry sherry or vermouth added, or a few torn parsley leaves. For a special touch, sprinkle some Frizzled Leeks onto each serving.

Yield: About 6 cups of delicious broth
Preparation time: 1 hour (20 minutes of work)

TOMATO-FENNEL CONSOMME

Fennel is a subtle presence that blends perfectly with tomatoes in this light, clean-tasting soup. Serve Tomato-Fennel Consommé hot or chilled; plain, or with just a few croutons floating on top. On hot summer afternoons, my friend Tina likes this ice-cold in a tall glass, with a splash of vodka.

Remove the leafy tops from the fennel, and set aside. Cut the fennel bulbs into chunks. Place them in a food processor with the onions, and pulse together until finely minced. (You can also do this by hand.)

Heat the oil in a medium-sized saucepan. Add the chopped onion-fennel mixture and the salt, and sauté over medium heat for about 10 minutes. Lightly rinse out the food processor bowl and set aside to use again later.

Add the water and tomatoes, and bring to a boil. Cover, lower the heat to a simmer, and cook for about 20 minutes. (A little longer wouldn't hurt. This is an inexact craft.)

Transfer the soup to the food processor and purée. Carefully strain into a large-ish bowl (if you plan to serve this cold) or another saucepan (if you're serving it hot). Don't press too hard on the vegetables, so the consommé stays clear. Season to taste with cayenne.

Heat or chill the soup, depending upon your taste and the weather. Garnish each serving with some of the feathery fennel tops, minced into tiny bits with scissors. You can also float some croutons on top, if you like.

Yield: About 6 cups (4 to 6 dainty servings)
Preparation time: 45 minutes, plus longer for chilling, if you want to serve it cold (15 minutes of work)

---

4 medium-sized fennel bulbs (about 4 pounds)

2 medium-sized onions (about 1 pound), peeled and cut into chunks

1 tablespoon olive oil

2½ teaspoons salt (less if using canned tomatoes)

4 cups water

6 medium-sized ripe tomatoes (about 2½ pounds), chopped—or 3 14½-ounce cans diced tomatoes

A pinch or two of cayenne (optional)

Croutons (optional)

....

★ *Although you can successfully make this soup all year long with a good brand of canned tomatoes, it's especially delicious made with fresh, ripe tomatoes at the peak of their season. This soup freezes beautifully.*

★ *The onion and fennel can be prepared a day or two ahead. Chop them together in a food processor (just a few bursts with the steel blade) and store in a sealed plastic bag in the refrigerator.*

★ *For a menu suggestion, see page 212.*

EGGFLOWER SOUP
WITH PASTA SHELLS

8 cups water

2 tablespoons Roasted Garlic Paste
(page xiv)

1 tablespoon peanut or canola oil

3 tablespoons minced fresh garlic

1½ teaspoons salt (maybe more,
to taste)

1 cup uncooked small pasta shells

2 large eggs

Black pepper to taste

2 teaspoons soy sauce

1 tablespoon Chinese sesame oil

3 to 4 tablespoons balsamic or
cider vinegar

¼ pound firm tofu, cut into small
cubes

Minced fresh scallions for the top

....

★ *This soup calls for Roasted Garlic
Paste, which takes very little effort.
Do this ahead of time.*

★ *You can prepare the soup, up to
the point of adding the pasta, well in
advance, and store it in the refrigerator. Shortly before serving, heat the
soup to a boil, and proceed with the
recipe.*

*My original vision for this soup was more Italian than Chinese. But as I
developed the recipe, it somehow took on a life of its own and turned sharply
eastward. The only remnants of its Italian roots are the roasted garlic, pasta
shells, and balsamic vinegar, all surprisingly compatible with the Asian ingredients in this East-meets-West, melting pot (so-to-speak) result. Please bear
with the mixed metaphor, and enjoy this comforting hot-and-sour spin-off.*

Place 1 to 2 cups of the water in a blender with the Roasted Garlic
Paste, and purée until smooth. Set aside.

Heat the peanut oil in a soup pot or Dutch oven. Add the fresh garlic and ½ teaspoon of the salt, and sauté over medium-low heat for
about 8 to 10 minutes, or until the garlic is aromatic, but not yet
turning brown.

Add the Roasted Garlic Paste mixture to the sauté, along with the
remaining water and the rest of the salt. Bring to a boil, then lower
the heat to a simmer. Partially cover, and cook for about 20 minutes. At this point, the soup can rest until just before serving time.

Shortly before serving, bring the soup to a rolling boil. Add the
pasta, and cook until it is just tender. Reduce the heat to a simmer.

Beat the eggs well in a small bowl, and drizzle them into the simmering soup, stirring as you drizzle. (They will "blossom" upon contact
with the hot soup; hence, the name.) Stir in all the remaining ingredients except the scallions, and let it simmer about 5 minutes longer.

Serve hot, topped with a few finely minced scallions.

Yield: 6 to 8 servings
Preparation time: 45 minutes (35 minutes of work)

POTATO SOUP
WITH ROSEMARY AND ROASTED GARLIC

Roasted garlic is a mild, rich presence in this low-keyed, creamy soup. It is used in combination with fresh garlic, which is cooked directly into the stock, creating a deep, complex flavor.

This soup contains a surprise ingredient: silken tofu, which is a seamlessly smooth variety that comes vacuum-packed in little cardboard boxes in many grocery stores. It gives the soup an incredible creaminess—better, in this case, than cream itself. Really!

Place the potatoes in a large saucepan or Dutch oven along with the garlic, water, onion, carrot, salt, and rosemary. Bring to a boil, then cover and simmer until the potatoes are very soft (about 20 to 30 minutes). Remove from heat; fish out and discard the rosemary.

Stir the Roasted Garlic Paste into the soup along with the silken tofu, mashed slightly or broken up into pieces. Transfer the soup—in several batches—to a blender or food processor, and purée each batch until very smooth. Return the purée to another pot, and stir well.

Heat the soup gently; adjust the salt, and add white pepper to taste. Serve hot, garnished with a sprig or two of fresh rosemary, if available.

Yield: 6 to 8 servings (possibly even more)
Preparation time: 50 minutes (20 minutes of work)

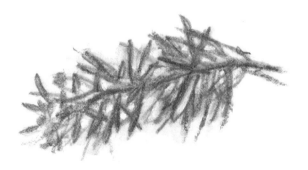

Ingredients

1½ pounds russet potatoes (about 4 medium-sized), peeled and cut into medium-sized chunks

8 large cloves garlic, peeled

6 cups water

2½ cups chopped onion

I large carrot, peeled and cut into large chunks

2 teaspoons salt

A few sprigs of fresh rosemary (or a teaball with about 2 teaspoons dried rosemary)

2 tablespoons Roasted Garlic Paste (page xiv)

I 10-ounce box silken tofu (soft variety)

White pepper to taste

Additional sprigs of rosemary for garnish (optional)

⋆ *Use fluffy russet potatoes, rather than creamier ones, like Yellow Finn or Yukon Gold. The former will whip up more cleanly, while the latter will become too gluey in the blender or food processor.*

⋆ *This soup keeps well for about 5 days if stored in a tightly covered container and refrigerated. It also freezes well.*

⋆ *For a menu suggestion, see page 213.*

CHICKPEA SOUP
WITH GOLDEN SPICES

I never get tired of chickpeas (aka garbanzo beans), especially in mashed or puréed form, as in this soup. It's warming and delicious, much resembling a heated-up version of hummus, the classic Middle Eastern spread.

2 cups uncooked chickpeas, soaked for at least 4 hours (or 4 15-ounce cans chickpeas)

1 tablespoon olive oil

2 cups minced onion

4 tablespoons minced garlic

2 teaspoons salt

1 large carrot, diced

A few threads of saffron (not too much—literally a pinch)

2 teaspoons lightly roasted cumin seeds (dry roasted or sautéed in a little olive oil)

2 teaspoons dry mustard

1/4 cup fresh lemon juice

Black pepper and cayenne to taste

2 to 3 tablespoons sesame tahini (optional)

OPTIONAL, FOR THE TOP:

2 medium-sized ripe tomatoes, peeled, seeded, and diced

A little minced cilantro, parsley, or mint

A drizzle of Chinese sesame oil

★ *If using dried chickpeas, you can soak and cook them well in advance.*

★ *This soup stores well in the refrigerator or freezer if packed in an airtight container.*

★ *For a menu suggestion, see page 211.*

Place the soaked, uncooked chickpeas in a large pot and cover with water by at least 2 inches. Bring to a boil, then partially cover and simmer for about 1½ hours, or until the chickpeas are very soft. (If you're using canned chickpeas, rinse and drain them, and set aside.)

Heat the olive oil in a soup pot or Dutch oven. Add the onion, half the garlic, half the salt, and the carrot, saffron, cumin seeds, and mustard. Sauté over medium heat for about 10 minutes, or until the carrot begins to soften.

Add the chickpeas and 4 cups water. (You can use their cooking water, if there's any left.) Bring it to a boil, lower the heat, and cook, covered, for about 20 minutes.

Add the remaining garlic and salt, along with the lemon juice, black pepper, and cayenne to taste. You can also add some sesame tahini at this point, if desired. Purée the soup in a blender or food processor until fairly smooth. (You might want to add a little extra water if it seems too thick.) Taste to adjust seasonings.

Serve hot, with a spoonful of diced tomato, a small amount of minced cilantro or mint, and possibly a drop or two of Chinese sesame oil on top of each serving, if desired.

Yield: 6 to 8 servings
Preparation time: About 1 hour (30 minutes of work)

Mollie Katzen's VEGETABLE HEAVEN

LENTIL SOUP
WITH A HINT OF FRUIT

The fruit that's doing the hinting here is the humble dried apricot, which might seem bizarre at first glance, or even at second glance. But something subtle and magical happens when the apricot flavor modestly blends into the soup. Try this easy, intensely seasoned, oil-free winner, and you'll see what I'm talking about.

Place the lentils and water in a soup pot or Dutch oven and bring to a boil. Cover, lower the heat to a simmer, and cook for about 15 minutes. Add the onion, cumin, and mustard, and continue to simmer, covered, until the lentils are very soft (about 15 more minutes). Add small amounts of additional water, if it seems too thick.

Add the garlic, apricots, and salt, cover, and let it simmer for another 15 minutes or so. Stir in the vinegar, black pepper, and cayenne to taste (and correct the salt too, if necessary). At this point the soup will keep for several days.

Serve hot, topped with a few extra slivers of dried apricot, a swirl of yogurt, and a sprig of cilantro or parsley, if desired.

Yield: 6 to 8 servings
Preparation time: 45 minutes (10 minutes of work)

2 cups green, red, or French lentils, rinsed and picked over

8 cups water (maybe more)

2 cups minced onion

2 teaspoons ground cumin

2 teaspoons dry mustard

2 tablespoons minced garlic

1 cup minced dried apricots

1½ to 2 teaspoons salt (to taste)

3 to 4 tablespoons balsamic vinegar (or to taste)

Black pepper and cayenne to taste

OPTIONAL GARNISHES:

Extra slivers of dried apricot

A swirl of yogurt

A sprig or two of cilantro or parsley

⋆ *This soup freezes well if stored in an airtight container.*

⋆ *For a menu suggestion, see page 212.*

TOMATILLO-CHILE SOUP

Although they look like miniature green tomatoes, tomatillos are actually a whole separate species, related to Cape gooseberries, of all things. Fresh, ripe tomatillos are firm and green, and covered with a husk that resembles brown paper. Just remove the husk, which comes off easily, and chop the fruit. Tomatillos have a wonderful, refreshing sourness that blends well with strong seasonings. Speaking of which, this soup is quite highly seasoned, and can make a delicious meal out of plain beans, rice, salad, and tortillas.

NOTE: If you can't find fresh tomatillos, buy them in cans from a Mexican market or the imported foods section of your grocery store. If you can't find canned either, you can substitute 6 cups chopped green tomatoes.

2 tablespoons olive oil

3 cups chopped onion

4 medium-sized fresh poblano and/or Anaheim chiles (or 2 bell peppers plus 1 7-ounce can diced green chiles), chopped

2 heaping tablespoons minced garlic

2½ teaspoons salt

2 tablespoons chile powder

6 cups husked, chopped tomatillos (about 2 pounds fresh, or 3 12-ounce cans, drained and chopped)

4 cups water

2 to 3 tablespoons sugar or honey

OPTIONAL TOPPINGS:

Sour cream

Torn cilantro leaves

Thin slices of avocado and/or ripe papaya

⋆ *If fresh poblano or Anaheim chiles are unavailable, use a combination of fresh bell peppers and canned green chiles.*

⋆ *This soup freezes well if stored in an airtight container.*

⋆ *For a menu suggestion, see page 213.*

Heat the olive oil in a soup pot or Dutch oven. Add the onion, and sauté over medium heat for about 5 minutes to give it a little head start.

Add the chiles (and/or peppers), garlic, salt, and chile powder, and mix well. Cover and cook over medium heat for about 5 minutes, stirring often.

Stir in the tomatillos, cover, and cook for another 10 minutes or so. Add the water and bring to a boil, then lower the heat to a simmer. Cover and cook about 10 minutes longer.

Purée in batches in a blender or food processor, and return to the pot. Add sugar or honey to taste, and correct the salt, if necessary.

Serve hot, garnished with some or all of the optional toppings, for a beautiful, cooling contrast.

Yield: 6 intense servings
Preparation time: 1 hour (20 minutes of work)

BIG, BOLD NOODLE SOUP

How can a dish be dark, mysterious, and filling, but spirited, uplifting, and light at the same time? I don't know, but while you're pondering, try this great soup.

Fresh Asian egg noodles (particularly the thick Shanghai variety or Japanese udon) are ideal here, but go ahead and use any kind of long pasta—fresh or dried—and your soup will be wonderful. Keep the cooked noodles separate and add them to each bowl just before ladling in the liquid. (Explanation: The noodles tend to expand greatly if left in the soup, leaving you to wonder who drank all the broth.)

Preliminary: Rinse the mushrooms and place them in a small bowl. Pour in 1½ cups boiling water and cover with a plate. Let stand at least 30 minutes. (This can be done several days ahead, and the mushrooms can just stay in the water until use.)

Combine the bouillon, star anise, and ginger in a soup pot, and bring to a boil. Turn the heat down, cover, and simmer for about 20 to 30 minutes. At this point, the broth can sit for up to several hours—or even overnight—before you proceed.

Remove the ginger and star anise with a slotted spoon. Strain the mushrooms over the soup, squeezing them firmly, so all of their soaking liquid goes in. Then slice the mushrooms thinly and add them to the soup as well.

Heat the soup to the boiling point, and add the mustard greens, bok choy, and scallions. Turn the heat down, and simmer for about 2 minutes.

Meanwhile cook the noodles in boiling water until just tender. Drain them in a colander, rinse, and drain again, so they won't clump. Divide the cooked noodles among the largest soup bowls you can find, and ladle the soup on top. Pass around the optional toppings on a small tray, so each person can customize his or her portion.

Yield: 6 to 8 soul-soothing servings
Preparation time: 50 minutes (15 minutes of work)

6 or 7 dried shiitake mushrooms

1½ cups boiling water

8 cups strong vegetable bouillon (page xiv)

6 star anise

4 or 5 large slices ginger

4 cups (packed) stemmed, chopped mustard greens (about half a large bunch)

4 cups chopped bok choy, stems included (2 to 3 small heads)

10 scallions, thinly sliced on the diagonal

1 pound fresh egg noodles—or ½ pound dried (about 3 or 4 cups cooked)

OPTIONS FOR THE TOP:

Soy sauce

Chile garlic paste, chile oil, or red pepper flakes

Chinese sesame oil

Torn cilantro leaves

★ *If you don't have access to mustard greens and bok choy, substitute other leafy greens with strong personalities, like kale, watercress, or spinach. The amounts are flexible.*

★ *The mushrooms, bouillon, and vegetables can be prepared way ahead of time.*

★ *For a menu suggestion, see page 212.*

TORTILLA SOUP
WITH ROASTED RED PEPPERS

A traditional tortilla soup usually relies upon chicken broth for its flavor. This outstanding vegetarian version is made with a delicious corn and cilantro stock instead, and features the inimitable flavors of roasted bell peppers and sautéed fresh chiles. Stir in a tiny bit of minced chipotle chiles (intensely flavored smoked jalapeños), and this soup will go over the top.

The Corn-Cilantro Stock

The Corn-Cilantro Stock

3½ cups frozen corn (or 3 ears of fresh corn, cobs and all)

16 scallions (about 2 bunches), cut into 1-inch lengths

2 handfuls fresh cilantro

6 cups water

1 teaspoon salt

Place everything in a large saucepan and bring to a boil. Partially cover, lower heat to a simmer, and cook gently for about 30 minutes. (A little longer is okay, but keep the lid on so not too much liquid evaporates.)

The Rest of the Soup

The Rest of the Soup

2 teaspoons olive oil

1 medium onion, minced (about 1½ cups)

1 medium-sized poblano chile, seeded and minced

1 medium-sized Anaheim chile, seeded and minced

1½ tablespoons minced garlic

1 teaspoon salt (possibly more, to taste)

4 medium-sized red peppers, roasted, peeled, seeded, and chopped (page 96)

2 medium-sized ripe tomatoes, peeled, seeded, and minced (page xiv)

2 tablespoons fresh lime juice

Cayenne to taste (optional)

Minced canned chipotle chiles (a teaspoon or less), optional

Tortilla Strips (recipe follows) —or commercial tortilla chips

Heat the oil in a soup pot or Dutch oven. Add the onion, chiles, garlic, and salt, and sauté for about 5 minutes over medium heat. Turn the heat down, cover, and cook, stirring occasionally, for another 5 to 10 minutes, or until all the vegetables are very tender.

Place the roasted bell peppers and the tomatoes in a blender or food processor with about 2 cups of the stock. (It's all right if some of the vegetables from the stock get in there, too.) Purée until smooth, then add this to the onion mixture. Strain in the rest of the stock, pressing every last bit of the liquid from the cooked vegetables.

Add lime juice; taste to correct salt and add a little cayenne or a very small amount of minced chipotles, if desired. Serve hot, topped with a generous handful of tortilla strips.

Mollie Katzen's VEGETABLE HEAVEN

Tortilla Strips

Set a medium-sized, heavy skillet over medium heat. Meanwhile, lightly brush both sides of each tortilla with oil. Cut the tortillas in half, then cut each half into thin strips.

Place the strips in the hot pan. Cook and stir gently for about 5 minutes, or until they are chewy-crisp. Remove from heat, drain on paper towels, and salt lightly. Sprinkle a few strips on top of each bowl of soup.

Yield: 6 or more servings
Preparation time: 1 hour (30 minutes of work)

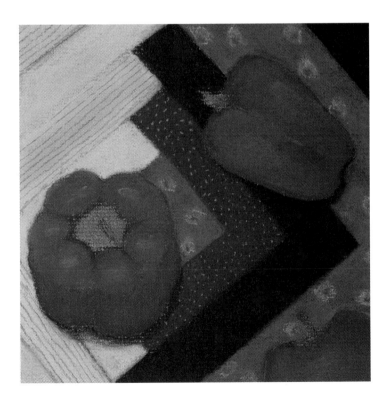

Tortilla Strips
4 or 5 thin corn tortillas
A little olive oil
Salt

★ The easy Corn-Cilantro Stock can be made well in advance.

★ The peppers and tomatoes can be prepared days ahead and stored together in a tightly covered container in the refrigerator. (They will give off some juices as they sit around. Put it all in the soup.)

★ A little bit of canned chipotle chiles goes a long way. After you open the can and take out a smidgen for this soup, you can store the rest in a tightly lidded jar in your refrigerator, and use it sparingly as a seasoning for all sorts of things. Even with frequent use, one can will probably last you about a year.

★ The chewy Tortilla Strips are wonderful on top of the soup, especially if they are freshly sautéed. Make them while the soup simmers. (You can also substitute a good brand of commercial tortilla chips.)

★ For a menu suggestion, see page 212.

ROOT VEGETABLE SOUP

1 tablespoon butter or vegetable oil

1½ cups chopped onion

1 heaping tablespoon minced garlic

3 to 4 tablespoons minced fresh ginger

1½ teaspoons salt

1 medium rutabaga, peeled and diced (about ½ pound)

2 small turnips, peeled and diced (about ½ pound)

1 medium sweet potato or yam, peeled and diced (about ¾ pound)

2 medium-small potatoes, peeled and diced (about ¾ pound)

1 8-inch parsnip, peeled and diced (about ¾ pound)

2 large carrots, peeled and diced

6 cups water

1 cinnamon stick

OPTIONAL:

A fine sprinkling of grated fresh horseradish

Toast

Red Onion and Shallot Marmalade (page 162)

....

★ *This soup freezes well if stored in an airtight container.*

★ *For a menu suggestion, see page 211.*

Rutabagas, turnips, and parsnips don't normally get a whole lot of attention, but this delicious soup, at long last, provides them their fifteen minutes of fame. I never thought something so earthy could be this beautiful: pale sunny yellow with spots of creamy white, gold, and bright orange peeking through. It's naturally sweet, too, and slightly hot from the ginger and the optional horseradish. Wait until your family or friends have taken a taste before you tell them what's in it—they'll be really surprised.

NOTE: The quantities given for the vegetables are all ballpark figures. Don't worry if your amounts vary slightly. Also, instead of peeling the vegetables, you can simply scrub them with a good stiff brush.

Melt the butter or heat the oil in a soup pot or Dutch oven. Add the onion, garlic, ginger, and ½ teaspoon salt, and sauté over low heat for about 10 minutes. Stir in the remaining vegetables and another teaspoon of salt. Cover and cook over medium heat for 10 more minutes.

Add the water and the cinnamon stick. Bring to a boil, then turn the heat way down. Cover and simmer for 10 minutes. Remove the cinnamon stick, cover again, and continue to simmer for about 5 more minutes, or until the vegetables are completely tender.

Place about a quarter of the vegetables and some of their cooking liquid in a food processor or blender, and process briefly to thicken (but not necessarily to purée) the soup. Return the processed batch to the rest of the soup, and stir it in. This treatment gives the soup a delightful, varied texture.

Serve hot, with a very light sprinkling of grated fresh horseradish on top (go easy), and slices of crisp toast spread thickly with Red Onion and Shallot Marmalade on the side, if desired.

Yield: 6 to 8 servings
Preparation time: About 1 hour (20 minutes of work)

BLACK-EYED PEA AND SQUASH SOUP
WITH SHIITAKE MUSHROOMS

Try this surprisingly elegant and wonderful soup during any season, but especially when those late autumn winds begin to blow. If you simply add a basket of whole-grain crackers, a platter of cheeses, a green salad, and a mug of apple cider, my bet is that everyone will be thoroughly satisfied.

Like other beans, black-eyed peas are easy to find, inexpensive, and highly nutritious. Where they really stand out from the crowd is in their exceptional flavor, relatively short cooking time, and attractive appearance (cream colored with a snazzy dark blotch). You can use fresh, frozen, or dried. Dried black-eyed peas cook better if soaked first for at least 4 hours.

NOTE: Cook the black-eyed peas up to several days ahead, if desired. Save time by preparing the other ingredients while the peas cook.

Place the soaked or fresh black-eyed peas in a saucepan and cover with water by at least 2 inches. Bring to a boil, turn the heat way down, and simmer, partially covered, until tender—about 30 minutes. Drain and set aside.

Melt the butter in a soup pot or Dutch oven. Add the onion, mustard, half the garlic, half the ginger, and half the salt. Sauté over medium heat for about 5 minutes. Stir in all the mushrooms and sauté for a few minutes, then add the sherry. Cover and cook over medium heat for about 10 minutes.

Add half the squash and all the water. Bring to a boil, then lower the heat to a simmer, and cover. Cook for about 10 minutes, then add the cinnamon, lemon juice, and vinegar, along with the black-eyed peas, the remaining garlic, ginger, squash, and salt. Cover again, and cook over low heat until the most recently added squash is just tender.

Season liberally with freshly ground black pepper, and taste to see if it needs more salt. Serve hot, topped with very finely minced parsley and/or scallions, if desired.

Yield: 6 to 8 servings
Preparation time: 1 hour

I cup dried black-eyed peas, soaked (or 2 cups fresh or frozen/defrosted)

I tablespoon butter

2 cups minced onion

2 tablespoons dry mustard

2 tablespoons minced garlic

2 tablespoons minced fresh ginger

2 teaspoons salt

I pound fresh domestic mushrooms, stemmed and sliced

10 shiitake mushrooms (fresh or dried and soaked), stemmed and thinly sliced

¼ cup dry sherry or vermouth (or Chinese rice wine)

I medium-sized (2-pound) butternut squash, peeled and cut into small dice (about 5 cups)

4 cups water

¼ teaspoon cinnamon

I tablespoon fresh lemon juice

I tablespoon cider vinegar

Fresh black pepper to taste

Finely minced fresh parsley and/or scallions for the top (optional)

★ You can use fresh or dried shiitake mushrooms. If using dried, soak them ahead of time in 2 cups hot water for about 30 minutes, then drain well.

★ This soup keeps well, if covered tightly and refrigerated, for up to 5 days. It also freezes well.

★ For a menu suggestion, see page 211.

SPINACH SOUP
WITH BASIL AND DILL

2 fist-sized russet potatoes (about 1 pound), cut into cubes (peeling optional)

2 cups chopped onion

1 heaping tablespoon minced garlic

6 cups water

1½ teaspoons salt (possibly more, to taste)

1 teaspoon dry mustard

2 10-ounce packages frozen chopped spinach, defrosted (or 2 pounds fresh spinach, cleaned and chopped)

½ cup minced fresh dill

A small handful of fresh basil leaves

Freshly ground black pepper to taste

OPTIONAL, FOR THE TOP:

A little yogurt

Mild paprika

⋯⋯⋯⋯⋯⋯⋯⋯⋯⋯⋯⋯

★ Go ahead and use frozen spinach—it works very well here. (Just remember to defrost it ahead of time.)

★ Don't substitute dried herbs for the fresh. It just won't be the same.

★ The potatoes and onion can be cooked up to several days ahead.

★ This soup freezes well if stored in an airtight container.

Easy, nonfat, bright green, and beautiful. Did I forget to mention delicious? What more could a soup hope to be?

Place the potatoes, onion, garlic, water, salt, and mustard in a soup pot or Dutch oven. Bring to a boil, then cover and simmer very slowly for about 20 minutes.

Use a food processor or a blender to purée the soup with all its solids, adding the spinach and fresh herbs along the way. You will definitely need to do this in several batches.

Return the soup to the pot and heat slowly. Serve hot, with a drizzle of yogurt and a dusting of mild paprika on top, if desired.

Yield: 6 or more servings
Preparation time: 50 minutes (25 minutes of work; slightly longer if made with fresh spinach)

Mollie Katzen's VEGETABLE HEAVEN

COCONUT-LEMON GRASS SOUP

It's good to know you can make a vegetarian version of this Thai classic (usually chicken-based) without compromising any of its personality—and without having to search for exotic, hard-to-find ingredients. The only unusual item here is lemon grass, for which you can substitute about 5 bags of lemon grass (or lemon verbena) tea.

NOTES: The vegetables are flexible, so if you can't find all of them, use just some, or substitute others. Also, the infusion can be made well ahead. In fact, it tastes best if made the day before and left to steep overnight.

The Infusion

Combine all the infusion ingredients in large saucepan and bring to a boil. Cover, remove from heat, and allow to infuse for at least 2 hours, but preferably overnight.

Strain the infusion into the soup (as indicated below). Or, if you are not planning to make the rest of the soup right away, strain the infusion into a jar with a tight-fitting lid, and refrigerate until use. It will keep up to a week. Let it warm to room temperature before adding it to the soup.

The Rest of the Soup

Heat the oil in a soup pot or Dutch oven. Add the onion, garlic, ginger, and about half the salt. Sauté over medium heat for about 5 minutes, or until the onion becomes translucent.

Stir in the cauliflower, carrot, cabbage, mushrooms, optional corn, and remaining salt, and cover. Continue to cook for about 10 more minutes, stirring occasionally. Stir in the zucchini or summer squash and bell pepper, and cook for just a minute or two longer.

Strain the infusion into the soup, and heat to not-quite-boiling. Turn the heat down, and simmer for just a minute or two. Stir in the tofu and basil, and add lemon juice to taste.

Serve hot, topped with a little cayenne, if you'd like it a touch hotter.

Yield: 6 to 8 servings
Total time: 1 hour, plus 2 to 24 hours for the infusion (20 minutes of work)

The Infusion

1½ cups dry white wine

4 14-ounce cans lowfat coconut milk

12 cloves garlic, peeled and bruised

6 stalks lemon grass, cut into 2-inch pieces and bruised

12 slices fresh ginger (¼-inch thick)

2 jalapeño chiles (3 inches long), cut in half

The Rest of the Soup

1 tablespoon vegetable oil

1½ cups minced onion

1 tablespoon minced garlic

1 tablespoon minced fresh ginger

2¼ teaspoons salt

2 cups cauliflower, broken into tiny florets

1 medium carrot, diced

2 cups chopped cabbage

About 10 small mushrooms, quartered

1 cup baby corn, cut into 1-inch sections (optional)

1 small zucchini or yellow summer squash, thinly sliced

1 small red bell pepper, in short, thin strips

⅓ pound tofu, diced

1½ cups (packed) basil leaves, coarsely chopped

1 to 3 tablespoons fresh lemon juice

Cayenne for the top (optional)

ZUPPA DI VERDURE

Color is the theme in this Italian vegetable soup, which is a light variation on the classic minestrone. If you have access to some ripe yellow or orange tomatoes, they will make it look especially beautiful. The vegetables are quite flexible, so if you can't get your hands on the ones listed below, just substitute something similar.

I love this soup with a spoonful of Tapenade and a sprinkling of grated cheese added just before serving. It's also good plain, with the Tapenade spread on slices of crisp toast and served on the side.

NOTE: This soup keeps for several days and reheats very well, as long as you don't boil or otherwise overcook it. It also freezes well if stored in an airtight container.

2 tablespoons olive oil

1 medium-sized onion, minced

1 medium-sized stalk celery, minced

1 large carrot, diced

2 teaspoons salt

About 10 large mushrooms, minced or sliced

A handful or two of fresh green beans, trimmed and cut into 1-inch pieces

3 tablespoons minced garlic

1 teaspoon dried oregano or marjoram (or 1 tablespoon fresh, if available)

2 to 3 stalks ruby chard, chopped (include stems, but keep them separate)

6 cups water

2 small (6-inch) zucchini, diced or sliced

½ cup (packed) minced fresh basil leaves

1 15-ounce can navy or pea beans, thoroughly rinsed and drained

3 medium-sized ripe tomatoes, peeled, seeded, and chopped

OPTIONAL GARNISHES:

Tapenade (page 161)

Grated pecorino or parmesan cheese (or a good blend of Italian cheeses)

Slices of crisp toast

Heat 1 tablespoon of the olive oil in a soup pot or Dutch oven. Add the onion, celery, carrot, and ½ teaspoon salt, and sauté over medium heat for about 5 minutes.

Stir in the mushrooms, green beans, garlic, oregano or marjoram, and another ½ teaspoon salt. Sauté for a few minutes more, then cover and cook over low heat for 15 minutes. Add the chard stems, and sauté again for a minute or two.

Pour in the water and the remaining salt. Bring to a boil, then lower the heat to a simmer. Cover and cook for 10 minutes.

Stir in the chard leaves, zucchini, basil, navy or pea beans, and tomatoes, and bring to a boil. Cover, remove from heat, and let the soup sit for about 10 minutes before serving.

Serve hot, topped with a spoonful of Tapenade, some grated cheese, and slices of crisp toast on the side, if desired.

Yield: 6 servings
Preparation time: 40 minutes (10 minutes of work)

★ For a menu suggestion, see page 211.

CREAMY SUNCHOKE SOUP

A native American vegetable, the sunchoke (also known as Jerusalem arti-choke) is the tuber of a pretty yellow sunflower. The tuber itself is knobby and homely, but it has a lovely, mild flavor and a fantastic crisp texture when eaten raw. It also cooks very nicely—baked, boiled and mashed, or sautéed. In this soup, the sunchokes are cooked until they are very soft, then puréed. Texture is critical here, so make sure you get the soup really smooth. (A good blender will do this better than a food processor.)

Peel the sunchokes, or just scrub them well with a stiff brush, and chop them coarsely.

Melt the butter or heat the oil in a soup pot or Dutch oven. Add the onion and salt, and stir well. Cover and cook for about 10 minutes over medium-low heat, stirring a few times. You want the onion to get very soft, but not brown.

Stir in the sunchokes, cover again, and cook for 5 minutes.

Add the water and sugar or honey, and bring to a boil. Turn the heat way down, cover, and simmer for 20 to 30 minutes, or until the sunchokes are tender enough to be pierced easily with a fork. Sunchokes tend to cook unevenly, so test more than one to make sure they are all very soft.

Purée bit by bit in a blender, adding the buttermilk in batches as you go. Return to a clean pot, add white pepper to taste, and adjust the salt, if necessary.

Heat very gently (don't boil), and serve hot, topped with a few crou-tons, if desired, and a dusting of mild paprika to give it a finished look.

Yield: About 6 servings
Preparation time: A little over an hour (15 minutes of work)

1½ pounds sunchokes

1 tablespoon butter or vegetable oil

2 cups minced onion

1 teaspoon salt (possibly more, to taste)

4 cups water

1 teaspoon sugar or honey

2 cups buttermilk

½ teaspoon white pepper (or to taste)

Croutons (optional)

Mild paprika for the top

⭐ *This soup will keep for several days if stored in an airtight container in the refrigerator.*

TUNISIAN TOMATO SOUP
WITH CHICKPEAS AND LENTILS

1 cup uncooked chickpeas, soaked overnight (or 1 to 2 15-ounce cans chickpeas)

1 cup uncooked lentils (any kind), rinsed and picked over

1 cinnamon stick

2 tablespoons olive oil

4 cups minced onion

2 tablespoons minced garlic

2 teaspoons salt

1 teaspoon turmeric

1½ teaspoons cumin seeds

2 teaspoons ground cumin

2 to 3 bay leaves

1 28-ounce can crushed tomatoes

Black pepper and cayenne to taste

3 tablespoons fresh lemon juice (or to taste)

OPTIONAL TOPPINGS:

Yogurt

Minced fresh parsley or mint

A few currants

⭐ *Streamline the preparation time by chopping the onions, mincing the garlic, and sautéing them with the seasonings while the legumes cook.*

⭐ *This soup freezes well if stored in an airtight container.*

⭐ *For a menu suggestion, see page 212.*

It seems like an ordinary list of ingredients, but when they are combined in this very satisfying soup, the flavors transcend the sum of their parts.

Place the soaked, uncooked chickpeas in a large pot and cover with water by 3 inches. Bring to a boil, lower heat to a simmer, partially cover, and cook for 1 hour. (If you're using canned chickpeas, rinse and drain them, and set them aside.)

Add the lentils and cinnamon stick, partially cover again, and cook for another 30 minutes, or until the chickpeas and lentils are perfectly tender, but not mushy. (If you're using canned chickpeas, just cook the lentils with the cinnamon stick in 7 cups water until tender—about 30 minutes.) Remove and discard the cinnamon stick, and drain the legumes, saving the water, if any is left.

Meanwhile, heat the oil in a soup pot or Dutch oven. Add the onion, garlic, salt, turmeric, cumin seeds, ground cumin, and bay leaves, and sauté over medium heat for 5 to 8 minutes, or until the onions are soft.

Add 6 cups of water (including the reserved cooking water from the lentils, if any) and the tomatoes, and bring to a boil. Lower the heat to a simmer, partially cover, and cook for another 15 minutes or so. (The timing does not need to be exact.) Fish out and discard the bay leaves.

Stir in the chickpeas and lentils, and cook for only about 5 minutes longer, so the legumes won't become mushy. Season to taste with black pepper, cayenne, and lemon juice.

Serve hot, topped with some yogurt, a sprinkling of parsley or mint, and currants, if desired.

Yield: 6 servings (maybe a little more)
Preparation time: About 80 minutes with dried chickpeas; 50 minutes with canned chickpeas (25 minutes of work either way)

A DOZEN TASTY BITES

Hail ye, small sweet courtesies of life,
for smooth do ye make the road of it.

—Laurence Sterne, *Tristram Shandy*

Y ou can serve these flavor-packed touches singly or in various combinations, as
miniature palate-teasing snacks, accompaniments to soups or sandwiches, or as downright remarkable salad garnishes. When you
have gone the extra mile (or I should say, the
extra inch) to create these delightful edible expe-
riences, you will light up the moment for your
family and friends, making them feel truly
loved.

Some (but not all) of these recipes require a
little bit of work, so consider inviting a friend
over and making them together while you visit.
It's a lovely way to spend some time.

A DOZEN TASTY BITES

ALMOND-STUFFED OLIVES AND DATES

It takes a little bit of work to assemble these bite-sized treats, but it's fun, especially if you turn on some music and make it a relaxing activity. You might say the process is as meaningful as the product here.

Almond-Stuffed Olives and Dates provide a truly special touch when added to any meal—before, during, or after—or served as a snack.

Preheat the oven to 325°F. Spread the almonds on an ungreased baking tray, and toast them in the oven until they turn light golden brown (about 15 minutes). Watch them carefully so they don't burn. When they look and smell just right to you, remove them from the oven, and allow to cool.

Meanwhile, pit the olives and dates. (The easiest way to remove the pit from a ripe olive is to make a little slit at one end, and squeeze. The pit should slip right out.)

Firmly insert one almond into each olive and date, pushing it in as far as possible, and wrapping the fruit around it.

Make a beautiful arrangement on a plate, cover tightly, and refrigerate until use.

Yield: 6 servings (2 dates and 4 olives per serving)
Preparation time: about 30 to 40 minutes

---

3 dozen blanched whole almonds

2 dozen oil-cured or Kalamata olives

1 dozen whole dates

★ *This recipe calls for blanched almonds. You can buy them already blanched, or do it yourself. Just soak them for a few minutes in a bowlful of boiling water, then rub off and discard the skins. You can do this, and then toast the almonds way ahead of time.*

★ *The riper the olives, the easier they are to pit and stuff. (Green olives cling to their pits, and you have to slice them off. Also, they are harder, and don't mold themselves around the almonds as well as riper olives.)*

★ *If you have sensitive skin, wear gloves when pitting olives.*

★ *For a menu suggestion, see page 213.*

MINIATURE POTATO DUMPLINGS
WITH SAGE AND CHIVES

1 pound potatoes

1½ cups unbleached white flour (plus a little extra)

1 teaspoon salt (plus a little extra to sprinkle on later)

2 to 3 tablespoons milk

1 to 2 tablespoons butter for sautéing

Dried rubbed sage

Minced fresh or freeze-dried chives

Crisp on the outside and chewy on the inside, these intensely flavored little mouthfuls are hard to stop eating. They make a magnificent if diminutive appetizer, and also go very well alongside almost any soup.

Boil the potatoes in plenty of water until soft. Drain, and set aside to cool.

When they are cool enough to comfortably handle, peel the potatoes with a sharp paring knife, and "rice" them in a ricer or the grating attachment of a food processor. (You should have about 3 cups cooked, riced potatoes.) Transfer to a medium-sized bowl.

Add 1½ cups flour and 1 teaspoon salt to the potatoes. Mix first with a spoon and then with your hand to make a dough. Add the milk a little at a time as needed, so the dough becomes soft and workable. You want it pliable but not sticky.

Put up a large pot of salted water to boil.

Meanwhile, lightly flour a clean, dry surface. Turn out the dough and push it together with your hands, but don't otherwise knead. Divide the dough in two, and roll each piece until it is about ½ inch thick. Use a plain dinner knife to cut 1-inch squares (or diamonds, or triangles, or rhomboids, or whatever).

Mollie Katzen's VEGETABLE HEAVEN

When the water boils, turn it down to a simmer, and add as many pieces of dough as will fit without crowding. They will soon rise to the surface of the simmering water. Cook them for 3 minutes, then scoop them out with a strainer or a slotted spoon and put them on a plate. Continue with another batch until all the dumplings are poached. At this point, they can be stored in an airtight container in the refrigerator for up to 3 days.

Heat a large nonstick skillet and add about a tablespoon of butter. When it is melted, add as many dumplings as will comfortably fit in a single layer and sprinkle lightly with salt. Lower the heat to medium, and sauté the dumplings on one side for 8 to 10 minutes, or until golden brown.

Sprinkle with the sage and chives, and turn the dumplings over. Sauté another 8 to 10 minutes, then transfer to a plate lined with paper towels. Serve as soon as possible.

Yield: 55 to 60 bite-sized treasures
Preparation time: 1 hour (30 minutes of work)

★ You can use any kind of potato for these. If you choose a baking variety, like a russet, the dumplings will come out fluffier, with a lighter potato flavor. Boiling varieties, like Yukon Gold or Yellow Finn, will yield denser dumplings with a richer potato flavor

★ For chewier, crisper dumplings, let them dry out on paper towels for about 20 to 30 minutes between poaching and sautéing.

★ Much of this recipe can be done well in advance. However, the dumplings taste best if served soon after they are sautéed.

★ For a menu suggestion, see page 211.

A DOZEN TASTY BITES

GREEN ONION WONTON STRIPS

Think of these as Chinese-style crackers. They go beautifully with just about any soup or salad, and are also a lovely appetizer, served plain or with a dip or sauce. This recipe scores big with children, who also love to help make the dough.

1⅓ cups unbleached white flour (possibly more)

3 medium-sized scallions, very finely minced

½ teaspoon salt

½ cup water

Extra flour for handling the dough

Vegetable oil for the pan

Chinese sesame oil

⭐ *You can easily whip up the dough in a food processor fitted with the steel blade. It will only take a few seconds.*

⭐ *Store these in an airtight container at room temperature for up to a week. (They'll <u>keep</u> that long, but probably won't <u>last</u> that long, if you know what I mean.)*

⭐ *For a menu suggestion, see page 212.*

Place the flour, scallions, and salt in a medium-sized bowl. Add the water, and stir until fairly well combined.

Transfer the dough to a clean, floured surface, and knead for a few minutes, adding additional flour, as needed, to keep it from sticking.

Divide the dough into 6 equal balls, and roll each one into a very thin circle, about 7 inches in diameter. Use plenty of flour, both on the rolling surface and the rolling pin. Stack the pancakes on a plate, sprinkling extra flour in between to keep them separate.

Heat a heavy skillet over medium heat, and brush it lightly with vegetable oil. Sauté each pancake for 5 minutes on each side, then brush the top surface with Chinese sesame oil. (If you'd like them crisper, sauté them a little longer.)

Cut the pancakes into strips (once down the middle, then about 8 cuts across).

Transfer to a plate, and cool for at least 10 minutes before serving.

Yield: About 90 bite-sized pieces (plenty for 6 people)
Preparation time: 35 minutes (15 minutes of work)

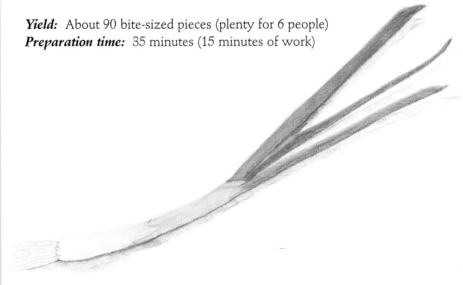

CROSTINI

In the United States, we eat toast with butter and cinnamon or jam for break-
fast or as a late-night comfort food. But in Italy, toast (crostini) is prepared and
eaten in a whole different context. It is a savory treat, brushed with garlic and
olive oil, and served with savory toppings—as an appetizer, antipasto, or mid-
day snack.

   It's fun to make a platter of assorted crostini. Garnish it lavishly, and serve
it to your delighted guests along with bowls of soup, for a wonderful light
supper.

Basic Crostini Recipe

Preheat the oven to 375°F. Combine the olive oil and garlic in a
small bowl, and set aside.

Cut the baguette into ½-inch slices, and brush each slice lightly on
both sides with the olive oil-garlic mixture. Lay the slices flat on an
ungreased baking tray and bake on the center rack of the oven until
the bread begins to crispen, but is still a little chewy (about 10 to
12 minutes).

Remove from the oven and serve hot, warm, or at room temperature, topped with whatever is appealing and available.

¼ to ⅓ cup extra virgin olive oil

2 small cloves garlic, minced or
   crushed

1 good-quality baguette, 2 to 3
   inches in diameter

Optional assorted toppings (list of
   suggestions follows)

POSSIBLE TOPPINGS:

Goat cheese, fresh mozzarella, or
   fresh ricotta cheese, with a leaf
   of basil and a small slice of ripe
   tomato

Tapenade (page 161)

Red Pepper-Walnut Paste (page 159)

Chimichurri (page 165)

Red Onion and Shallot Marmalade
   (page 162)

GuacaMollie (page 158)

Leftover Roasted Eggplant Salad
   (page 8)

Leftover Roasted Vegetables
   (pages 96 through 99) with a
   drizzle of Vinaigrette (page173)

Anything else you can think of

PARMESAN CRISPS

Cheese crackers in the most literal sense, these are about as crisp as crispy gets. You simply melt thin little piles of plain parmesan cheese in a heavy skillet—without oil, butter, or any additional seasoning—then cook them until crisp. Use Parmesan Crisps as you would any cheese-flavored cracker—for snacking or garnishing. It's especially fun to crumble these on top of pasta dishes and green salads.

Place a cast-iron skillet (or a similar heavy skillet, ideally nonstick) over medium heat.

Measure out the cheese by heaping tablespoons, and place each spoonful in a little pile in the pan. Spread each mound into a 2½-inch round. It's okay if they are close together.

Sauté the wafers on each side for about 3 minutes, or until golden brown and crisp. Transfer to a plate and allow to cool for a few minutes. (You will definitely need to cook these in several batches.)

Yield: About 25 wafers
Preparation time: About 15 minutes

½ **pound grated parmesan cheese**

★ *Store Parmesan Crisps in a covered container (no refrigeration necessary). Theoretically, they'll keep for weeks, but you will probably eat them all much sooner than that.*

★ *For a menu suggestion, see page 211.*

BAKED COATED NUTS
SWEET OR SAVORY

Here are two different approaches to enhancing nuts. Either version makes a great snack or an impressive garnish for vegetable dishes, salads, or grains. Try putting out a bowlful of sweet or savory Baked Coated Nuts at the end of a large meal, with or after dessert. It's a loving touch.
  NOTE: Each batch yields 4 cups.

Sweet Coated Nuts

Preheat the oven to 400°F. Lightly grease a baking tray or a jelly roll pan with vegetable oil.

Place the egg whites in a shallow pan (like a pie pan), and beat in the salt and sugar. Add the nuts in several installments, and stir each batch until they are thoroughly coated.

Transfer the coated nuts to the prepared pan, and spread them out in a single layer. Bake for 15 to 20 minutes, stirring frequently, until they are golden brown.

Remove the nuts from the oven, and let them cool on the tray. When they are cool, transfer them to a bowl for instant pleasure, or to a container with a tight-fitting lid for delayed gratification.

Preparation time: 25 to 30 minutes (10 minutes of work)

Savory Coated Nuts

Preheat the oven to 275°F. Lightly grease a baking tray.

Beat together the eggs, soy sauce, and salt in a medium-large bowl. Add the nuts and stir until they are thoroughly moistened. Let stand 5 minutes.

Spread the wheat germ on a large piece of waxed paper. Use a slotted spoon to scoop up the nuts a few at a time, plop them down onto the wheat germ, and roll them around until they are well coated.

Arrange the nuts on the prepared tray in a single layer. (It's okay if some of them are clustered together.) Bake undisturbed for 1¼ hours. Cool on the tray, then store in a tightly lidded jar.

Preparation time: 1½ hours (15 minutes of work)

Sweet Coated Nuts

A little vegetable oil for the pan

2 egg whites

½ teaspoon salt

4 to 6 tablespoons sugar

4 cups walnut or pecan halves

Savory Coated Nuts

A little oil for the baking tray

2 large eggs

2 tablespoons soy sauce

1 teaspoon salt

2 cups wheat germ

4 cups nuts (any combination of whole almonds, cashew pieces, walnuts, or pecans)

⋆ *These keep well in an airtight container in the refrigerator or freezer, if they get the opportunity.*

KALE CRUNCH

Try these fascinating, sophisticated "chips" for snacking or for sprinkling on just about any savory dish.

Baking kale is an interesting process. First, the leaves become bright green and soften, then they begin to turn crisp. In between, they go through a chewy-crisp stage, which is also delicious. So the baking time is flexible. Just keep checking the kale until it is done the way you like it.

Preheat the oven to 350°F. Line a large baking tray with foil, then brush or spray it with oil.

Add the kale, and spread it out as much as possible.

Bake for 10 minutes, mixing it up once or twice during that time. Sprinkle with parmesan, if desired, and bake for 10 to 15 minutes longer, stirring occasionally, until it's as crisp as you like it. The kale will continue to shrink and crispen the longer it bakes. If you watch it closely and stir it often enough, you can get it quite crisp without burning it.

Remove the tray from the oven, and let the kale cool on the tray.

Yield: 2 to 4 cups (depending on how long you leave it in the oven)
Preparation time: 30 minutes (10 minutes of work)

A little olive oil or oil spray for the baking tray

1 giant bunch fresh kale, stemmed and minced (about 1 pound)

2 to 3 tablespoons grated parmesan cheese (optional)

★ *Kale Crunch will keep for a week or two in a covered container—no refrigeration necessary.*

★ *For a menu suggestion, see page 211.*

FRIZZLED LEEKS

A chewy-crisp flavor enhancer for many salads and soups, Frizzled Leeks keep well for over a week if stored in a tightly covered container in the refrigerator.

Clean the leeks thoroughly and slice them paper-thin, either in rounds or half-rounds. Dry on paper towels, and set aside.

Preheat the oven to 400°F. Line a baking tray with foil, and place a double thickness of paper towels on a dinner plate.

Heat the oil in a medium-sized skillet over medium-high heat for 30 seconds or so. Add the leeks to the hot oil, and sauté for 5 minutes, stirring frequently with a long-handled fork or with chopsticks.

Transfer the leeks to the foil-lined baking tray, and bake for 15 minutes, stirring them about every 5 minutes. (They can easily burn if you get distracted and forget to watch them closely. So don't answer the phone until they're done.)

Transfer the leeks to the paper towel-lined plate, and spread them out in a single layer. Sprinkle lightly with salt, and let cool for about 15 minutes.

Store in a tightly covered container, and use as desired.

Yield: 2 cups
Preparation time: 25 minutes (10 minutes of your full attention, plus 15 minutes of intermittent stirring)

8 leeks, 1-inch in diameter
   (about 1½ pounds)
2 tablespoons olive oil
Salt to taste

★ *Try these on Roasted Eggplant Salad (page 8) Vegetarian Salade Niçoise (page 15) Rich Mushroom Broth (page 30) or on anything else you can think of.*

★ *For a menu suggestion, see page 212.*

CHERRY TOMATO CHEWIES

Transform ordinary cherry tomatoes into a delicacy. The process is similar to making oven-dried tomatoes, but some moisture is left in, so the tomatoes become wonderfully chewy, retaining and intensifying their natural sweet and tart qualities.

Olive oil for the baking tray

1 pound cherry tomatoes
    (1-inch-diameter)

⋯⋯⋯⋯⋯⋯⋯⋯⋯⋯

★ *Serve Cherry Tomato Chewies as a garnish, for snacks, or on sandwiches or grains. Float them in soups, or sprinkle them on top of a platter of roasted vegetables. They are truly delightful and versatile.*

★ *Cherry tomatoes are at their peak during the summer, when you might not want your oven on for two hours. So maybe you'd like the option of making these in the winter instead. No problem! Just cut the fresh tomatoes in half and freeze them until solid in a single layer on a plate or tray. Then gather them into a plastic bag, seal, and store indefinitely in the freezer. You don't need to defrost them before they go into the oven.*

★ *For a menu suggestion, see page 211.*

Preheat the oven to 275°F. Line a baking tray with foil and brush it generously with olive oil.

Cut the tomatoes in half, and arrange them cut side up in a single layer on the prepared tray. (It's okay if they are touching.)

Bake for 2 to 6 hours, jostling them loose and moving them slightly every half hour or so, so they don't stick and/or burn. Don't actually turn them over. They come out best if left facing up for the duration of the baking.

Transfer the tomatoes to a platter lined with a double thickness of paper towels and cool for at least 30 minutes. Store them in a tightly covered container in the refrigerator for softer, moister Chewies, or leave them uncovered and out of the refrigerator, and they will dry out a bit more and become somewhat crispy. They're lovely both ways.

Yield: 1½ cups Chewies (easily multiplied)
Preparation time: Up to 7 hours (10 minutes of work)

MUSHROOM PICKLES

Here's a lemony wake-up call for your taste buds, just in case they've been getting bored lately.

Combine the water, lemon juice, salt, thyme, peppercorns, coriander, and garlic in a medium-sized saucepan. Heat the mixture just to a boil, then stir in the honey until it dissolves, and turn the heat down to a simmer.

Add the mushrooms, and cook uncovered over very low heat for about 15 minutes. Cool to room temperature, then transfer to a tightly lidded container and chill.

Yield: 4 to 6 tasty little servings
Preparation time: 30 minutes, plus time to chill (10 minutes of work)

¾ cup water

¼ cup fresh lemon juice

1 teaspoon salt

A few sprigs of fresh thyme

1 teaspoon peppercorns

1 teaspoon coriander seeds

6 small whole garlic cloves

2 tablespoons honey

1½ pounds button mushrooms (the smallest you can find), cleaned and stemmed

★ *Mushroom Pickles will keep for a week or more, if kept tightly covered in the refrigerator.*

★ *These go beautifully with a sandwich or a bowl of soup.*

CARROT PICKLES

Light, refreshing, and ridiculously easy, these not only keep well, but actually get better over time.

Serve Carrot Pickles with any salad, sandwich, or main dish. Or just open the jar and nibble while you're trying to figure out what else to cook.

1½ cups water

¼ cup balsamic vinegar

1 teaspoon salt

1 tablespoon mustard seeds

2 tablespoons honey

1½ pounds baby carrots

6 to 8 medium-sized cloves garlic

2 large sprigs of fresh dill
(possibly more)

Place the water in a medium-sized saucepan with 2 tablespoons of the vinegar, and the salt and mustard seeds. Heat just to boiling, then stir in the honey until it dissolves.

Add the carrots, garlic, and dill, and lower the heat to a simmer. Cook uncovered for about 10 minutes, or until the carrots are as tender as you like them.

Cool to room temperature, then add the remaining 2 tablespoons vinegar and another sprig or two of dill, if desired.

Transfer to a tightly lidded container and chill.

Yield: 12 servings, or more (depending greatly on the context)
Preparation time: 25 minutes, plus time to chill (5 minutes of work)

PICKLED RED ONIONS

Red onions have a secret talent: they turn a beautiful, bright shade of pur-plish pink when doused with hot water and then stay crunchy and delicious seemingly forever.

Serve Pickled Red Onions in every imaginable context: next to or over hot or cold bean and grain dishes, with (or in) salads or sandwiches, on toast or crackers, with hors d'oeuvres—you name it.

Peel the onions and slice them as thin as you possibly can. Transfer them to a medium-sized bowl.

Pour the boiling water into the bowl, and let the onions soak in the boiling water for 5 minutes. Drain thoroughly in a colander.

While the onions sit in the colander, combine the marinade ingredients in the same bowl, and mix well. Stir in the onions, and let them sit in the marinade for about 10 minutes.

Transfer the onions with all the liquid to a jar with a tight-fitting lid, and chill until very cold.

Yield: About 3½ cups
Preparation time: 20 minutes, plus time to chill (10 minutes of work)

2 medium-sized red onions (about 1 pound)

4 cups boiling water

Marinade

½ cup cider vinegar or unseasoned rice vinegar

½ cup water

3 tablespoons honey or sugar

½ to 1 teaspoon salt

1 teaspoon peppercorns

½ teaspoon whole cloves (optional)

★ *These keep for months if stored in a tightly-lidded jar in the refrigerator.*

★ *For a menu suggestion, see page 212.*

SIDE-BY-SIDE DISHES

Beans, Grains, and Vegetables

One pleasure of the cook is that now and then you learn all over again.

—**Frances Mayes**, *Under the Tuscan Sun*

*U*nlike the "old days," when I used to make one large, heavy entrée and several smaller dishes to serve "on the side," this is the way I cook now: I make several simple dishes out of beans, grains, and vegetables, and serve them together in various configurations. Side-by-Side meals (as I call these) have a fresh, spontaneous quality, with each component receiving equal emphasis. And they are actually easier to prepare than the old center-of-the-plate model.

The Side-By-Side format works very well for vegetarian meals, as the beans and grains provide complementary proteins. And because many of the seemingly disparate dishes in this section go surprisingly well together, you can use the following table of contents as a menu-planning guide. Just mix 'n match, as the saying goes. You might come up with some fantastic combinations.

SIDE-BY-SIDE DISHES
Beans, Grains, and Vegetables

ROASTED BEANS
WITH GARLIC AND OLIVES

3 tablespoons extra virgin olive oil

1 1-pound package frozen lima beans (or 3 to 4 cups fresh favas, shelled and peeled)

6 large cloves garlic, peeled and halved (or quartered lengthwise)

1 heaping cup green olives, pitted and sliced

1 to 2 tablespoons minced fresh herbs (1 to 2 teaspoons dried): summer savory, marjoram, thyme, and/or sage

Salt and pepper to taste

....

I like to make this with only one or two herbs, to keep it simple. My favorite combination is sage and savory, but you can use whatever combination of herbs appeals to you.

Try to use a top-quality extra virgin olive oil in this recipe. It really makes a difference.

Serve this with any combination of grains and vegetables, or even by itself as a nutritious, very unusual snack.

For a menu suggestion, look at page 213.

Try this new twist on the Baked Bean Concept. You simply toss the beans with garlic, olives, and seasonings in a pan, cover, and roast everything together in the oven.

This dish is especially convenient because it can be made with frozen lima beans, straight from the freezer. It requires only a few minutes of your efforts, then bakes into a fabulous dish all by itself with no further help from you. If you can get fresh fava beans and have the time to shell and peel them, by all means use them instead of the frozen limas. The finished dish will be just that much more special.

Preheat the oven to 375°F. Spread 2 tablespoons olive oil into a 6 x 9-inch baking pan or an oval gratin pan.

Toss everything together directly into the pan and sprinkle with a little salt and pepper. Cover the pan tightly with foil.

Bake for 50 minutes or until the garlic is tender when pierced with a toothpick or a fork. Transfer to a bowl, and stir. If desired, you can drizzle on a little extra olive oil and add more salt and pepper to taste.

Serve hot, warm, or at room temperature.

Yield: 4 to 5 servings (depending on what goes with it)
Preparation time: 1 hour (10 minutes of work)

GREEN AND WHITE BEANS
UNDER GARLIC MASHED POTATOES

The ideal beans for this special, savory deep-dish entrée are Christmas limas or Great Northern beans, available dried in many stores. If you can't find them, substitute with a smaller, more common variety of dried lima bean, or use frozen, defrosted lima beans.

Cook the soaked beans in plenty of gently simmering water for approximately 1 to 1¼ hours. Start checking the beans after about 45 minutes of cooking, so they don't overcook and become too soft. (If you are using frozen lima beans, boil them in plenty of water until they are tender.) Transfer to a colander, rinse under cold water, drain well, and set aside.

Meanwhile, boil the potatoes until very soft. Drain, transfer to a medium-large bowl, and add the butter, milk, 1 tablespoon of the garlic, and ½ teaspoon salt. Mash well and set aside.

Heat the olive oil in a large, deep sauté pan or a Dutch oven. Add the leeks, ½ teaspoon salt, and thyme. Stir, cover, and cook over medium-low heat for about 10 minutes. Add the remaining tablespoon garlic, and cook for just 5 minutes, stirring.

Sprinkle in the flour, nutmeg, and black pepper to taste, and stir well. Add the water, stir again, and cook for about 5 more minutes. Stir in the cooked limas, and the green beans, spinach, and remaining ½ teaspoon salt, and cook for a minute or two—just long enough for the spinach to begin to wilt. Remove from heat. The green beans will be barely cooked.

Preheat the oven to 375°F. Transfer the bean mixture to a large oval gratin pan or a 9 x 13-inch baking pan. Spread the potatoes over the beans and vegetables—all the way to the edge. Sprinkle the grated cheese over the top, and pat it into place. If desired, add a light dusting of paprika. Bake uncovered for 35 to 40 minutes—or until golden brown on top. Serve hot.

Yield: 6 servings (possibly more, depending on what goes with it)
Preparation time: 1¾ hours (30 minutes of work)

1½ cups dried white beans, soaked (or 2 1-pound bags frozen lima beans)

2 pounds potatoes, peeled and cubed

1 tablespoon butter

6 tablespoons milk

2 heaping tablespoons minced garlic

1½ teaspoons salt

1½ tablespoons olive oil

2 cups chopped leeks (squeaky clean)

1 teaspoon dried thyme

2 tablespoons flour

½ teaspoon nutmeg

Black pepper

1 cup water

1 pound green beans, trimmed and cut into 1½-inch pieces

1 pound spinach (or a 10-ounce package frozen, chopped spinach, defrosted and drained)

¾ cup grated gruyère cheese

Paprika for the top (optional)

. . . .

Soak the dried beans ahead of time for at least 4 hours.

To streamline preparation time, cook the potatoes and leeks while the limas are cooking.

This dish reheats beautifully in an oven or microwave—the gruyère cheese comes alive.

For a menu suggestion, see page 212.

SOFT LENTILS
WITH ROASTED TOMATOES AND CARAMELIZED ONIONS

Oil or oil spray for the pan

1 tablespoon olive oil

1 tablespoon butter

3 cups minced onion

1½ teaspoons salt

1 cup minced roasted tomatoes
   (or 1 cup diced canned tomatoes)

1 tablespoon brown sugar

1 tablespoon balsamic vinegar

8 cups well-cooked lentils

Black pepper to taste

Pitted, sliced green olives
   (optional garnish)

· ·

About the lentils: Red lentils cook more quickly and are a prettier color than the green or French varieties. That said, you can use any kind of lentil for this dish, and it will come out fine.

Both the lentils and the tomatoes can be prepared well ahead of time.

About the tomatoes: Roast about 6 plum or Roma tomatoes—or 3 large beefsteak tomatoes—as per the instructions on page 98. Peel, seed, and mince them, then measure out 1 cup to use in this dish. If you're short on time, you can substitute 1 cup canned diced tomatoes.

Serve Soft Lentils with any kind of plain grain or pasta—or simply with bread and a salad. For a more elaborate scheme, see the menu suggestion on page 211.

It sounds complicated, but this dish is actually a snap to make. All the components can be prepared well ahead of time with almost no effort, then you just combine everything and bake it. The results are heavenly.

   NOTE: To get 8 cups of cooked lentils for this dish, begin with 4 cups dried. Rinse them well, place them in a pot with 10 cups of water, bring to a boil, then simmer until very soft (20 minutes for red lentils; 30 to 40 minutes for green or French). After you measure out the 8 cups needed for this recipe, you will probably have some left over. You can add the extra lentils to a vegetable soup, a salad, or some cooked grains.

Preheat the oven to 350°F. Lightly oil—or oil-spray—a shallow 9 x 13-inch casserole dish or a large oval gratin pan.

Heat the olive oil in a large, deep skillet or Dutch oven, then add the butter and let it melt into the oil. Stir in the onion and salt, and cook, covered, over low heat for about 30 minutes, stirring often. The onions should be very soft and golden. Add the tomatoes, cover, and cook for another 15 to 20 minutes, stirring frequently.

Add all the remaining ingredients except the olives, and stir well. Transfer to the prepared baking pan, cover tightly with foil, and bake for about 45 minutes, or until heated through.

Serve hot, topped with a scattering of sliced green olives, if desired.

Yield: 6 servings
Cooking time: 1½ hours (15 minutes of work)

PERSIAN KIDNEY BEANS

It looks especially pretty when this soothing dish is sprinkled with minced red chiles and orange and lime zest just before serving. Try it with plain basmati rice, or with any component of Persian Layered Pilafs (page 84). For an unusual lunch treat, serve Persian Kidney Beans in pita bread with Mediterranean Yogurt (page 169).

Heat the oil in a deep saucepan or Dutch oven. Add the onion, and sauté for about 5 minutes over medium heat. Add the garlic, salt, cumin, and cinnamon, and sauté for about 5 minutes longer over slightly lower heat.

Stir in the juices and tomato paste until well combined. Cook for about 10 minutes, uncovered, over very low heat.

Add the beans, citrus zests, and a little hot pepper, and stir gently. Bring to a boil, cover, and reduce heat. Cook for about 20 minutes, keeping the heat low, and stirring often.

Taste to adjust the seasonings, then serve hot, topped with a little more zest and some minced chiles or red pepper flakes.

Yield: 6 to 8 servings
Preparation time: 45 minutes (10 minutes of work)

1 tablespoon olive oil

2 cups minced onion

1 tablespoon minced garlic

1 ½ teaspoons salt

1 ½ teaspoons ground cumin

¼ teaspoon cinnamon

1 ½ cups orange juice
(possibly more)

¼ cup fresh lime juice

2 tablespoons tomato paste

About 8 cups cooked kidney beans
(5 or 6 15-ounce cans, rinsed
and drained)

½ teaspoon lime zest (plus a little
extra for the top)

½ teaspoon orange zest (ditto for
the top)

Hot pepper (minced fresh jalapeño
chiles or red pepper flakes)

Grate the zest before squeezing the citrus juices—it's much easier this way.

FIRECRACKER
RED BEANS

"These beans have more flavor than they know what to do with."
—My husband Carl

2 tablespoons olive oil

3 cups minced onion

2 tablespoons minced fresh ginger

2 teaspoons fennel seeds

2 tablespoons minced garlic

½ teaspoon allspice

1 teaspoon dried thyme

1½ to 2 teaspoons salt

1 cup dry sherry or vermouth

2 tablespoons prepared mustard

¼ cup ketchup

1 teaspoon minced chipotle chiles

1 cup water

¼ cup almond butter

2 tablespoons brown sugar

½ cup boiling water

About 6 cups cooked small red
  beans and/or kidney beans
  (3 or 4 15-ounce cans, rinsed
  and drained)

Wedges of lime

Influenced by Jamaican-style "jerk" spices, these feisty baked beans are full of contrasting flavors—aromatic, pungent seasonings, bitter sherry or vermouth, tart lime juice, a little bit of sweetening, and a combination of hot touches that create a slow burn.

Small red beans (called "peas") are traditional in Jamaica, but kidney beans work just as well. A combination of the two is quite attractive. Serve this with plain white rice, or for a colorful flavorfest that will give people's taste buds a real workout, pair Firecracker Red Beans with Spiced Pineapple Pilaf (page 86).

Heat the oil in a large, deep skillet or a Dutch oven. When it is very hot, add the onion, ginger, and fennel seeds, and sauté over strong heat for about 5 minutes. Turn the heat down to medium, and add the garlic, allspice, thyme, and 1½ teaspoons salt. Cover and cook for about 3 minutes over medium-low heat.

Stir in the sherry or vermouth, mustard, ketchup, minced chipotle, and 1 cup water. Cover and cook for another 10 minutes.

Place the almond butter and brown sugar in a small bowl. Add the boiling water, and mash with a spoon until it becomes a uniform mixture. Stir this into the sauce, and cook uncovered over low heat for about 5 minutes. (NOTE: You can leave the sauce as it is if you like it textured, but if you prefer it smooth, transfer to a blender and purée.)

Preheat the oven to 325°F. Place the beans in a 9 x 13-inch baking dish or an equivalent casserole, and pour in all the sauce. Cover tightly with foil, and bake for 45 minutes. Remove the pan from the oven, and let it sit for about 15 to 20 minutes, still tightly covered, so the beans can continue to absorb the liquid. Serve hot or warm, with squeezable wedges of lime on the side.

Yield: 6 intense, fascinating servings
Preparation time: 2 hours (40 minutes of work)

※ *Chipotle chiles (smoked jalapeños) are available canned in adobo sauce in the imported foods section of your grocery store, or in Latin American markets. They are very strong flavored and keep forever if stored in a tightly lidded container in the refrigerator.*

※ *This dish reheats well, so you can make it up to several days ahead.*

※ *For a complete menu suggestion, see page 212.*

Mollie Katzen's VEGETABLE HEAVEN

BLACK BEANS
IN MANGO SAUCE

All you need are a couple of perfectly ripe mangoes, and you're up and running with this quick, exotic dish. To make it into a complete meal, just add some plain steamed broccoli and rice.

Wonderful though they are to eat, mangoes can be difficult to cut up without their turning to mush. The good news here is that in this dish, it doesn't matter, because the mangoes get mashed anyway. So just cut them open, scrape out the flesh, and mince as best you can.

Heat the oil in a medium-sized skillet. Add 1¾ cups of the onion, and the garlic, chile, ginger, cumin seeds, and salt. Sauté over medium-high heat for about 3 minutes.

Turn the heat down to medium-low, and add the black beans and about half the lime juice. Sauté for about 5 more minutes, or until everything has mingled nicely, and the beans are heated through. Mash the beans slightly with the back of the spoon, and transfer to a bowl.

Stir the remaining lime juice and about half of the chopped mangoes directly into the hot beans, mashing the mangoes a little as you stir. Grind in some black pepper, then cover and let stand for about 15 minutes to let the sauce develop.

Serve warm, at room temperature, or even cold, topped with the remaining red onion and mango, and some minced cilantro, if desired. For a finishing touch, tuck a juicy wedge of lime into the side of each serving.

Yield: About 6 servings, depending on what else is served
Preparation time: About 45 minutes (30 minutes of light work)

1½ tablespoons olive oil

2 cups minced red onion

1 tablespoon minced garlic

1 3-inch jalapeño chile, seeded and minced

1½ tablespoons minced fresh ginger

1½ teaspoons cumin seeds

1½ teaspoons salt

About 6 cups cooked black beans (3 15-ounce cans, rinsed and drained)

6 tablespoons fresh lime juice

2 large ripe mangoes, minced

Freshly ground black pepper to taste

Minced fresh cilantro (optional)

Squeezable wedges of lime

For a complete menu suggestion, see page 211.

DREAMY WHITE BEANS
WITH OLIVE OIL, GARLIC, AND HERBS

They really <u>are</u> dreamy: pure, rich, and deeply infused with rosemary, sage, and garlic. Serve Dreamy White Beans plain, or to confer transcendence, drizzle them lightly with olive oil and balsamic vinegar just before eating. You'll want to make these again soon.

2 cups dried white pea or navy beans, soaked (or 4 15-ounce cans, rinsed and drained)

2 large sprigs rosemary

About 12 sage leaves, tied together with a bag tie or string

1½ tablespoons minced garlic

1¼ teaspoons salt (or to taste)

Freshly ground black pepper

OPTIONAL, FOR THE TOP:

Extra virgin olive oil

Balsamic vinegar

Minced parsley

....

I don't recommend substituting dried rosemary and sage for the fresh. Much of the intensity will be lost.

You can make this dish with canned beans, if that's what you have on hand. However, you won't actually save cooking time by doing so, because you'll need to simmer the canned beans for about as long as the dried, soaked ones will need to cook.

It's fine to make this ahead of time, and reheat it in a microwave or a regular oven.

Place the soaked, uncooked beans in a large pot and cover with water by 2 inches. Add the rosemary and sage, and bring to a boil. Lower the heat, and simmer until tender (about 30 minutes). If you are using canned beans, place them in a pot with 2 cups cold water and the herbs, bring to a boil, then lower the heat and simmer for 30 minutes. Remove and discard the herbs, and drain the beans, saving the water.

Add the garlic to the hot beans. Mash or partially purée some of the beans, using some (or all) of their cooking water, until they acquire a smooth, thick consistency. (The amount of water is flexible, so do this according to your own judgment.)

Season to taste with salt and a generous amount of freshly ground black pepper. Serve topped with a drizzle of extra virgin olive oil, a small splash of balsamic vinegar, and a sprinkling of minced parsley, if desired.

Yield: About 6 servings
Preparation time: 40 minutes (10 minutes of work)

Mollie Katzen's VEGETABLE HEAVEN

SANTA FE STEW

Brimming with more spunk than you can shake a stick at, this great stew goes well with warmed corn tortillas (the thick kind, if possible). You probably won't want anything else.

Heat the oil in a large, deep skillet or Dutch oven. Add the onion, 1 teaspoon of the salt, cumin, and cinnamon. Cook over very low heat until the onion is soft (about 10 minutes), stirring frequently.

Stir in the garlic, chiles, and chile powder. Cover, and cook for about 5 minutes over medium-low heat, stirring occasionally. Add the water, cover, and cook another 15 minutes.

Stir in the squash, the remaining teaspoon of salt, and the lime juice. Cover, and cook over low heat for 15 minutes longer, or until the squash is perfectly tender, but not mushy.

Gently stir in the beans, cover, and cook for only about 5 more minutes. Taste to see if it needs more lime juice.

Serve hot, topped with a little sour cream or Chipotle Cream, a generous sprinkling of lightly toasted pepitas, and a little bit of minced cilantro or parsley, if desired.

Yield: 4 to 6 servings
Preparation time: 1 hour (15 minutes of work)

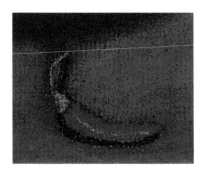

2 tablespoons olive oil

3 cups chopped onion

2 teaspoons salt

2 teaspoons cumin seeds

½ teaspoon cinnamon

4 to 5 tablespoons garlic, minced

2 medium-sized Anaheim chiles, minced

2 medium-sized poblano chiles, minced

2 tablespoons chile powder

2 cups water

1 medium-sized (2-pound) butternut squash, peeled, seeded, and chopped (about 5 cups)

4 to 5 tablespoons lime juice (possibly more, to taste)

1½ to 3 cups cooked pinto beans (1 or 2 15-ounce cans, rinsed and drained)

OPTIONAL TOPPINGS:

Sour cream or Chipotle Cream (page 166)

Lightly toasted pepitas (aka pumpkin seeds)

Minced fresh cilantro and/or parsley

You can make this more or less "beany" by adding anywhere from ½ to 3 cups of cooked beans (1 or 2 15-ounce cans).

This recipe calls for a combination of fresh Anaheim and poblano chiles. If you can't find these, substitute 2 bell peppers and a 7-ounce can of diced green chiles.

For a complete menu suggestion, see page 213.

BASIC SOYBURGERS
"DON'T KNOCK 'EM TILL YOU TRY 'EM"

1½ to 2 cups cooked soybeans
(1 15-ounce can, rinsed and
drained)

½ cup mashed tofu

1 teaspoon salt

1 to 2 large cloves garlic

1 cup minced onion

2 minced scallions

A handful of parsley

2 to 3 tablespoons minced fresh
dill (or 2 teaspoons dried)

2 tablespoons cider vinegar

2 teaspoons dry mustard

2 cups fine bread crumbs or cooked
short-grain brown rice

Vegetable oil for the pan

• •

Soak and cook dried soybeans
ahead of time, or buy canned soybeans in a natural foods store.

Soyburgers can be made with fine
bread crumbs or with cooked short-
grain brown rice. With rice, you have
a wheat-free option, and the burgers
will come out crumblier, but crunchi-
er. With bread crumbs, they hold
together better. The burgers taste great
both ways. (If you're using rice, don't
forget to cook it in advance.)

*You can buy many types of "veggie burgers" these days, but just in case
you'd prefer to make them yourself—and therefore know exactly what's in
them—here is the original concept. These simple, good, inexpensive burgers
can be assembled and sautéed in just 30 minutes, so it's not nearly as much
work as it might seem.*

*Serve Soyburgers with or without toasted buns, accompanied by all the tra-
ditional burger trimmings—mustard, ketchup, mayonnaise, onion, tomato,
pickles, etc. These burgers taste especially delicious when spread lavishly
with Red Pepper-Walnut Paste (page 159).*

*NOTE: You can freeze the uncooked patties. Just wrap each burger tightly
in plastic wrap, then store all the individually wrapped patties together in a
sealed plastic bag in the freezer. You can defrost one at a time, as needed,
and sauté to order.*

Place everything except the bread crumbs (or rice) and cooking oil
in a food processor and purée until fairly smooth.

Transfer to a bowl, and add the bread crumbs or rice. Stir until well
combined.

Form into patties about 4 inches in diameter and ½ inch thick,
using about ½ cup of the mixture for each patty.

Heat a heavy nonstick skillet and brush with oil. When the pan is
hot, add the burgers, turn the heat down to medium, and cook for
about 10 minutes on each side. Watch them carefully so they get
nice and brown, but don't burn.

Serve hot, in burger style (see serving suggestions above).

Yield: 6 to 8 4-inch burgers
Preparation time: 30 minutes after the soybeans are cooked
(10 minutes of work)

TUSCAN BEAN AND PASTA STEW

Canned beans and tomatoes, and frozen spinach, make this an ideal throw-together-after-work dish for a hungry family.

Heat a large pot of salted water for the pasta. When it boils rapidly, add the pasta, give it a stir, and cook until tender. Drain, and set aside.

Meanwhile, heat the oil in large, deep saucepan or Dutch oven. Add the onion and half the garlic, and sauté for about 5 minutes over medium heat, stirring often. Add ½ teaspoon of the salt and the dried herbs, and sauté for about 10 minutes longer. NOTE: If you're using fresh basil add it later.

Add the spinach to the onion, along with the tomatoes and remaining garlic and salt. Stir, cover, and let stew over medium heat for about 10 minutes, stirring once or twice.

If you're using fresh basil, stir it in now, along with the beans and cooked pasta. Don't cook the stew any further at this point—just heat it gently before serving. When it is heated through, add a generous amount of freshly ground black pepper, a few tablespoons of grated parmesan, and the vinegar.

Serve hot, in bowls, and pass around the pepper mill, some extra cheese, and a cruet of additional vinegar. This also tastes good at room temperature.

Yield: 4 to 6 servings
Preparation time: About 45 minutes (30 minutes of work)

3 cups uncooked pasta (macaroni, small shells, fusilli—any shape in this general size range)

1 to 2 tablespoons olive oil

2 cups minced onion

1 tablespoon minced garlic

1½ teaspoons salt

1 teaspoon dried thyme

1 teaspoon dried rubbed sage

1 tablespoon dried basil (or 3 tablespoons minced fresh basil)

2 10-ounce packages frozen chopped spinach, defrosted and drained (or 2 pounds fresh spinach—cleaned, stemmed, and chopped)

2 14½-ounce cans diced tomatoes

2 15-ounce cans cannellini beans, rinsed and drained

Freshly ground black pepper

2 or 3 tablespoons grated parmesan cheese (plus more for the top)

2 teaspoons red wine vinegar (plus more for the top)

* * * * * * * * * * * * * * * * * * * *

✶ *You can save time by doing everything else while the pasta cooks.*

✶ *This dish can be made in advance and gently reheated in a microwave.*

STOVETOP CASSOULET

Although it tastes like autumn itself, you can make Stovetop Cassoulet any time of the year. Unlike the traditional French cassoulet, which is full of meat and needs to be baked, this version is vegetarian, and cooks in a pot on top of the stove. It is similar to the French dish, though, in its deep, rich flavor laced with herbs and wine. Serve this with large steamed artichokes, some Horse-radish Aioli (page 168) to dip them in, and a loaf of crusty sourdough bread. A light fruit dessert or a sorbet is all you'll need to complete the meal.

Bring a large saucepan of water to a boil. Trim and discard the stem ends from the shallots, drop the shallots into the boiling water for about 1 minute, transfer them to a colander, and refresh under cold running water. (This procedure makes them easier to peel.) Drain well. Peel, then chop them or mince them in a food processor.

Heat the olive oil and melt 1 tablespoon of the butter together in a large, deep skillet with a lid or a Dutch oven. Add the shallots, stir, and cook uncovered over medium-low heat for about 10 minutes. Stir in the potatoes until they are well coated with the butter and oil. Cover and cook over medium-low heat for about 5 minutes, then add the salt, cover again, and cook for 10 minutes more.

Stir in the herbs, wine, carrots, and garlic. Cover, and cook for about 15 minutes over low heat. Add the bouillon and beans, and bring to a boil. Lower heat, cover, and cook until the potatoes and carrots are completely tender (about 25 minutes). Taste to see if it needs more salt, and grind in a good amount of fresh black pepper.

Stir in the mustard greens, cover, and remove from heat. Let it sit for about 10 minutes longer before serving.

Meanwhile, melt the remaining tablespoon of butter in a medium-sized skillet. Add the bread crumbs, and sauté over medium heat for about 10 minutes, or until the crumbs are toasty.

Serve the cassoulet hot, with a generous spoonful of bread crumbs on top. Pass the pepper grinder for a finishing touch.

Yield: 6 servings
Preparation time: 1½ hours after beans are cooked (15 minutes of work)

---

1 pound shallots

1 tablespoon olive oil

2 tablespoons butter

1 pound very small potatoes, halved—or about 3 cups diced potatoes

1¼ teaspoons salt (possibly more later)

1 teaspoon dried rubbed sage

1 teaspoon dried marjoram or oregano

1 teaspoon dried thyme

1 cup dry red wine

2 to 3 cups baby carrots

1 tablespoon minced garlic

1½ cups vegetable bouillon (page xiv)

About 6 cups cooked white pea or navy beans (3 to 4 15-ounce cans, rinsed and drained)

Freshly ground black pepper to taste

2 to 3 packed cups chopped fresh mustard greens (½ pound)

3 cups good, coarse bread crumbs

Mustard greens are especially delicious, but if you can't find them, substitute other leafy greens: escarole, collards, kale, or chard.

The best small potatoes to use in this dish are tiny Yukon Gold "creamers," if available.

This keeps well in an airtight container in the refrigerator. Reheat in a microwave or a regular oven.

CHICKPEA AND SWEET POTATO KOFTAS

Koftas are little patties or balls made from ground or mashed vegetables. In traditional East Indian cooking, they are usually deep-fried, and served in a creamy, savory sauce. In this recipe, the koftas are shaped into patties, similar to felafel, then sautéed or baked, instead of deep-fried. These delicious little circles are also quite pretty: a deep shade of golden yellow, punctuated by nuggets of bright green peas. For a great lunch, serve them in pitas, with minced tomatoes and cucumbers and some yogurt. They also taste wonderful topped with Mediterranean Yogurt (page 169).

Peel and dice the sweet potato or yam, and cook it in boiling water until soft—about 10 minutes, depending on the size of the pieces. Drain well. (Or cook the whole sweet potato in the microwave until soft, then peel.) You should have about 1½ cups of cooked sweet potato. Transfer to a food processor.

Add all the other ingredients, except the flour, peas, and oil. Purée until fairly smooth. (The mixture might be very thick, depending on the sweet potato or yam, so be patient with this process.) Transfer to a bowl.

Stir in the flour until it is thoroughly incorporated, then gently stir in the peas. Form into large or small patties. To make them uniform and professional looking, use a ¼-cup measure to scoop up the mixture, then pat each one down until it is about ½-inch thick and 2½ inches in diameter.

Place a skillet over medium heat and add a little bit of oil. When the oil is very hot, add the patties, and sauté for about 8 to 10 minutes on each side, or until lightly browned and heated through. Serve hot, warm, or at room temperature.

Yield: About 16 2½-inch patties (4 main-dish servings; 6 appetizer servings)
Preparation time: 35 to 40 minutes

- I medium-sized sweet potato or garnet yam (3/4 pound)
- I½ to 2 cups cooked chickpeas (I 15-ounce can, rinsed and drained)
- I large clove garlic
- 2 scallions, cut into I-inch pieces
- 2 teaspoons lightly toasted cumin seeds
- I tablespoon minced fresh ginger
- I teaspoon salt
- 2 tablespoons fresh lemon juice
- Freshly ground black pepper to taste
- 6 tablespoons unbleached white flour
- I cup peas (fresh or frozen)
- Vegetable or olive oil for sautéing

....

If you are using frozen peas, you don't need to defrost them first.

Alternative Method: If you are in a hurry and don't have the time to form patties and sauté them, you can make this into a small casserole instead. Omit the flour, and just spread the mixture into a lightly oiled 8 x 8-inch pan. Top with a few bread crumbs, and bake uncovered at 350°F for about 30 minutes, or until heated through. This will yield about 4 servings.

For a complete menu suggestion, see page 212.

PILAF-STYLE BASMATI RICE

8 to 10 cups water
  (it doesn't need to be exact)

1 tablespoon salt

2 or 3 cups uncooked basmati rice,
  white or brown

1 tablespoon vegetable oil or
  melted butter

Basmati rice is my favorite choice for pilafs, because it has a fantastic nutty taste, an excellent texture, and great versatility. An aromatic rice, originally from Northern India and Pakistan, it is now grown in the United States as well. The word basmati means "queen of fragrance," and the minute you drop these grains into a potful of boiling water and take a whiff, you'll know why.

This is the best way I have found to cook basmati rice for pilafs: First you boil it in a large quantity of salted water until it is mostly cooked, then you drain the rice, transfer it to a shallow pan, cover tightly, and bake it until done. This takes about the same amount of time as the old-fashioned stovetop method, but more reliably produces perfectly separate, fluffy rice, ready to combine with whatever additional ingredients are called for. (Several pilaf recipes follow.) Two additional benefits: a) You are spared having to worry about proportions of rice to water; and b) You can prepare the other pilaf ingredients while the rice cooks, and after the rice is done, add everything else to it, right in the same pan.

These instructions will work for any amount of basmati rice, white or brown. NOTE: For a medium recipe, use 2 cups uncooked rice; for a large recipe, use 3 cups uncooked rice.

Preheat the oven to 350°F. Put the water and salt in a large saucepan, and bring to a rolling boil. Meanwhile, place the rice in a strainer and rinse several times under cold running water.

Add the rice to the boiling water and let it boil rapidly, 10 minutes for white, 30 for brown , or until the rice is just tender to the bite (in other words, almost done). Drain the rice in a colander over the sink, and rinse with warm running water.

Brush the oil or melted butter over the bottom surface of a 9 x 13-inch pan (or a 10 x 13-inch pan, if you have one, for the large batch), and spread out the rice in an even layer. Tightly cover the pan with foil, and bake 10-15 minutes for white basmati, or 20-25 minutes for brown, or until the rice is done to your liking.

Carefully stir in whatever special ingredients the pilaf recipe calls for, and cover the pan tightly until serving time. Serve hot, warm, or at room temperature. (Reheat in a 350°F oven to the desired temperature, if necessary.)

Yield: About 6 cups cooked rice (medium batch); about 9 cups cooked rice (large batch)

Preparation time: 25 minutes for white basmati; 55 minutes for brown (5 to 10 minutes of work)

WILD RICE PILAF
WITH ORANGES AND CHERRIES

Botanically speaking, wild rice is actually the seed of an aquatic grass and not a true member of the rice family. Whatever its classification, with its dark, mysterious qualities and strong, earthy flavor, wild rice combines beautifully with aromatic basmati rice and a few touches of fruit and herbs to make this lovely dish. Serve it at any temperature and at any time of day.

1 cup uncooked wild rice

2½ cups water

1 medium recipe Pilaf-Style Basmati Rice (page 80)

4 or 5 oranges

1 teaspoon minced garlic (optional)

1¼ teaspoons salt

½ to ¾ cup dried cherries, halved or left whole

½ cup fresh or frozen/defrosted cherries, pitted and halved (optional)

1 to 2 tablespoons fresh lemon juice

Black pepper to taste

¼ cup minced fresh chives or scallions

3 to 4 tablespoons minced fresh mint

OPTIONAL TOPPINGS:

Strips of orange peel

Minced parsley for the top

⋆ *You can cook both the wild rice and the basmati well ahead of time. Prepare the oranges ahead, too. The longer they sit, the more juice you'll get.*

⋆ *If you're using frozen cherries, defrost and drain them thoroughly before adding to the rice. Save the juice for drizzling on pound cake or vanilla yogurt.*

⋆ *For a complete menu suggestion, see page 212.*

Place the wild rice in a medium-sized saucepan and add 2½ cups water. Cover the pan and heat to a boil. Lower the heat to the slowest possible simmer, and cook, covered and undisturbed, until tender. This will take about 1¼ to 1½ hours. While the wild rice is simmering, prepare the Pilaf-Style Basmati Rice.

While the rice cooks, prepare the oranges. First, cut off a few lovely strips of peel to use for garnish, if desired. Then grate enough zest to amply fill ½ teaspoon. Set the zest and strips aside. Cut and discard all the remaining skin from the oranges, then hold each orange over a bowl as you cut the sections away from the membrane—one by one, with a serrated knife, using a gentle sawing motion. After you have sectioned all the oranges, squeeze in as much of the juice from the remaining membranes into the bowl as possible, then discard the membranes.

When the wild rice is cooked, fluff it thoroughly with a fork to let the steam escape, then add it to the cooked basmati rice, still in its baking pan. Gently stir in the garlic, salt, cherries, lemon juice, grated orange zest, and about half of the orange sections. (Fluff the pilaf with a fork as you stir.)

Strain out ⅔ cup of the orange juice, and stir this in as well. Add black pepper to taste. Cover and let it stand for at least 30 minutes, to let the flavors mingle. (It can also stand longer—it keeps well, covered and refrigerated, for up to 5 days.)

Serve warm, at room temperature, or cold. (If you want to serve it warm, place the covered pan back in a 350°F oven for about 20 minutes, or until heated.) Shortly before serving, stir in the chives or scallions and the mint. Place the reserved orange sections on top, and sprinkle with strips of orange peel and a little minced parsley, if desired.

Yield: About 6 servings
Preparation time: 2 hours (15 minutes of work)

Mollie Katzen's VEGETABLE HEAVEN

COCONUT RICE
WITH GINGER, CHILES, AND LIME

Tart, lively rice is an easy and unexpected way to spruce up a meal. This pilaf does just that, with touches of flavor and heat that are surprising, yet subtle.

Begin preparing a large batch of Pilaf-Style Basmati Rice.

Meanwhile, heat the oil in a medium-sized skillet. Add the onion, and sauté over medium heat for about 10 minutes. Stir in the chiles, ginger, garlic, and ½ teaspoon salt, lower the heat, and continue to cook slowly for about 10 minutes longer.

Carefully stir the sautéed mixture into the rice, fluffing the rice with a fork as you stir, and gradually adding the remaining salt, lime zest, lime juice to taste, and most of the toasted coconut. (Save a little coconut for the top.) When everything is well combined, taste to see if it needs more salt. Cover the pan tightly, so the rice won't dry out, and reheat in a 350°F oven, if desired, before serving.

Serve hot, warm, or at room temperature, topped with the reserved coconut, and with some or all of the intriguing optional garnishes.

Yield: 8 or more servings
Preparation time: 30 minutes with white basmati; 1 hour with brown
 (15 minutes of work)

1 large recipe Pilaf-Style Basmati Rice (page 80)

1 tablespoon peanut or vegetable oil

2 cups minced onion

2 to 3 serrano or jalapeño chiles, seeded and minced

2 tablespoons minced fresh ginger

2 tablespoons minced garlic

1¼ teaspoons salt (possibly more, to taste)

1¼ teaspoons grated lime zest

4 to 5 tablespoons fresh lime juice

1 cup shredded unsweetened coconut, lightly toasted

OPTIONAL GARNISHES:

A handful of torn cilantro leaves

Wedges of lime

Slices of kiwifruit

....

 Sauté the onion and chiles while the rice cooks. Add everything directly to the rice, and stir it up right in the baking pan.

 Zest the limes before squeezing the juice.

 For a menu suggestion, see page 211.

PERSIAN LAYERED PILAFS

After looking through several beautifully illustrated Persian cookbooks, I became infatuated by the photographs of numerous rice dishes, each one more glorious than the next. Inspired, I made a large batch of rice, divided it into three bowls, and seasoned each one differently: onion, saffron, and pretty green flecks of scallion and parsley in one; grated carrots and cumin in another; and a bright magenta blend of beets, garlic, dill, and raspberry vinegar in the third.

My friend Tina suggested piling them in layers and sprinkling pistachio nuts on top, and this spectacular triple-decker pilaf was born.

Begin preparing the rice. While it cooks, prepare the three mixtures on the opposite page.

When the rice is cooked, divide it into three medium-sized ceramic or heatproof glass bowls. Stir one filling into each bowl of rice, mixing thoroughly. Cover each bowl until serving time.

Arrange the pilafs in three layers on a large platter, and top with pistachio nuts.

NOTE: You can also make a molded dish by firmly pressing one pilaf at a time into a large, lightly oiled soufflé dish. Cover tightly, and reheat in a 350°F oven for about 30 minutes. To serve the mold, invert onto a plate, and top with pistachios.

Yield: 8 or more servings
Preparation time: 1 hour (30 to 40 minutes of work)

I large recipe Pilaf-Style Basmati Rice (page 80)

I recipe Onion-Garlic-Saffron Mixture (recipe opposite)

I recipe Carrot-Cumin Mixture (recipe opposite)

I recipe Beet Mixture (recipe opposite)

I cup minced, toasted pistachio nuts

....

The beets can be cooked and peeled days ahead.

Use the food processor to mince the scallions and parsley and to grate the carrots.

Use the same skillet to cook the vegetables for each layer, but don't bother to clean it between batches.

You can assemble the three bowls of seasoned rice up to a day ahead of time. Cover them tightly and refrigerate.

Make this for a special occasion—it serves a lot of people—and your guests will talk about it for weeks. (For a complete menu, see page 213.)

On the other hand, if you're planning a simple meal for 4 to 6 people, you can easily adapt any one of these layers to serve all by itself. Just double the amounts of your chosen seasoning mixture, and add it to a medium batch of Pilaf-Style Basmati Rice (page 80).

Onion-Garlic-Saffron Mixture

Heat the olive oil in a small skillet. Add the onion and salt, and cook over high heat for about 5 minutes.

Lower the heat, add the garlic and dissolved saffron, and cook for about 5 minutes longer over low heat.

Remove from heat, and stir in the scallions and parsley.

Carrot-Cumin Mixture

Heat the olive oil in a medium-sized skillet. Add the garlic, and sauté for about 10 seconds over low heat. Add the cumin, carrots, and salt, and cook for another 8 to 10 minutes, or until the carrots are tender. If the mixture appears to be sticking, add up to 3 tablespoons water or orange juice.

Remove from heat, and stir in the raisins and about 6 to 8 grinds of fresh black pepper.

Beet Mixture

Heat the olive oil in a small skillet. Add the garlic and cook over low heat for about 10 seconds. (Don't let it turn color, or it will become bitter.)

Add the beets and salt, and sauté for about 5 minutes longer.

Remove from heat and stir in the dill, vinegar, honey, and a little black pepper to taste.

Onion-Garlic-Saffron Mixture

1 tablespoon olive oil

1½ cups minced onion

½ teaspoon salt

1 tablespoon minced garlic

3 strands saffron, dissolved in 1 tablespoon hot water

4 scallions, finely minced

3 tablespoons minced parsley

Carrot-Cumin Mixture

1 tablespoon olive oil

1 teaspoon minced garlic

1 teaspoon ground cumin

3 cups grated carrot (about 4 medium carrots)

½ teaspoon salt

2 to 3 tablespoons water or orange juice, as needed

¼ cup golden raisins

Freshly ground black pepper

Beet Mixture

1 tablespoon olive oil

1 tablespoon minced garlic

3 small beets, cooked until tender, peeled and finely minced (1½ cups minced)

½ teaspoon salt

2 tablespoons minced fresh dill (or 2 teaspoons dried dill)

2 tablespoons raspberry vinegar

1 tablespoon honey

Freshly ground black pepper

SPICED PINEAPPLE PILAF

2 tablespoons butter

2 teaspoons mustard seeds

1½ tablespoons minced
    fresh ginger

1½ tablespoons minced fresh garlic

1¼ teaspoons salt

½ teaspoon turmeric

¼ teaspoon allspice

¼ teaspoon nutmeg

1 20-ounce can crushed pineapple
    (packed in juice)

1 large recipe Pilaf-Style Basmati
    Rice (page 80)

3 to 4 tablespoons cider vinegar or
    unseasoned rice vinegar

Cayenne for the top

• • • • • • • • • • • • • • • • • • • •

Begin cooking the rice first. Prepare the spiced pineapple while the rice is cooking.

Serve Spiced Pineapple Pilaf with Firecracker Red Beans (page 72) and/or a colorful mélange of steamed vegetables (broccoli, carrots, red peppers, etc.)

I get a kick out of serving this very pretty yellow pilaf to people without first telling them what's in it. It has a very unusual combination of seasonings: ginger, turmeric, garlic, mustard seeds, allspice, and nutmeg—all bound together by the sweet-tart presence of pineapple. After several bites, everyone comments on how interesting it tastes. After several more bites, the consensus is, "This is really good." I guess you might say this dish sneaks up on you quietly.

Melt the butter in a small saucepan. Add the mustard seeds and ginger, and cook over medium-low heat for about 3 minutes, stirring frequently. Add the garlic, ½ teaspoon salt, turmeric, allspice, and nutmeg, and sauté for about 1 more minute, or until the garlic is just about to turn golden. Add 1½ cups of the pineapple (including its juice) and cook for about 5 minutes longer.

Transfer this mixture to the cooked rice, add the vinegar and remaining salt, and mix everything in well. The rice is ready to serve at this point, but it tastes even better if heated through with the seasonings mixed in. Just cover the pan tightly with foil, and place it in a 350°F oven for about 30 minutes.

Serve hot or warm, topped with the remaining pineapple and a fine dusting of cayenne. It will look very pretty.

Yield: 8 or more servings

Preparation time: 30 minutes with white basmati; 1 hour with brown
    (30 minutes of work either way)

THREE-PART HOMINY

Lovely for supper, and also good reheated for breakfast, this easy, inexpensive dish is like a highly-seasoned Southwestern-style polenta. Fresh corn shaved straight from the cob is very special in here, but frozen corn will also work perfectly well.

Hominy is the name given to dried whole corn kernels that have been boiled with lye or lime to remove the outer skin. It is quite chewy and tender, and gives this dish a great texture. Hominy comes in cans and is available in most supermarkets. Grits traditionally were made from ground hominy, but nowadays, the word "grits" usually refers to coarse white cornmeal. Look for the quick-cooking kind in the cereal section.

Melt the butter or heat the oil in a large, deep skillet or Dutch oven. Add the onion, and sauté over medium heat for 5 minutes. Stir in half the garlic, ½ teaspoon of the salt, the chile, and the bell pepper. Cover, and cook over low heat for 10 minutes.

Stir in the grits and the remaining salt, and sauté for a minute or two. Then pour in the water and bring to a boil. Lower the heat, cover, and simmer until the grits are tender (about 5 minutes).

Fluff with a fork, and stir in the remaining garlic, and the corn and hominy. Cover, remove from heat, and let it stand for 5 minutes. Then fluff with a fork again, and taste to adjust the salt. Grind in some black pepper, and serve hot.

Yield: 6 servings
Preparation time: 35 minutes (15 minutes of work)

---

1 tablespoon butter or olive oil

1½ cups finely minced onion

1 tablespoon minced garlic

1½ teaspoons salt

1 medium-sized poblano or Anaheim chile, seeded and minced (about 1 cup)

Half a medium-sized red bell pepper, minced (about ½ cup)

2 cups uncooked grits

6 cups hot water

3 cups fresh or frozen corn (3 ears or a 1-pound package frozen/defrosted)

1 15-ounce can white or yellow hominy, rinsed and drained

Freshly ground black pepper

....

✴ You can substitute a 7-ounce can of diced green chiles for the fresh poblano or Anaheim chile.

✴ Reheat leftover Three-Part Hominy in a microwave. Or, for a special treat, you can form patties and sauté them in a little butter or olive oil over medium heat (or on a grill) for about 2 minutes on each side, or until heated through on the inside and crispy on the outside.

MILLET AND QUINOA
WITH CASHEWS
AND SUNFLOWER SEEDS

Crunchy, nutty, toasty . . . and easy. It's always nice to put these humble, highly nutritious grains to good use.

1½ cups millet

½ cup quinoa

3 cups water

¾ teaspoon salt

1 cup sunflower seeds

1 cup cashew nuts

. . . .

The purpose of fluffing the millet and quinoa so much is to ensure that you end up with a bowlful of tender, separate grains, instead of mush. So get out that fork, and seriously fluff. It will be worth it.

Delicious though it is, this dish is somewhat lacking in the visual department, so garnish it with something colorful, like citrus wedges, grated carrots, minced parsley, or cherry tomatoes.

Place the millet and quinoa in a strainer, and rinse thoroughly under cold running water. Transfer the grains to a medium-sized saucepan, and add the water and ½ teaspoon of the salt. Cover and bring to a boil. Turn the heat down as far as it will go, and simmer, covered, for 15 minutes.

Meanwhile, place the sunflower seeds in a blender and pulse a few times until they are coarsely ground. Add the cashews and pulse a few more times, until the mixture resembles a very rough meal.

Place the nut-seed mixture in a heavy skillet (cast-iron is ideal) and dry-roast over medium-low heat, stirring frequently, until the mixture is light golden brown and gives off a toasty aroma. This will take about 10 minutes, but watch the pan carefully so the nuts and seeds don't suddenly burn.

Back to the grains. Stir the millet and quinoa from the bottom of the pot with a fork, and keep fluffing the grains for a minute or two, then cover again, and continue to cook for about 5 minutes longer, or until the grains are perfectly tender.

Transfer the grains to a bowl, and fluff with a fork—all the way to the bottom of the bowl—to let steam escape. Let stand uncovered for about 15 minutes, repeating the fluffing procedure every few minutes or so.

Stir in the toasted cashews and sunflower seeds, and serve warm, or at room temperature.

Yield: About 6 servings
Preparation time: 35 minutes (15 minutes of work)

MIXED-UP GRAINS

After all those fancy pilafs, this easy, highly textured combo offers a refreshing change of pace. Once cooked, the wheat becomes roly-poly, and the rye puffs up and turns a lovely shade of warm brown. The wild rice bursts open, releasing an irresistible earthy flavor, and revealing a creamy-colored interior. You can also add some barley, for extra sweetness. And prepare to chew!

What I like most about mixing these grains is that they all cook for the same amount of time—and therefore, in the same pot. And they do it on their own, so you can get other things done in the meantime.

Rinse all the grains together in a strainer. Transfer them to a medium-large saucepan with 5¾ cups water (6¾ cups if you are including the optional barley). Bring to a boil, cover, and simmer over the lowest possible heat for 1½ hours.

Check the grains to see if they are done to your liking. (This is a chewy pilaf.) If you would like them somewhat softer, cook them covered for another 10 to 15 minutes. However, if they seem about right, but there is still some water left in the pot, just turn up the heat a little, and cook them uncovered, stirring often, for about 5 to 10 minutes longer. The water will evaporate, but the grains will not overcook. (Alternatively, you can drain out any extra water by placing the cooked grains in a colander in the sink and leaving them there for 10 minutes or so.)

Add minced red onion, if desired, and salt to taste. Fluff with a fork, and serve.

Yield: About 6 servings
Preparation time: 1¾ hours (about 5 minutes of work)

1 cup whole rye
  (also called rye berries)
1 cup white (soft) wheat berries
½ cup wild rice
½ cup pearl barley (optional)
5¾ to 6¾ cups water
½ cup minced red onion (optional)
½ teaspoon salt (or to taste)

This grain combo goes well with Roasted Onions (page 96), and/or Green Salad with Blue Cheese, Walnuts, and Figs (page 19).

Don't rule out the possibility of eating this for breakfast.

COUSCOUS
WITH TOUCHES OF ORANGE, DILL, AND PISTACHIO

2 cups quick-cooking couscous (not whole-wheat)

3 cups boiling water

Salt to taste

1 medium-sized juice orange

3 to 4 tablespoons finely minced fresh dill (or 1 tablespoon dried dill)

½ cup minced, toasted pistachio nuts

....

Serve this dish with Moroccan Roasted Vegetable Stew (page 100). Also, check out the larger, more expansive menu on page 213.

Couscous is actually a tiny pasta (sometimes referred to as "North African pasta") made from semolina wheat. Cooking couscous by traditional methods requires several steaming processes to attain a light and fluffy result. Recently, quick-cooking varieties, requiring only a brief soaking in hot water have become available. Whole-wheat quick-cooking couscous invariably becomes mush, and I wouldn't recommend it for anything other than a good, hot breakfast cereal. But the light-colored quick-cooking kind is quite good, and if handled correctly, can make an ethereal pilaf, accessible to the busy, working cook.

For more information about couscous, including great cultural information, anecdotes, and details/directions on the authentic, traditional way to cook it, I highly recommend the definitive work by Paula Wolfert, Couscous and Other Good Food from Morocco.

Place the couscous in a medium-sized bowl. Pour in the boiling water, and cover the bowl with a plate. Let stand for 15 to 20 minutes, or until the couscous is tender. Fluff thoroughly with a fork and add salt to taste.

Grate the zest from the orange and then squeeze out all the juice. Add both the zest and juice to the couscous, along with the dill. Mix well, making sure there are no clumps of couscous left on the bottom of the bowl. Cover tightly, and set aside until serving time.

This dish can be served at room temperature, hot, or warm. (Heat just before serving in a microwave or a regular oven at 325°F, if desired.) Sprinkle lightly with pistachios before serving.

Yield: 4 to 6 servings
Preparation time: 20 minutes (5 minutes of work)

Mollie Katzen's VEGETABLE HEAVEN

KASHA VARNISHKES

Buckwheat combined with pasta and seasoned simply with onion—this is the kind of food that, according to my mother, keeps body and soul together. It's also very quick and easy. If you have any left over, try it cold, as a snack.

Put up a medium-sized saucepan of water to boil for the pasta. Preheat the oven to 350°F.

Melt the butter or heat the oil in a large, deep, skillet with an oven-proof handle and a cover. Add the onion, and sauté over medium heat for about 5 minutes. Add the kasha or buckwheat groats and the salt, and sauté for about 10 minutes, stirring frequently.

Pour in 2½ cups boiling water; cover and cook over low heat for about 10 minutes. (Meanwhile, cook the pasta in plenty of boiling water until al dente, and drain.)

Stir the pasta into the kasha, cover, and bake for 30 minutes.

Remove the pan from the oven, and stir in the optional scallions and dill, if desired. Serve hot or warm, with any or all of the optional garnishes.

Yield: 6 healthy portions
Preparation time: About 1 hour (15 minutes of work)

1 tablespoon butter or oil

1½ cups minced onion

2 cups uncooked kasha or buckwheat groats

1½ teaspoons salt

2½ cups boiling water

1 to 2 cups uncooked small farfalle (bow-tie pasta)

2 to 3 scallions, minced (optional)

A handful of minced fresh dill (optional)

OPTIONAL GARNISHES:

Chopped or grated hard-boiled eggs

Yogurt or sour cream, with a little prepared horseradish mixed in

Kasha simply refers to buckwheat that has been dry-roasted. Kasha and plain buckwheat groats can be used interchangeably.

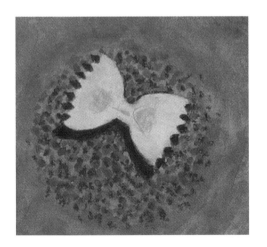

AFTER-WORK BULGUR SPECIAL
AND OPTIONAL STUFFED PEPPERS

1 cup coarse bulgur

1¾ cups boiling water

2 tablespoons minced fresh dill
(or 1 teaspoon dried dill)

3 scallions, finely minced

½ cup lightly toasted pine nuts

A small handful of currants

½ teaspoon salt (or more, to taste)

Black pepper to taste

A drizzle of extra virgin olive oil

2 tablespoons fresh lemon juice
(or to taste)

2 or 3 medium-sized red or yellow
bell peppers (optional)

We all need an option like this—and often. It's quick, and good, and utterly nutritious, and goes with just about everything.

Before You Go to Work: Place the bulgur in a large bowl. (Make sure it's large enough for the bulgur to expand, which it will greatly do.) Pour in the boiling water, cover tightly with foil, and go to work.

When You Come Home: Remove the foil; fluff the bulgur with a fork. Add the remaining ingredients; mix and serve. It's good at room temperature, but you can also reheat it, covered, in a 350°F oven for about 30 minutes—or in a microwave.

Optional Presentation: Halve and hollow out 2 or 3 medium-sized red or yellow bell peppers and fill with the bulgur mix. Cover and place in the microwave (high power) for 2 minutes. Voilà! Dinner.

Yield: About 6 servings (easily doubled—just be sure you use a large enough bowl)

Preparation time: A few minutes before work; a few more minutes when you get home.

FANTASTIC BULGUR DISH

Based very loosely on a Turkish bulgur dish called "kisir," this tomatoey, garlicky, slightly peppery preparation is delicious plain, but downright fabulous when served with a healthy dollop of Red Pepper-Walnut Paste. The paste is easy to prepare, but must be done ahead. So keep this in mind when you notice that red bell peppers are on special in your local produce department.

Heat 1 tablespoon olive oil in a large, deep, nonstick skillet. Add the cherry tomatoes, and sauté over high heat for about 5 minutes.

Stir in the dried tomatoes and ¾ teaspoon salt. Continue cooking over high heat for about 2 to 3 minutes longer. (The cherry tomatoes might begin to pop open from the heat, and that's just fine.)

Turn the heat down. Add the garlic and bulgur—and a little more oil, if it seems dry—and sauté over medium-low heat for about 2 minutes. Stir in the water, bring to a boil, then turn down the heat as far as possible. Cover and simmer for 35 minutes or until the bulgur is tender.

Transfer to a serving bowl, and fluff with a fork to let the steam escape, so the bulgur won't become mushy. Taste to adjust salt, and add red pepper flakes, lemon juice, honey, and black pepper to taste.

Serve hot or warm, with a generous spoonful of Red Pepper-Walnut Paste on top, and a wedge of lemon on the side, if desired.

Yield: 4 to 6 servings
Preparation time: 45 minutes (10 minutes of work)

---

1 tablespoon olive oil
(plus a little more, as needed)

2 cups tiny cherry tomatoes
(½ pound)—yellow ones,
if available

½ cup dried tomatoes, minced
(1 ounce)

¾ teaspoon salt (possibly more)

1 tablespoon minced garlic

1½ cups coarse bulgur

2 cups water

¼ teaspoon red pepper flakes

1 to 2 tablespoons fresh lemon
juice

2 to 3 teaspoons honey

Freshly ground black pepper
to taste

OPTIONAL GARNISHES:

2 to 3 tablespoons Red Pepper-
Walnut Paste (page 159)

Wedges of lemon

....

Use plain dried tomatoes, not packed in oil. Soak them well ahead of time. Plain kitchen scissors are the best gadget for cutting them up.

Tiny yellow cherry tomatoes look and work best in this dish. If you can only get larger ones, cut them in half. If you can only get red ones, that will be beautiful too.

For a menu suggestion, see page 212.

BULGUR NOODLES
WITH MY GRANDMOTHER'S ONIONS

3 to 4 tablespoons olive oil

4 cups minced onion

Salt to taste

About 1½ cups broken spaghetti
  or vermicelli (in 1½-inch pieces)

1½ cups coarse bulgur

2½ cups vegetable bouillon
  (page xiv)

....

  *You'll need two pans for this—
a medium-sized skillet to cook the
onion topping, and a larger, deeper
one for the bulgur and noodles.*

  *The onion enhancement gets a
head start, then cooks mostly by
itself, with just an occasional stir
from you. The bulgur and noodles
cook fairly independently, also, making this an easy, light-work dish.*

*If you want to get your kids to eat more whole grains, this might be the way
to go. In this dish, bulgur and spaghetti are sautéed together with onions,
then steamed until tender, and enhanced with extra fried onions, the kind my
grandmother's kitchen smelled of, much to our pleasure.*

Heat 2 tablespoons of the oil in a medium-sized skillet. Add 3 cups of
the minced onion, and begin cooking them over high heat, stirring
occasionally. After about 10 minutes, salt them lightly, and turn the
heat to medium-low. Keep them cooking while you proceed.

Heat another tablespoon of oil in a heavy nonstick sauté pan or
Dutch oven. Add the remaining cup of onion and cook over medium heat, stirring, for about 5 minutes. Add the spaghetti or vermicelli, and sauté for about 10 minutes. You might need to drizzle in
small amounts of additional oil, if it begins to stick.

Add the bulgur to the pasta and stir for a few minutes, then pour
in the bouillon. Bring to a boil, cover, and lower the heat to a simmer. Open the lid after about 15 minutes, and fluff from the bottom of the pan with a fork. Cover again, and cook for about 10
more minutes. Leaving the cover on, remove the pan from the heat
and let it sit for about 10 minutes longer. (By the way, the panful of
onions has been slowly cooking away this entire time, right? Just
checking.)

Transfer the bulgur mixture to a bowl, fluff with a fork, and add salt
to taste. Finally, remove the panful of onions from the stove and scrape
every last bit into the bulgur and noodles. Stir until well combined and
serve right away. This also tastes good warm or at room temperature.
In fact, it's very hard to stop eating at any temperature.

Yield: 6 cups
Preparation time: About 1 hour (10 minutes of work)

MUSHROOM-BARLEY "RISOTTO"

A true risotto is made with Arborio rice—a plump, starchy variety that makes its own creamy sauce while it cooks. The allure of a risotto is its texture: the cooked grains become tender, yet remain somewhat firm at the same time. Barley, although not in the least traditional for this purpose, makes a wonderful alternative "risotto." Whereas Arborio rice is expensive and requires constant stirring, barley is cheaper, easier to find, and requires far less fuss. It has a similar quality to Arborio rice in that when it is done, the tender grains retain a delightful chewiness in the center, and the cooking liquid is transformed into a smooth sauce.

Place the dried shiitake mushrooms in a medium-sized bowl, and pour in 2 cups of hot water, then let it sit for 20 to 30 minutes, or until the mushrooms are very soft. Place a few layers of cheesecloth in a strainer over a second bowl, and strain the mushrooms, pressing out and saving all their liquid. Stem and thinly slice the shiitakes, and set aside.

Meanwhile, melt the butter or heat the oil in a large saucepan or a Dutch oven over medium heat. Add the onion and half the garlic, and sauté for about 5 minutes. Add the fresh mushrooms and salt, and stir well. Cover and cook for about 15 minutes.

Stir in the barley and sauté for a minute or two, keeping the heat at medium. Pour in the wine, cover, and turn down the heat. Simmer until the liquid is absorbed (10 minutes). Add the sliced shiitakes and their liquid. Stir, cover, and cook over low heat until the liquid is absorbed (another 10 to 12 minutes).

Pour in 2 cups of the additional water. Stir, cover, and simmer until the water is absorbed (about 10 minutes). Then pour in the last 2 cups of water, stirring in the remaining garlic and the vinegar at the same time. Cover one more time, and cook until all the liquid is gone (10 minutes again). Grind in some black pepper, and stir from the bottom to let steam escape.

Serve hot, lightly topped with minced, toasted pecans and a little bit of minced fresh dill, if desired.

Yield: 6 to 8 servings
Preparation time: About 1 hour (10 minutes of work)

12 dried shiitake mushrooms

2 cups hot water

1 tablespoon butter or oil

2 cups minced onion

2 tablespoons minced garlic

1 pound fresh domestic mushrooms, minced

1½ teaspoons salt

2 cups pearl barley, rinsed

1 cup dry sherry, vermouth, or Chinese rice wine

About 4 cups additional water (added gradually)

3 tablespoons cider vinegar

Black pepper to taste

OPTIONAL, FOR THE TOP:

Minced toasted pecans

A tiny bit of minced fresh dill

⋆ *Risotto is usually made with a richly flavored stock. In this recipe, you soak dried shiitake mushrooms, then use the soaking water, which has become strongly infused, as part of the liquid. For extra flavor, you can replace some or all of the additional water with Rich Mushroom Broth (page 30) or with vegetable bouillon (page xiv). If you use the bouillon, reduce the salt by about ½ teaspoon.*

⋆ *The mushrooms can be soaked way in advance, or while you cook the fresh mushrooms and the barley.*

ROASTED VEGETABLES

Do you often yearn for some exquisitely prepared vegetables, but you don't have the time or patience to fuss around with them? Consider roasting your vegetables—any and all of them. The dry, high heat of the roasting process causes the vegetables to cook from their own inner moisture, intensifying their flavor, and enhancing their natural, rich sweetness.

Trendy though roasting is, it's actually very simple—and has been a standard cooking procedure of ordinary cooks for years. Just cut your favorite vegetables into big careless pieces (or leave some whole—see the various instructions that follow) and spread them out on an oiled tray. Place the tray in the oven, and basically leave it alone while you do other things for 20 or 30 minutes. When the vegetables come out of the oven, they're more than just ready. They're transformed.

Serve roasted vegetables plain or with a splash of citrus juice or vinegar. Try swirling them with Balsamic Drizzle (page 172) or dipping them into many of the various sauces, pastes, or vinaigrettes from the Never a Bland Moment chapter (page 155).

You can also add dried or minced fresh herbs—or savory seeds, like cumin, mustard, or caraway. (If you're adding fresh herbs, sprinkle them on during the last 5 minutes of roasting.)

What follows is a series of general instructions, rather than recipes with given amounts. The quantities are up to you—just be sure the vegetables are spread in a single layer on the baking tray. And while figuring quantities, don't forget that the vegetables will shrink during the roasting process. So plan accordingly.

NOTE: Olive oil is the best oil to use for roasting vegetables.

Roasted Onions and Shallots

Preheat the oven to 375°F and lightly oil a baking tray. Without bothering to peel them, cut medium-sized onions into quarters, and smaller onions and shallots in half. Swish the onions and/or shallots around on the oiled tray to coat the open sides with oil. Roast for anywhere from 20-30 minutes (yellow onions) or for 10 minutes (red onions and shallots). Serve at any temperature with just about anything.

Roasted Bell Peppers

Preheat the oven to 375°F. Place as many bell peppers as will fit on an ungreased tray and roast near the top of the oven. Using tongs, turn the peppers every 5 to 10 minutes for about 35 to 40 minutes, or until the skins blacken and separate from the flesh. Transfer the peppers to a glass or ceramic bowl and cover with a plate. Let sit for 30 minutes before peeling, seeding, and slicing. Save the delicious juices that accumulate in the bottom of the bowl for soups or sauces—or to just drink.

NOTE: If you prefer to char the peppers, you can broil them directly under the heat at 500°F instead. Turn them frequently and watch them carefully, as this process will go a lot more quickly than roasting at a lower temperature.

Roasted Artichokes

Preheat the oven to 375°F. Use medium-sized (3-inch-diameter) artichokes; cut them in half lengthwise, and scrape out the choke. Liberally brush the open sides with lemon juice, then place the artichokes cut side down on a generously oiled tray. Splash a few tablespoons of water on the tray near the artichokes, and cover the tray tightly with foil. Roast for about 30 minutes, or until the leaves come off easily, and the heart is tender when poked gently with a fork. Remove from oven, and turn over to face up. Sprinkle lightly with salt while still hot, then cool for at least 10 minutes before serving.

Roasted Potatoes

The ideal potatoes for roasting are a medium-waxy variety, like Yukon Golds. Preheat the oven to 400°F. Choose potatoes that are about 1½ inches in diameter, and cut them in half. Oil the tray and place potatoes cut side down. Roast for 15 minutes, then turn the potatoes over and roast for 15 minutes longer on their backs. Sprinkle lightly with salt while still hot, then serve at any temperature. NOTE: You can also roast the potatoes whole. Just increase the roasting time on each side by about 10 minutes. They're done when a fork slides in easily.

Roasted Green or Wax Beans

Preheat the oven to 375°F. Trim the beans, spread them out on an oiled baking tray, and roll them around in the oil so they get thoroughly, but lightly coated. Roast for 5 to 8 minutes, shaking the pan once or twice during the process to move the beans around. Remove from the oven, and sprinkle lightly with salt while the beans are still hot. Serve at any temperature.

Roasted Beets

Use small or medium-sized beets (1- to 2-inch-diameter). Trim the greens but leave on the stems. Preheat the oven to 375°F. Place the beets in a small pan with a splash of water, and cover tightly with foil. Roast for 1 hour, or possibly longer. They're done when a fork slides in easily. Cool to room temperature, then rub off the skins. NOTE: If you are roasting red and yellow beets at the same time, keep them separate, so the yellow ones won't get irreparably stained.

Roasted Winter Squash and Sweet Potatoes

Preheat the oven to 375°F. Cut the vegetables into pieces ¾ inch thick. (Peeling is optional.) Spread out the vegetables on an oiled tray and brush the open sides with a little extra oil. Salt lightly, cover tightly with foil and roast for 30 minutes, or until just tender. (For a crisper texture, remove the foil and move the tray to the top of the oven for the last 10 minutes of roasting.) Transfer the vegetables to a bowl and cover until serving time, so they won't dry out.

Roasted Eggplant, Zucchini, or Summer Squash

If an eggplant has shiny, tight skin, leave it on. Otherwise, peel it. Cut larger globe eggplants in 1-inch slices and smaller ones down the center lengthwise.

Slice short zucchini and summer squash in half lengthwise, and cut pattypan squash in half around the middle. (Tiny summer squashes can be left whole.)

Preheat the oven to 375°F. Bake on an oiled tray for about 20 minutes each, or until easily pierced with a fork. Salt lightly while still hot, and serve at any temperature.

Roasted Asparagus or Mushrooms

Preheat the oven to 400°F. Roll asparagus and/or whole small mushrooms (stemmed or not) around on an oiled tray until they are lightly coated. Roast for only 5 to 10 minutes, or until just tender. (Asparagus cooks very fast, so keep an eye on it. In just a couple of minutes, it can go from too crunchy to overly soft. Naturally, you want it somewhere in between.) Salt lightly while still hot, and serve at any temperature.

Roasted Cauliflower, Broccoli, Cabbage, or Brussels Sprouts

In all of the following cases: preheat the oven to 375°F, roast the vegetables on an oiled tray, salt lightly while still hot, and serve at any temperature.

Cauliflower: Break into 1½-inch florets, and roast for about 15 minutes.

Broccoli: Cut into 2-inch chunks (include the peeled stems) and roast for 20 to 25 minutes, depending on the thickness of the pieces.

Cabbage (surprisingly sweet!): Cut into 2-inch wedges and roast for about 20 minutes.

Brussels sprouts: Leave smaller ones whole; cut larger ones in half. Roast for 15 to 20 minutes, depending on the size.

Roasted Carrots or Parsnips

Preheat the oven to 375°F. Cut larger carrots or parsnips into 2-inch lengths; leave small ones whole. Roll the vegetables around on an oiled baking tray until they are lightly coated, then roast for 30 minutes, or until done to your liking. Serve at any temperature.

Roasted Tomatoes

The best types of tomatoes to roast are plum (Roma) tomatoes and large beefsteak tomatoes that are not too ripe. Cut out the stems first, then place the whole tomatoes (skins intact) on a lightly oiled baking tray. Preheat the oven to 400°F, and roast the tomatoes for 30 to 40 minutes. Riper tomatoes will roast more quickly.

If desired, you can drain off juices intermittently during the roasting process, enabling the tomatoes to cook from inner, rather than from expelled, liquid. (The latter causes them to stew, rather than roast.) Cool to room temperature, then remove skins.

Roasted Fennel, Celery Hearts, Bok Choy, or Leeks

For all of the following: preheat the oven to 400°F, roast the vegetables for 15 minutes on each side on an oiled tray, and brush any open sides with a little extra oil as well. After removing from the oven, salt lightly while still hot, and serve at any temperature.

Fennel and Celery Hearts: Clean them well, then cut into wedges.

Bok Choy: For smaller bok choy, leave the stems intact. For larger ones, cut in half or quarters lengthwise.

Leeks: Trim the root ends. Leave slender leeks whole; cut thicker ones in half lengthwise. Give the leeks a bath in several changes of cold water, digging into the crevices to get out all the dirt. Dry thoroughly before proceeding.

SIDE-BY-SIDE DISHES

MOROCCAN ROASTED VEGETABLE STEW

A little olive oil

2 medium-sized onions, in 1-inch chunks

½ pound baby carrots

Salt to taste

1 tablespoon cumin seeds

1 tablespoon mustard seeds

1 medium-sized garlic bulb

6 medium-sized tomatoes, not too ripe

4 large red and/or yellow bell peppers

1 cinnamon stick

1½ cups cooked chickpeas (1 15-ounce can, rinsed and drained)

3 tablespoons fresh lemon juice (possibly more)

Freshly ground black pepper

I suppose it's a contradiction in terms to make a stew in the oven, but this is probably the most delicious contradiction you'll ever eat. It's remarkably easy, too. The vegetables all fit onto two trays, and you can roast everything at the same time, assuming your oven has two racks. Very little labor is involved, so you can go about your business while the vegetables essentially cook themselves.

Preheat the oven to 375°F. Line two large baking trays with foil, and brush them with olive oil. Scatter the onions and carrots onto one tray, drizzle them with extra oil, and sprinkle with cumin, mustard seeds, and a little salt. Place the garlic bulb on one corner of the tray. Core the tomatoes, and arrange them on the second tray with the bell peppers.

Place the first tray on the lower rack in the oven, and the second tray on the upper rack. Bake the onions, carrots, etc., for about 30 to 35 minutes, stirring a few times, until the carrots are just tender. Remove the tray from the oven and set aside to cool.

Bake the tomatoes and peppers for about 45 minutes, turning the peppers with tongs every 10 minutes or so, so they blister evenly. (You don't have to turn the tomatoes.) Transfer to a large, heat-proof glass bowl, and add the cinnamon stick. Cover the bowl with foil or a plate, and let stand for about 30 minutes.

Mollie Katzen's VEGETABLE HEAVEN

Carefully lift out the peppers, leaving as much of their liquid in the bowl as possible, and remove their skins, seeds, and stems. (This will be a slippery operation, but otherwise easy.) Cut the peppers into strips and return them to the bowl. Then lift out the tomatoes, and pull off and discard the skins. Chop the pulp, and return it to the bowl. Fish out and discard the cinnamon stick.

When they are cool enough to handle, separate all the roasted garlic cloves, and squeeze the pulp into the bowlful of peppers and tomatoes. Scrape in the onions and carrots (including all the cumin and mustard seeds), and stir in the chickpeas and lemon juice. Taste to adjust the salt and lemon juice, and grind in some black pepper. Mix well.

Cover the bowl, and heat the stew in a 350°F oven for about 30 minutes, or in a microwave for 5 to 10 minutes. Serve hot, over or next to couscous, and garnished with minced parsley and wedges of lemon, if desired.

Yield: 4 to 6 servings
Preparation time: 1 hour (15 minutes of work)

OPTIONAL GARNISHES:

Minced fresh parsley

Squeezable wedges of lemon

....

⋆ *Serve Moroccan Roasted Vegetable Stew with plain rice or couscous, or with Couscous with Touches of Orange, Dill, and Pistachio (page 90).*

⋆ *For a more elaborate menu suggestion see page 213.*

SIZZLING LONG BEANS
WITH GARLIC AND CHILES

2 teaspoons Chinese sesame oil

1 pound Chinese long beans, cut into your desired length

¼ teaspoon salt

2 tablespoons minced garlic

3-inch jalapeño chile, thinly sliced (seeding optional)

• •

If you can't find Chinese long beans, you can substitute any variety of green beans. Trim them first.

If you seed the chile it will be milder.

For a menu suggestion, see page 213.

When I was growing up, frozen, "French-cut" green beans were my very favorite vegetable. I didn't see a fresh green bean until I was twelve, when I visited a friend whose mom had a vegetable garden, which I thought was very exotic. Even then, I couldn't have dreamed of the fresh bean varieties I would encounter in farmers' markets years later in California. Chinese long beans—and they are really long—are the most fun to prepare. You don't have to trim them, simply cut them into whatever length you desire.

Place a medium-sized wok over high heat. After about 30 seconds—or when the pan is good and hot—add the oil and the beans. Stir-fry for about 3 minutes over strong heat, then sprinkle in the salt. Stir-fry for about 3 more minutes until the beans are just barely done. This depends on their thickness, and on your taste.

Stir in the garlic and minced chile, and stir-fry for about 1 or 2 minutes longer. Serve hot or warm, with rice.

Yield: 2 to 3 servings (easily doubled if you have a large enough wok)
Preparation time: 15 minutes

Mollie Katzen's VEGETABLE HEAVEN

GREEN BEANS AND TOFU
IN CRUNCHY THAI PEANUT SAUCE

Prepare yourself for a virtual explosion of flavor and texture! And keep in mind that the fresher and firmer the green beans, the better this will taste.

Serve this with jasmine or basmati rice. (Put up the rice to cook before you begin.)

Place the peanuts in a blender, and grind briefly until they form a coarse meal. Set aside.

Heat a medium-sized heavy skillet. Add 1 tablespoon of the oil and the ginger and garlic. Sauté for a few minutes over medium heat, then add the crushed peanuts and the lemon zest. Cook over medium-low heat for 10 to 15 minutes, stirring often, until the peanuts are lightly toasted. Remove from the heat and set aside.

As the peanut mixture is cooking, heat a large wok or deep skillet. Drizzle in a little oil. When it is very hot, add the tofu cubes and ½ teaspoon salt. Cook over high heat for 10 to 15 minutes, stirring occasionally. Sprinkle with lemon juice, reduce the heat, and cook for a few minutes longer. Transfer the tofu to the pan containing the peanut mixture, and set aside.

Scrape out the wok or skillet if necessary, and return it to the heat. Let it get very hot, then add the remaining scant tablespoon of oil. When the oil is hot, add the green beans. (The pan should sizzle when the beans hit.) Stir-fry over high heat for about 5 minutes, then sprinkle with the remaining ½ teaspoon salt and some red pepper flakes.

Stir-fry for just a few minutes longer, or until the beans are divinely tender-crisp (mostly crisp, but just tender enough). Add the peanut-tofu mixture and toss everything together. Serve right away, over rice.

Yield: 4 to 6 servings (maybe fewer—this is hard to stop eating!)
Preparation time: 20 to 30 minutes (10 minutes of work)

1½ cups peanuts (unsalted or lightly salted)

2½ tablespoons peanut or vegetable oil

2 tablespoons minced fresh ginger

1 tablespoon minced garlic

½ teaspoon grated lemon zest

1 pound firm tofu, cut into small cubes

1 teaspoon salt

1 tablespoon fresh lemon juice

1 pound fresh green beans, trimmed and cut into 1½-inch pieces

Red pepper flakes to taste

⋆ *You'll need two pans: a medium-sized heavy skillet to sauté the peanut mixture, and a large, deep wok or skillet for the tofu and green beans. You can have both pans going at the same time.*

⋆ *The tofu cubes will be even firmer if you boil them for about 10 minutes ahead of time. Drain well before adding to the hot oil.*

BITTER GREENS
WITH SWEET ONIONS
AND SOUR CHERRIES

1 cup fresh sour cherries, pitted
(or canned unsweetened sour
cherries, drained)

2 to 3 teaspoons sugar

1 tablespoon vegetable oil

3 cups sliced onion
(a sweet variety, like Vidalia
or Maui, if available)

1¼ teaspoons salt

3 large bunches fresh greens,
stemmed if necessary, and
coarsely chopped (about
12 cups)

1 cup dried sour cherries (optional)

....

⭑ *Unsweetened sour cherries from a
can work beautifully here, but if you
have access to fresh sour cherries
(and you have a good pitting gadget), by all means use them.*

⭑ *You can also use dried sour cherries,
soaked for 15 minutes in hot water, and
drained.*

⭑ *This dish gives off a lot of cooking
liquid, but it is too pretty and delicious to let evaporate. So just include
some with each serving, especially if
you are pairing this dish with pasta
or rice.*

⭑ *For a menu suggestion, see page 212.*

*I love the taste of sour or tart fruit in savory dishes, especially in this very
unusual one, where the flavors of the greens, onions, and cherries are all
equally strong. The result is surprisingly balanced and smooth.*

*My favorite combination of greens for this dish is collards, red mustard,
arugula, and kale. The amount of greens listed might seem enormous, but don't
forget they will cook way down.*

Place the fresh or canned cherries in a small bowl and sprinkle them
with sugar. Let sit for about 10 minutes.

Heat the oil in a large, deep skillet or Dutch oven. Add the onion
and ½ teaspoon of the salt, and sauté over high heat for about 5
minutes. Turn the heat to medium, cover the pan, and let the onion
cook until very tender (about 10 more minutes).

Begin adding the greens in batches (as much as will fit), sprinkling
each addition with about ¼ teaspoon salt. Stir and cover between
additions, letting the greens cook down for about 5 minutes each
time, to make room for the next batch.

When all the greens are added and have wilted, stir in the sour
cherries and cook for just about 5 minutes longer. Transfer to a platter, and sprinkle the dried cherries on top, if desired. Serve hot or
warm, being sure to include some of the delicious cooking juices
with each serving.

Yield: 4 to 6 servings
Preparation time: 40 minutes (15 minutes of work)

Mollie Katzen's VEGETABLE HEAVEN

BITTER GREENS
WITH SWEET ONIONS
AND TART CHEESE

A variation on the preceding recipe, this version contains more onions, and substitutes feta cheese for the sour cherries. Superb on any short, substantial pasta, it also tastes good by itself, with a big chunk of crusty bread to mop up the juices.

Try a combination of kale, escarole or chard, and mustard greens to complement the pungent flavor of the cheese.

Heat the oil in a large, deep skillet or Dutch oven. Add the onion and salt lightly. Sauté over high heat for about 5 minutes, then turn the heat to medium, cover, and let the onion cook until very tender (about 10 more minutes).

Add the greens in batches, sprinkling lightly with salt after each addition. (Same as in the opposite recipe, but with less salt.)

When all the greens have wilted, stir in the feta, and cook for about 2 minutes longer. Taste to adjust salt. (Some feta cheeses are saltier than others.)

Transfer to a platter, and grind on a generous amount of black pepper. Serve hot or warm, on or next to pasta or grains, or by itself.

Yield: 4 to 6 servings
Preparation time: 40 minutes (15 minutes of work)

---

2 tablespoons olive oil

4 cups sliced onion (a sweet variety, like Vidalia or Maui, if available)

Salt to taste

3 large bunches fresh greens, stemmed if necessary, and coarsely chopped (about 12 cups)

½ to ¾ pound feta cheese, crumbled

Freshly ground black pepper

....

Vidalia onions are terrific, but if you can't find them, just use regular ones.

For a menu suggestion, see page 212.

SESAME CARROTS
ON A BED OF SOFT CABBAGE

2 teaspoons Chinese sesame oil

3 cups baby carrots

1 teaspoon salt

2 tablespoons unseasoned rice vinegar

2 tablespoons honey

2 teaspoons sesame tahini

1 large clove garlic, minced

1 teaspoon vegetable oil

3 cups chopped onion

6 cups chopped napa or savoy cabbage

Freshly ground black pepper

⋯⋯⋯⋯⋯⋯⋯⋯⋯⋯⋯⋯⋯⋯⋯

✷ To streamline preparation, have all the ingredients ready and right at hand before you start cooking. Use two pans, and cook the two components of this dish side by side to save time. This won't add much to the cleanup, because nonstick pans are so easy to wash.

✷ Mix the tahini from the bottom of the container before using it, so it will be smooth enough to blend into the sauce and effectively coat the carrots.

Here is a tasty two-layered vegetable dish that seems to appeal to people of all ages. Use the smallest baby carrots you can find. (If they're really small, you can use them whole, so there will be less chopping to do.)

Heat a nonstick wok or a large, deep nonstick skillet, and add the sesame oil, carrots, and ½ teaspoon of the salt. Stir-fry over medium-high heat for about 5 minutes. Cover, and cook for another 5 minutes.

Turn the heat down to medium, and add the vinegar. Cover again, and cook for an additional 5 minutes. Stir in the honey, tahini, and garlic, and cook uncovered, stirring frequently, for 5 to 8 more minutes, or until the carrots are tender and starting to brown.

At the same time, heat a second non-stick wok or skillet, and add the vegetable oil, the onion, and the remaining ½ teaspoon salt. Stir-fry over medium heat for 10 minutes, then add the cabbage. Keep the heat high, and stir-fry another 5 minutes or so, or until the cabbage wilts. (It will still be slightly crunchy.) Transfer to a serving platter.

Spoon the carrots on top of the cabbage. Grind some black pepper over the top, and serve hot, warm, or at room temperature.

Yield: 4 to 6 servings
Preparation time: 15 minutes

CAULIFLOWER
IN TOMATO CURRY

Add this flavorful quickie to your growing repertoire of wholesome make-after-work meals.

This is a basic recipe to which you can add other vegetables, if you have the inclination and the inventory. Try including thin slices of a small eggplant or zucchini, or some cleaned, stemmed spinach leaves.

Place the potato in a medium-sized saucepan and cover with water. Bring to a boil and cook until tender. Drain and set aside.

NOTE: You can save the potato water and use it to cook the cauliflower.

Meanwhile, heat the oil in a large, deep skillet or Dutch oven. Add the onion, ginger, and ½ teaspoon salt, and cook, covered, over medium-low heat for about 10 minutes. Add the spices and garlic, and sauté for about 5 minutes. Stir in the water, cauliflower, and another ½ teaspoon of the salt. Cover, and cook over medium heat for about 10 minutes, or until the cauliflower is tender.

Stir in the tomatoes, potatoes, and remaining salt. Cover again, and simmer for 10 to 15 more minutes over low heat.

Serve hot, with rice, and any of the accompaniments suggested, if desired.

Yield: 6 servings
Preparation time: 30 minutes (10 minutes of work)

---

1 medium potato, cut into small dice (peeling optional)

1 tablespoon vegetable or peanut oil

1½ cups chopped onion

4 thin slices fresh ginger, cut on the diagonal—about 2 inches long

1¼ teaspoons salt

½ teaspoon ground cumin

½ teaspoon turmeric

¼ teaspoon allspice

½ teaspoon ground fennel

1 tablespoon minced garlic

½ cup water

4 cups chopped cauliflower (about 1½ pounds)

A 1-pound 12-ounce can crushed tomatoes

....

Put up some basmati rice to cook first, then start boiling the potatoes. If you prepare everything else while the rice and potatoes are cooking, dinner will be ready in 30 minutes.

Any or all of the following would make great accompaniments: yogurt, toasted cashews, raisins, Indian pickles or chutney, or toasted coconut.

You can make this up to several days ahead—it reheats very well.

SUGAR SNAP PEAS
WITH A SINGLE HERB

1 pound fresh sugar snap peas

2 teaspoons butter

Salt and pepper to taste

1 to 2 tablespoons minced fresh
savory, tarragon, mint, marjoram,
or thyme (pick just one)

....

Choose only the freshest, tightest
sugar snaps, so they can cook
very quickly and still be crisp, yet
sublimely tender.

Dried herbs will work in this
recipe if you can't get fresh ones.

For a menu suggestion, see page 213.

Sugar snaps—those chubby, edible-pod peas—are so good raw or lightly cooked, I don't like to gussy them up too much. In this recipe, all you do is sauté them lightly in butter, sprinkle in a little salt and pepper, and add just a touch of a single herb (you get to choose which one). There. I just told you the whole recipe.

This is a great choice for cooks who hate to chop. Just snip the chosen herb with scissors.

Remove the tops from the peas, and pull off the strings.

Melt the butter in a skillet over medium-high heat. Add the peas, keeping the heat fairly high. Cook quickly for about 1 minute. Sprinkle with salt, pepper, and the herb of your choice. Cook quickly for about 1 minute longer.

Transfer to a bowl and eat as soon as possible, while they are still bright green, puffy, and hot.

Yield: 4 to 6 servings
Preparation time: About 5 minutes

Mollie Katzen's VEGETABLE HEAVEN

PEA SHOOTS
WITH GARLIC

Early in the season, when pea vines have just a few leaves and tendrils, the shoots themselves are delightful to eat. The pleasures of cooking with pea shoots have long been known to Chinese cooks, but are a relatively new discovery in the West. If you don't grow your own peas, look for fresh pea shoots at a farmers' market or a good greengrocer.

Pea shoots can be eaten raw in salads, or stir-fried very briefly in a hot pan. They have a good strong flavor and a wonderful crunchy texture. Best of all, they require no chopping. Just rinse and drain them, and they're ready to go.

I call this The Fastest Stir-Fry in the East-West.

Heat a wok or large, deep skillet. When it is very hot, add the oil and the pea shoots, and stir-fry over medium heat for about 2 or 3 minutes.

Add the garlic and salt, and stir-fry for about 2 to 3 minutes longer, attempting to distribute the garlic as evenly as possible through the tangle of shoots (tongs work beautifully for this.) Remove from heat as soon as the pea shoots are wilted and have turned a deep green. Serve hot or warm.

Yield: 4 to 6 servings
Preparation time: Less than 10 minutes

1 tablespoon peanut or
   vegetable oil

1 pound pea shoots, rinsed
   and drained

2 tablespoons minced garlic

½ teaspoon salt

Carrots, julienned

For a menu suggestion, see page 213.

SWEET POTATOES AND SPINACH

IN SPICED ORANGE SAUCE

2 to 3 tablespoons vegetable oil and/or butter

3 cups chopped onion

3 tablespoons Persian Allspice (recipe follows), or 3 tablespoons regular allspice

2 teaspoons salt

2½ tablespoons minced garlic

8 cups peeled, cubed sweet potatoes or yams (about 3 pounds)

3 cups orange juice

1½ cups dried sugar plums or prunes, pitted and sliced

1 pound fresh spinach, cleaned and stemmed (or 1 10-ounce package frozen leaf spinach, defrosted)

Persian Allspice

1 tablespoon coriander seeds

1 to 2 teaspoons cardamom pods

1 tablespoon cumin seeds

2 teaspoons cinnamon

2 teaspoons turmeric

2 teaspoons ground ginger

½ teaspoon ground cloves

¼ teaspoon black pepper

....

✶ Make the Persian Allspice ahead of time. If you use an electric spice grinder, this will take just a minute or two.

✶ Get the rice going before you begin.

✶ You can use fresh plums, peaches or nectarines in place of the dried sugar plums or prunes.

✶ For a menu suggestion, see page 213.

I modeled this dish after a traditional Persian stew called Koresh. Adapted from the family recipe of a friend of mine, sweet potatoes are steeped in orange juice and deeply infused with the heavenly flavor of homemade Persian Allspice. Serve this with plain basmati rice, or with any of the pilafs on pages 82 to 84.

NOTE: If you're short on time, substitute commercial, prepared allspice for the Persian Allspice.

Heat the oil and/or melt the butter in a large, deep pot or a Dutch oven. Add the onion, 3 tablespoons Persian Allspice, (or regular allspice), and 1 teaspoon of the salt, and sauté for about 5 minutes over medium heat.

Stir in the garlic, sweet potatoes or yams, orange juice, and remaining salt. Cover and cook over medium heat, stirring occasionally, until the sweet potatoes are tender—about 30 minutes, depending on the size and shape of the pieces.

Add the fruit and the spinach, and give it a good stir. Cover and cook over low heat for 10 minutes longer.

Serve hot, over—or next to—plain cooked basmati rice or a pilaf.

Yield: 6 to 8 servings, depending upon how many other dishes you are serving
Preparation time: 1 hour (15 minutes of work)

Persian Allspice

Grind everything together in a spice grinder until it becomes a fairly uniform powder. This makes enough for 2 batches of stew.

BRUSSELS SPROUTS
IN CREAMY MUSTARD SAUCE

In their prime, Brussels sprouts are incredibly buttery, sweet, and tender —high on my list of favorite vegetables. However, they really must be served only when they are very fresh, young, and in season. Otherwise, they will probably be tough and bitter, further tarnishing their undeserved bad reputation.

Whisk together the sauce ingredients in a medium-sized bowl. Cover and let the mixture come to room temperature. (You can also heat it gently in the microwave for about 40 seconds.) Set aside.

Quarter or mince the Brussels sprouts, unless they are very small, in which case leave them whole.

Melt the butter in a large skillet. Add the Brussels sprouts and sprinkle lightly with salt. Stir, cover, and cook over medium heat until quite tender (8 to 10 minutes). When they are done to your liking, transfer them to a serving bowl or small platter, and pour the sauce over the top. Serve right away.

Yield: 4 to 6 servings
Preparation time: 15 minutes

Sauce

1½ cups yogurt

2 tablespoons Dijon mustard

2 tablespoons real maple syrup or honey

¼ to ½ teaspoon salt

1 tablespoon minced fresh dill (or 1 teaspoon dried dill)

Freshly ground black pepper to taste

1 to 1½ pounds Brussels sprouts

1 tablespoon butter

Salt to taste

....

If you prefer not to cook the Brussels sprouts in butter, you can just steam them instead.

The sauce also doubles as a great topping for broiled fish or roasted potatoes.

ASPARAGUS
IN WARM TARRAGON-PECAN VINAIGRETTE

1½ pounds fresh asparagus (the thinner, the better)

2 tablespoons balsamic or cider vinegar

2 teaspoons sugar

2 tablespoons olive oil

1 cup minced pecans

1 tablespoon minced garlic

¾ teaspoon salt

1 to 2 tablespoons minced fresh tarragon (or 2 teaspoons dried)

Black pepper to taste

....

This dish tastes best within an hour of being made. Serve it over or next to rice, if desired.

If you are not a vegetarian, try this with grilled salmon.

For a menu suggestion, see page 211.

Asparagus has a passionate affinity for tarragon. Throw in some pecans for good measure, and this becomes a delicious welcoming party for the spring season.

Break off and discard the tough bottom ends of the asparagus, then slice the stalks on the diagonal into 1½-inch pieces. Set aside.

Combine the vinegar and sugar in a small bowl and mix until the sugar dissolves. Set aside.

Heat the oil in a large skillet. Add the pecans, and sauté over medium-low heat for about 10 minutes, or until they are fragrant and lightly toasted. Be careful not to let them burn.

Turn the heat to medium-high, and add the asparagus, garlic, and ½ teaspoon of the salt. Stir-fry for about 3 to 5 minutes, or until the asparagus is just barely tender. (Thicker asparagus will take longer.)

Add the vinegar mixture to the asparagus, stirring well. Cook over high heat for only about 30 seconds longer, then remove from heat.

Stir in the tarragon, the remaining salt, and black pepper to taste. Serve hot, warm, or at room temperature.

Yield: 4 to 6 servings
Preparation time: 20 minutes

WHIPPED SWEET POTATOES

WITH LIME

I love to experiment by throwing different kinds of vegetables over (or into) the coals when the outdoor grill is fired up. My favorite is the plain old sweet potato, which somehow transforms itself into a superb delicacy when bundled in foil and mercilessly tossed into the glowing inferno. The insides of the sweet potato become buttery beyond description, and its natural sweetness deepens. All you need to add, for an utterly divine result, is a healthy drizzle of fresh lime juice. That's all! No butter, and absolutely no marshmallows.

Of course, you are not going to be tossing yams into fires on any kind of regular basis, but the good new is this: the lime juice trick also works on sweet potatoes that have been baked, boiled, or microwaved. Just scoop them out of their skins, mash or whip them until smooth, and drizzle on fresh lime juice to taste. People will ask you for the recipe, and you'll tell them there really isn't one.

However, here's a recipe-of-sorts, just in case you need a guideline:

Cook the sweet potatoes your favorite way (peeled or not, whole or cut, baked, nuked, or boiled—or grilled in the coals, if you're lucky).

If you cooked the sweet potatoes whole and unpeeled, scoop out the insides. Mash by hand, or whip with a handheld electric mixer.

Add fresh lime juice to taste, and a little salt, if desired.

Serve hot or very warm, for lunch, dinner, or snacks.

Yield: Customize your own (see amounts above)
Preparation time: Just a few minutes after the sweet potatoes are cooked

---

Sweet potatoes or yams (1 medium-sized one per person)

Fresh lime juice (a few squirts per person)

Salt to taste (altogether optional)

....

For a menu suggestion, see page 213.

BROCCOLI-STUFFED MUSHROOMS

1½ pounds broccoli

1 small onion (about ¼ pound)

1½ tablespoons olive oil

¼ teaspoon salt (possibly more, to taste)

1½ cups grated gruyère or emmenthaler cheese (about ¾ pound)

Black pepper to taste

4 portobello mushrooms (4-inch-diameter)—or 14 to 16 domestic mushrooms (2-inch-diameter)

....

☆ If you make these with portobello mushrooms, you'll end up with portions large enough to be a meal unto themselves.

☆ For a menu suggestion, see page 211.

Stuffed mushrooms were very fashionable when I was first learning to cook. They were a special treat, made with domestic mushrooms (portobellos hadn't been discovered yet), and the stuffing usually consisted of something very rich, like buttered bread crumbs and cheese.

Here is a modern version of this retro concept, streamlined and de-fatted to please the busy, health-minded modern cook (who hadn't been invented yet, either).

Shave the outer skins from the broccoli stalks with a good vegetable peeler. Cut off the topmost florets, leaving a bit of stem, so you'll have something to "plant," and set aside. Cut the shaved stems and the onion into chunks, place them in a food processor, and process until finely minced. You might have to do this in batches.

Heat ½ tablespoon of oil in a medium-large skillet with an oven-proof handle. Add the broccoli florets and a pinch of salt. Stir-fry over medium heat for just a few minutes, or until the florets are bright green and tender-crisp. Transfer to a bowl, and set aside.

Without cleaning it, heat the skillet again. Add another ½ tablespoon of oil, the minced broccoli-onion mixture, and ¼ teaspoon salt. Sauté over medium-high heat for 5 minutes, then transfer to a bowl and stir in 1 cup of the grated cheese. Grind in some black pepper.

Remove and discard the mushrooms stems, and peel the mushrooms, if necessary. If you're using portobello mushrooms, scrape out the soft insides of the mushroom cap with a spoon if desired. Divide the filling evenly among the hollowed-out mushrooms, and arrange a tight cluster of broccoli florets right in the top of each one. Meanwhile, preheat the broiler.

Wipe out the skillet with a paper towel, and return it to the stove. Turn the heat to medium, and add the remaining ½ tablespoon oil. Place the filled mushrooms in the pan, cover, and cook undisturbed for about 10 to 15 minutes, or until the mushrooms are cooked through. Sprinkle the remaining cheese over the tops, and place the entire skillet under the broiler for 3 to 5 minutes, or until the cheese is thoroughly melted and lightly browned. Serve hot, warm, or at room temperature.

Yield: 4 to 6 servings, depending on the context
Preparation time: 50 minutes (20 minutes of work)

Mollie Katzen's VEGETABLE HEAVEN

BROILED BABY ZUCCHINI BOATS

WITH PARMESAN CRUST

Usher in the zucchini season with these neat little vessels. They're tender and moist with a pungent, crunchy top. You might also attract a few young children to zucchini in the process. Let them sprinkle on the cheese and this may actually interest them in eating the final result.

Preheat the broiler. Melt the butter in a large cast-iron skillet or something similar with an ovenproof handle. Add the garlic, and sauté over medium-low heat for about 30 seconds, being careful to let the garlic brown.

Place the zucchini halves facedown in the garlic butter and sprinkle lightly with salt and pepper. Sauté over medium high heat for about 5 minutes, or until the zucchini are just slightly tender when poked gently with a fork.

Turn the zucchini over, and sprinkle generously with parmesan. (Don't worry if the parmesan spills into the pan. It will melt into additional, delicious crust.) Cook for just a minute or two longer, then transfer the skillet to the broiler.

Broil for about 3 to 5 minutes, or until the cheese is melted and golden brown. Serve hot, and don't forget to scrape up the spilled parmesan from the bottom of the pan.

Yield: 4 to 6 servings
Preparation time: 15 minutes

1 tablespoon butter

2 teaspoons minced garlic

4 small zucchini and/or summer squash (slender ones, about 6 inches long), halved lengthwise

Salt and pepper

Grated parmesan

TIDY LITTLE MAIN DISHES

Lunch, Brunch, and Supper

Bergman, acknowledging a lack of expertise in the field, agreed to search out a Spanish-speaking tamale specialist who would know for certain how to find the best green-corn tamales in New Mexico. A few days later he called to inform me that I might be looking for blue-corn tamales, since green and blue are the same word in Navajo. I began to worry that I had chosen the wrong tamale man.

"I didn't ask for a scholarly footnote," I told him. "I need tamales."

—Calvin Trillin, *Alice, Let's Eat*

Savory Corn Cakes for breakfast or supper, Magic Carrot Flans for high tea with an old friend, Golden Rice Pie with its fantastic spinach filling for a family gathering on a chilly Sunday afternoon, Olive Waffles at midnight ... sometimes this is all we need to satisfy a certain nameless craving. A single baked dish cut into wedges or squares, a special something sautéed on the griddle, or just a humble sandwich, simply assembled and eaten out of hand—this can be the most perfect food in the world. Eat these special preparations by themselves, or serve them with salads, condiments, or soups, any time of day or night.

TIDY LITTLE MAIN DISHES
Lunch, Brunch, and Supper

OLIVE WAFFLES

Yes, Olive Waffles. Or pancakes, if you are so inclined. These savory skillet breads are wonderful for spontaneous late suppers or evening snacks, especially when served with GuacaMollie, or as the Russians serve blini—with a little sour cream and caviar or smoked salmon.

NOTE: The batter keeps fairly well for a few days if covered tightly and refrigerated, so you can make the waffles "to order," when the craving hits.

Separate the eggs, placing the whites in a large bowl and the yolks in a medium-sized one.

Combine the flours, baking soda, baking powder, and salt in a medium-sized bowl. Make a well in the center, and add the olives and rosemary.

Add the buttermilk and olive oil to the egg yolks, and whisk together until uniform. Pour this mixture into the well in the center of the dry ingredients, and mix briefly until blended.

Beat the egg whites until stiff, and fold them into the batter, along with the olives and the rosemary.

Bake on a hot, lightly greased waffle iron until golden and crisp. (For pancakes, cook on a skillet or griddle for about 3 to 4 minutes on each side.) Serve hot, with the topping(s) of your choice.

Yield: 4 to 5 servings
Preparation time: 10 minutes, plus about 4 minutes to cook each waffle (depending on the waffle iron) and about 8 minutes per batch of pancakes.

3 large eggs

1 1/4 cups unbleached white flour

1/2 cup whole wheat flour

1 teaspoon baking soda

1/2 teaspoon baking powder

1/4 teaspoon salt

1/2 cup minced pitted Kalamata olives

1/2 teaspoon crumbled dried (or 2 teaspoons minced fresh) rosemary

1 1/2 cups buttermilk

1 tablespoon olive oil

A little butter or oil for the waffle iron

MANY POSSIBLE TOPPINGS:

GuacaMollie (page 158)

Sour cream

Caviar or strips of smoked salmon

Dried Tomato Pesto (page 160)

Chimichurri (page 165)

Mediterranean Yogurt (page 169)

★ *Use a nonstick waffle iron (or a nonstick skillet, if you're making pancakes).*

★ *Store leftover waffles or pancakes in sealed plastic bags in the refrigerator. They reheat beautifully in a toaster oven.*

★ *For a menu suggestion, see page 212.*

SAVORY CORN CAKES

You can whip up these little gems in just 20 minutes, any time of day or night. They can be a breakfast or light supper in and of themselves, or a first course or side dish for a more complex meal.

2 teaspoons butter

¼ cup finely minced red bell pepper

2 cups corn

¼ cup minced scallions

½ cup cornmeal

½ cup unbleached white flour

I teaspoon baking powder

½ teaspoon baking soda

½ teaspoon salt

2 large eggs

I cup buttermilk

Oil or butter for the pan

OPTIONAL TOPPINGS:

Cilantro leaves

Chipotle Cream (page 166)

GuacaMollie (page 158)

Melt the butter in a small skillet. Add the bell pepper and corn, and sauté over medium heat for about 10 minutes. Remove from heat, stir in the scallions, and set aside.

Combine the cornmeal, flour, baking powder, baking soda, and salt in a medium-sized bowl. Make a well in the center.

Beat together the eggs and buttermilk until frothy. Pour this and the corn mixture into the well in the center of the dry ingredients, and stir briefly until everything is combined. Don't overmix.

Lightly grease a hot skillet or griddle with butter or oil, and fry the corn cakes for about 2 minutes on each side, or until golden. Serve hot, topped with a few cilantro leaves and a drizzle of room-temperature Chipotle Cream, or a dollop of GuacaMollie, if desired.

Yield: About a dozen 4-inch corn cakes
Preparation time: 20 minutes

★ *Frozen, defrosted corn works perfectly well in these pancakes. Canned corn is also okay, just as long as it doesn't contain sugar. Rinse and drain it thoroughly first.*

★ *For a menu suggestion, see page 211.*

FRIED GREEN TOMATO PILLOWS

Traditional fried green tomatoes are very light, and are usually served as a side dish or a snack. Attempting to create a fried green tomato variation substantial enough to be a light brunch or supper entrée, I came up with these fantastic cornmeal batter-coated puffs. Serve them with any one of several toppings alongside some cooked greens or a tossed salad, and everyone will be happy for hours.

Combine the flour, cornmeal, baking powder, salt, and cayenne in a medium-sized bowl and stir until well combined. Make a well in the center.

In a separate bowl, beat together the milk and eggs until frothy, and pour this into the well in the center of the flour/cornmeal mixture. Stir until thoroughly combined, but don't overmix.

Core the tomatoes and cut them into ½-inch rounds. (Meanwhile begin heating a little oil or melting a little butter in a skillet over medium heat.)

Add the tomato slices to the batter one by one, pushing them around gently with a spoon until they are well coated. Lift them from the batter with the spoon, and add them to the hot skillet. (You might need to spoon a little extra batter on top of each tomato, so no bald spots are peeking through.) Fry on both sides until crispy and golden, and serve hot, topped with sour cream, yogurt, Chipotle Cream or Chimichurri.

Yield: 4 to 6 servings
Preparation time: 20 to 30 minutes

1 cup unbleached white flour

1 cup cornmeal

2 teaspoons baking powder

¾ teaspoon salt

⅛ teaspoon cayenne

1 cup milk

2 large eggs

2 large unripe tomatoes, in ½-inch slices (about 1 pound)

A little oil or butter for the pan

OPTIONAL GARNISHES:

Sour cream or yogurt

Chipotle Cream (page 166)

Chimichurri (page 165)

⋆ You can make the batter up to several days ahead and store it in an airtight container in the refrigerator. If necessary, thin it with a little extra milk before coating the tomatoes.

⋆ If you can't get bona fide green tomatoes, just use the least ripe ones you can find. For those of you who grow your own, this won't be a problem.

⋆ For a menu suggestion, see page 213.

MAGIC CARROT FLANS

As these fragrant custards bake, they turn a creamy shade of yellow on the outside and a beautiful deep rust color on the inside. It's like magic.

1 tablespoon butter

1½ cups minced onion

1¼ teaspoon salt

1 tablespoon minced garlic

1 tablespoon dried thyme

1 tablespoon dried rubbed sage

4 cups fresh carrot juice

6 large eggs

1 cup milk (lowfat or soy okay)

A little melted butter or oil spray for the ramekins

1 medium-sized carrot, julienned and lightly steamed

Sprigs of fresh flowering thyme (optional)

★ *Use fresh carrot juice (the kind you find in a deli or health food store refrigerator), rather than canned. Or better yet, press your own in a juicer, if you have one.*

★ *Serve Magic Carrot Flans for supper or brunch, with Crostini (page 55) and a Frisée and Mushroom Salad (page 18).*

★ *The flans keep well if stored in a tightly-covered container in the refrigerator, and can be reheated in a microwave at a low power. However, the magical color will not hold.*

Preheat the oven to 350°F. Place a folded kitchen towel neatly in the bottom of a 9 x 13-inch baking pan. Grease or oil-spray four 12-ounce or six 8-ounce ramekins, custard cups, or ovenproof bowls, and place them on top of the towel.*

Melt the butter in a skillet or sauté pan over medium heat. Add the onion and ½ teaspoon salt, and sauté for 8 to 10 minutes, or until soft and translucent. Stir in another ¾ teaspoon salt, the garlic, and the herbs, and sauté for about 2 minutes longer. Add the carrot juice, bring to a boil, then turn the heat way down. Simmer uncovered until the carrot juice is reduced by about half. This should take 10 to 12 minutes. Remove from heat and set aside.

Combine the eggs and milk in a medium-large bowl, and beat slowly with a fork. (If you beat it too vigorously, you will incorporate air bubbles, and the custard won't be as smooth.)

Place a fine sieve or a cheesecloth-lined strainer over the bowl, and strain the carrot juice mixture into the eggs and milk, pressing all the liquid from—then discarding—the solids. Gently stir until thoroughly blended.

Stir from the bottom one more time so it won't separate, and immediately ladle the custard into the ramekins. Pour hot (not boiling) water into the baking pan until it reaches halfway up the sides. Bake 45 minutes to 1 hour, or until the custards are just set.

Remove the ramekins from the pan, let them cool for 5 minutes, then loosen the sides with a dinner knife, and unmold onto a plate. Serve hot, warm, or at room temperature, garnished with steamed, julienned carrots and sprigs of fresh flowering thyme, if available.

The purpose of the water in the pan—and the towel underneath—is to surround the baking custards with constant, moist heat, so they will cook evenly and acquire a fantastically smooth texture.

Yield: 4 to 6 servings
Preparation time: 1½ hours (15 minutes of work)

CAULIFLOWER KUKUS

A kuku is a Persian-style omelette that is filled with vegetables and baked in a shallow pan. In this fun version, the eggs and vegetables are divided into individual portions and baked in large muffin cups, giving the final product a delightful shape. Sturdy, yet tender, these kukus are a perfect entrée for brunch or a light supper.

Preheat oven to 350°F. Generously grease or oil-spray the bottoms and sides of six 4-inch muffin cups or twelve 2½-inch muffin cups (preferably nonstick).

Heat 1 tablespoon olive oil in a large skillet and add the onion and bay leaves. Sauté for just a few minutes, then add ½ teaspoon salt. Sauté for 8 to 10 minutes longer, or until the onion is very soft.

Add the garlic and cauliflower; stir and cover. Cook over medium heat until the cauliflower is tender (about 8 to 10 minutes). Remove from heat, and discard the bay leaves.

Cut the tomato in half, and squeeze out and discard the seeds. Chop the tomato into 1-inch pieces and add them to the cauliflower, along with the bread crumbs.

Divide the vegetables evenly among the muffin pans, sprinkle with black pepper and feta cheese, and set aside.

Beat the eggs with a whisk or in a blender until smooth and frothy. Stir in the remaining ½ teaspoon salt and the parsley. Ladle the egg mixture into the pans, distributing it as evenly as possible.

Bake for 35 to 40 minutes, or until solid in the center when a knife is inserted. Allow to cool in the pans for about 10 minutes before removing and serving.

Yield: 6 large or 12 small kukus
Preparation time: 1½ hours (30 minutes of work)

Butter, oil, or oil spray for the pans

1 tablespoon olive oil

2 cups minced onion

2 bay leaves

1 teaspoon salt

1 tablespoon minced garlic

6 cups small cauliflowerets
  (1 large head)

1 medium-sized ripe tomato

¼ cup fine bread crumbs

Black pepper to taste

1 cup crumbled feta cheese
  (about ⅓ pound)

1 dozen large eggs

¼ cup minced fresh parsley

★ *Try packing the kukus as a portable lunch. They're good at any temperature.*

★ *Nonstick pans work best for these, and even they should be lightly oiled. (Don't use paper liners—they will stick.) Six-ounce ramekins will also work, but grease them really well first.*

★ *For a complete menu, see page 212.*

FRITTATA
WITH RED ONIONS, ROASTED GARLIC, GREENS, AND GOAT CHEESE

Do you sometimes need an omelette that's more than just an omelette? Do you need it to be complex, thick, and colorful, and to come out of the oven steaming, aromatic, and golden? Maybe you need this recipe.

1 tablespoon plus 2 teaspoons olive oil

1½ cups thinly sliced red onion (about 1 medium onion)

1 teaspoon salt

2 teaspoons minced fresh rosemary (or a scant teaspoon dried)

8 large collard greens and/or Swiss chard leaves, chopped small

1 tablespoon Roasted Garlic Paste (page xiv)

8 large eggs

Freshly ground black pepper

4 ounces goat cheese, crumbled

POSSIBLE TOPPINGS:

Smoky Hot Sauce (page 167)

Roasted Tomato-Garlic Sauce (page 164)

Horseradish Aioli (page 168)

★ *Ruby chard looks especially pretty in this frittata. You can include the minced stalks, as well as the leaves.*

★ *This recipe calls for Roasted Garlic Paste, so be sure to prepare some well in advance.*

★ *For variations, experiment using leftover cooked vegetables. Thinly sliced potatoes are especially good.*

Heat 1 tablespoon of olive oil in a 9-inch skillet with an ovenproof handle, and add the onion, ½ teaspoon salt, and rosemary. Sauté for about 10 minutes over medium heat.

Stir in the chopped greens and the remaining ½ teaspoon salt, and sauté for another minute or two, or until the greens are wilted but still brightly colored. Remove from heat, stir in the Roasted Garlic Paste, and set aside.

Break the eggs into a large bowl, and beat well with a whisk. Add the sautéed vegetables, some black pepper, and the goat cheese, and stir with a spoon until blended.

Wipe the skillet clean and return it to the stove. Preheat the broiler.

Heat the remaining 2 teaspoons of oil in the same skillet over medium-high heat. Tilt the pan in all directions to be sure the entire bottom surface is coated. When the oil is very hot, pour in the vegetable-egg mixture and cook for 3 to 4 minutes, or until the eggs are set on the bottom.

Transfer the skillet to the preheated broiler, and broil for about 3 minutes, or until the frittata is firm in the center. Run a flexible rubber spatula around the edge of the frittata to loosen it from the skillet, and slide or invert it onto a large, round plate.

Serve hot, warm, or at room temperature, cut into wedges and topped with Smoky Hot Sauce or Roasted Tomato-Garlic Sauce. Frittata is also delicious served cold in a sandwich, with Horseradish Aioli and slices of ripe tomato.

Yield: 4 to 6 servings
Preparation time: 30 minutes

Mollie Katzen's VEGETABLE HEAVEN

FRENCH PICNIC TART
WITH POTATOES, RED PEPPERS, SAGE, AND GRUYÈRE

Transport yourself to the French countryside without even leaving your house. With this beautiful, authentic-tasting tart, you'll feel like you're really there.

Prepare the "Perfect Ten" Tart Crust and fit it into a 10-inch spring-form tart pan. Set aside.

Preheat the oven to 375°F. Place the potatoes in a medium-sized saucepan, cover them with water, and bring to a boil. Cook until just tender but still intact (about 10 to 15 minutes). Drain and set aside.

While the potatoes are cooking, heat the oil in a medium-sized skillet over high heat. Add the onion and salt, turn the heat down, and cook slowly over low heat until the onion is translucent and tender (10 to 15 minutes). Remove from heat, sprinkle generously with black pepper, and set aside.

Spread about 1 cup of the cheese into the bottom of the unbaked crust. Spoon the cooked onion over the cheese and sprinkle with sage.

When the potatoes are cool enough to handle, peel them with a sharp paring knife, and cut them into slices. Arrange the potato slices to overlap in concentric circles, covering the onion and sage, then create an artful arrangement of bell pepper slices on top of the potatoes. Sprinkle with the remaining cheese and a little extra black pepper.

Set the tart on a baking tray for easy handling, and bake for 35 to 40 minutes, or until the crust is golden around the edges. (Move the tray to the lowest shelf of the oven for the last 5 minutes, to be sure the bottom crust is cooked through and crisp.)

Remove the tray from the oven, slide the tart off the tray, and let it sit for at least 10 minutes. To serve, remove the rim and cut the tart into wedges. Serve hot, warm, or at room temperature.

Yield: 4 main-dish servings (more as a side dish)
Preparation time (after the crust is made): 1 hour (30 minutes of work)

---

1 unbaked "Perfect Ten" Tart Crust (page 191)

1 pound small red potatoes

1 to 2 tablespoons olive oil

1 large onion, thinly sliced (about 2 cups)

½ teaspoon salt

Freshly ground black pepper to taste

1½ cups grated gruyère or emmenthaler cheese (¼ pound)

2 tablespoons minced fresh sage (or 2 teaspoons dried rubbed sage)

½ medium-sized red bell pepper, thinly sliced

....

★ *Prepare the crust well ahead of time, cover tightly, and refrigerate or freeze. You don't need to defrost it before assembling the tart.*

★ *You can streamline preparations by cooking the onion and potatoes at the same time. This can be done in advance.*

★ *For an elegant, full-fledged menu, see page 212.*

GOLDEN RICE PIE
WITH SPINACH FILLING

If you love rice dishes with a distinct flair, try this one. Brown basmati rice is blended with a tart, lemony custard, layered with boldly seasoned spinach, and baked in a mold until golden brown. For an exotic finishing touch, sprinkle some pine nuts and pomegranate seeds over the top of each serving.

3 cups uncooked brown basmati rice

4 1/2 cups water

2 tablespoons olive oil

4 cups minced onion

1/2 teaspoon salt

2 tablespoons minced garlic

2 teaspoons ground cumin

1/2 teaspoon ground coriander

1/2 teaspoon cinnamon

1/4 teaspoon nutmeg

I pound spinach, cleaned, stemmed, and minced

1/2 teaspoon salt

2 cups lowfat yogurt

I large egg

I tablespoon grated lemon zest

I tablespoon fresh lemon juice

I teaspoon salt

1/8 teaspoon white pepper

Butter for the baking dish

Lightly toasted pine nuts for garnish

Pomegranate seeds (optional)

★ To streamline preparation time, cook the onions and rice at the same time.

★ You will thank yourself for grating the lemon zest before juicing the lemon.

★ This is a great choice for potluck dinners—it travels well and feeds a crowd.

★ For a menu suggestion, see page 212.

Place the rice and water in a saucepan with a tight-fitting lid, and bring to a boil. Reduce heat to a simmer, cover, and cook over very low heat until tender (about 20 to 30 minutes). Fluff with a fork to let steam escape, and set aside to cool a little.

While the rice is cooking, heat the olive oil in a large, deep skillet. When it is very hot, add the onion and 1/2 teaspoon salt, and turn the heat to medium-low. Stir and cook for about 5 minutes, then cover the pan and let the onion cook for 30 minutes longer. Stir in the garlic and spices, and cook for about 5 more minutes. Turn the heat way up and add the spinach and another 1/2 teaspoon salt. Stir-fry for just a few minutes, or until all the liquid has evaporated. Remove from heat.

Preheat the oven to 350°F. Generously butter a 2-quart lidded casserole about 10 inches in diameter and 2 to 3 inches deep.

Place the yogurt, egg, lemon zest, and lemon juice in a large bowl and sprinkle in 1 teaspoon salt and the white pepper. Beat well, add the rice and mix thoroughly.

Firmly press half the rice into the buttered casserole. Lift the spinach mixture from the skillet with a slotted spoon and spread it over the rice, then top the spinach with the remaining rice, smoothing it firmly into place. Cover the casserole with foil or a tight-fitting lid that has been buttered.

Bake for 45 minutes in the center rack of the oven, then for another 10 minutes on the bottom shelf. Remove from the oven, and let it sit for about 10 minutes, then invert the pie onto a platter. It will have a beautiful golden crust.

Serve hot or warm, cut into wedges, and sprinkled with toasted pine nuts and a few pomegranate seeds, if available.

Yield: 8 or more servings
Preparation time: 2 hours (35 minutes of work)

Mollie Katzen's VEGETABLE HEAVEN

EGGPLANT STRATA
WITH ZUCCHINI AND ROASTED RED PEPPERS

Actually, this is a Tidy Big Main Dish—enough for a crowd. Serve Eggplant Strata with fresh crusty bread to mop up the juices, and a small green salad on the side, and everyone will be happy.

NOTE: Make the Roasted Tomato-Garlic Sauce—and roast and peel the bell peppers—a day or two ahead of time, and the final preparations will be quite easy. The eggplant and zucchini don't need precooking, so just slice them, layer everything, and bake.

Preheat the oven to 350°F. Lightly oil a 9 x 13-inch pan.

In a medium-sized bowl, combine the ricotta, parmesan or pecorino, salt, pepper, cayenne, scallions, and rosemary, and mix well.

Spread a double layer of eggplant slices in the bottom of the prepared pan, followed by a single layer of zucchini. Spoon on half the ricotta mixture in small mounds, then lay half the roasted pepper strips on top. Cover the peppers with half of the smoked mozzarella slices, and ladle on half the Roasted Tomato-Garlic Sauce.

Spread a single layer of eggplant on top of the sauce, then repeat all the other layers, ending with the remaining sauce on top of the mozzarella. Bake uncovered for 1½ hours. (Cover lightly with foil if the top becomes too brown.)

Remove the pan from the oven, and let it sit for at least 15 minutes before serving. Cut into squares and serve hot, warm, or at room temperature.

Yield: 10 to 12 servings
Preparation time: 2 hours, after the sauce is made and the peppers are roasted (30 minutes of work)

A little oil for the pan

I pound ricotta cheese

I cup grated parmesan or pecorino cheese

I teaspoon salt

½ teaspoon black pepper

A pinch of cayenne

1½ cups minced scallions (about 2 bunches)

2 tablespoons minced fresh rosemary (or 2 teaspoons crumbled dried rosemary)

I recipe Roasted Tomato-Garlic Sauce (page 164)

2 pounds eggplant, in ½-inch slices, round or lengthwise (peeling optional)

4 small zucchini (about I pound), cut into thin circles

3 medium-sized red bell peppers, roasted, peeled, and cut into wide strips (page 96)

I pound smoked mozzarella cheese, thinly sliced

⭐ *You can freeze the baked strata in individual portions for easy reheating in a microwave. Just be sure to wrap them tightly, and label them clearly, so you won't forget what they are.*

⭐ *This recipe can easily be divided in half and baked in a smaller pan.*

GIANT MUSHROOM POPOVER

1 tablespoon butter

½ cup finely minced onion

½ pound fresh domestic mushrooms, stemmed and thinly sliced

¼ pound fresh shiitake mushrooms, stemmed and minced

1 large clove garlic, minced

¾ teaspoon salt

2 tablespoons dry sherry

3 large eggs

1 cup milk

1 cup unbleached white flour

⋆ Serve the Giant Mushroom Popover with a green salad or some fresh fruit for a refreshingly uncomplicated meal.

⋆ For a more elaborate menu suggestion, see page 211.

Here's how to roll out of bed in the morning and have something wonderful to eat before your brain kicks in (or after work, when your brain has already checked out). Make the mushroom mixture the day before and store it in a tightly covered container in the refrigerator. The next morning/afternoon, all you need to do is heat the mushrooms in an ovenproof skillet, prepare and add the egg mixture, and bake. The popover will puff up, and turn golden and magnificent all on its own.

Preheat the oven to 375°F. Melt the butter in a 10-inch ovenproof skillet. Add the onion and sauté over medium heat for 5 minutes.

Stir in the mushrooms, garlic, and salt, and sauté for another 5 minutes. Add the sherry, and cook uncovered for 10 minutes longer.

Meanwhile, place the eggs, milk, and flour in a blender, and whip them into a smooth batter. Pour this over the mushroom mixture in the skillet, and transfer the pan to the center of the oven.

Bake for 25 to 30 minutes, or until set. Cut into wedges and serve hot or warm.

Yield: 2 to 3 servings (easily doubled, if you have a second skillet)
Preparation time: 50 minutes (20 minutes of work, most of which can be done ahead)

Mollie Katzen's VEGETABLE HEAVEN

SPOON BREAD

Spoon Bread is a soft, custardy corn bread that can literally be eaten with a spoon. Some recipes call for separating the eggs, beating the whites until stiff, and then folding everything together, much as you would with a soufflé. This quick version skips all those steps, but the results are just as light.

Preheat the oven to 400°F. Lightly grease or generously spray an 8 x 8-inch baking pan.

Pour the milk into a medium-sized saucepan, and bring it just to a boil over medium heat. Immediately turn the heat down, and whisk steadily as you sprinkle in the cornmeal. Cook for 5 minutes over low heat, stirring constantly. Remove from heat, and stir in the salt, black pepper, scallions, and red pepper flakes, if desired.

Beat the eggs well, and stir them into the hot cornmeal mixture, along with the optional cheese (or not). Mix well, then transfer the batter to the prepared pan.

Bake for 30 minutes, or until firm in the center. Cut into squares, and serve hot with the topping of your choice.

Yield: 4 main-dish servings (6 side-dish servings)
Preparation time: 40 minutes (10 minutes of work)

Oil, butter, or oil spray for the pan

3 cups milk

1 cup white or yellow cornmeal

1 teaspoon salt (a little less if adding cheese)

¼ teaspoon black pepper

1 cup minced scallions (about 1 bunch)

Red pepper flakes to taste (optional)

4 large eggs

⅓ cup grated cheese, sharp or mild (parmesan, cheddar, or jack), optional

OPTIONAL TOPPINGS:

Summer Fruit Salsa (page 157)

Smoky Hot Sauce (page 167)

Mollie's Special Lowfat Mushroom Gravy (page 171)

Chipotle Cream (page 166)

⭐ *Serve Spoon Bread plain or topped with any number of sauces (see above), and with an accompaniment of cooked greens, for lunch or supper.*

SCALLOPED POTATOES
THREE VARIATIONS

Potatoes have finally come into their own, now that they are considered complex carbohydrates and sources of fiber, rather than simply a "starch."

My current favorite way to prepare potatoes is the old-fashioned scalloped method, but with upscale seasonings (roasted garlic, balsamic vinegar, chipotle chiles, etc.). Served with just a bowl of soup and a cooked green vegetable or salad, any of the following Scalloped Potatoes recipes makes a gratifying supper. And if you have some left over, try it for breakfast.

I. Scalloped Potatoes with Shallots and Mushrooms

Preheat the oven to 375°F. Oil or oil-spray a 9 x 13-inch baking pan.

Heat 1 to 2 tablespoons of olive oil in a medium-sized skillet. Add the shallots and cook over medium heat for 10 minutes, or until softened. Add the mushrooms, salt, and pepper, and sauté for an additional 10 minutes. Stir in the vinegar, and cook for 10 minutes longer, or until the liquid is mostly evaporated. Remove from heat, stir in the milk, and set aside.

Place about ⅓ of the potato slices in the bottom of the prepared pan, spreading them out in an even layer. Pour about ⅓ of the mushroom sauce over the top, then repeat with two more layers each of potatoes and sauce. Press the potatoes down with the back of a spoon, and jiggle the pan to let everything settle, and to make sure all the potatoes are well coated with the sauce.

Cover the pan tightly with foil, and bake for 30 minutes. Remove the foil, and bake uncovered for another 30 minutes. Sprinkle on the cheese (or not), and bake for a final 15 minutes. Remove the pan from the oven, and let it sit for 5 to 10 minutes before serving. This gives the potatoes a chance to completely absorb the sauce.

Yield: 6 to 8 servings
Preparation time: 1¾ hours (40 minutes of work)

Scalloped Potatoes with Shallots and Mushrooms

Oil or oil spray for the pan

1 to 2 tablespoons olive oil

8 medium-sized shallots (about 12 ounces), peeled and finely minced

⅔ pound mushrooms, chopped small

1 teaspoon salt

⅛ teaspoon black pepper

2 tablespoons balsamic vinegar

2½ cups milk (any kind)

2 pounds Yellow Finn or Yukon Gold potatoes, very thinly sliced (peeling optional)

½ cup grated hard cheese (parmesan, pecorino, gruyère, etc.), optional

You can use any kind of milk, including lowfat or soy. For a deceptively rich, creamy taste, try using canned evaporated skim milk.

II. Scalloped Potatoes with Roasted Garlic and Thyme

Preheat the oven to 375°F. Oil or oil-spray a 9 x 13-inch baking pan.

Combine the milk, salt, pepper, cayenne, Roasted Garlic Paste, and thyme in a blender or food processor, and buzz for a few seconds until the garlic is well distributed.

Layer the potatoes and sauce as described in the preceding recipe. Bake in the same fashion, adding the cheese, if desired, for the final 15 minutes of baking. Serve hot or warm, topped with mysterious swirls of Balsamic Drizzle, if desired.

Yield: 6 to 8 servings
Preparation time: 1 hour, 20 minutes (10 minutes of work)

III. "Killer" Scalloped Sweet and White Potatoes with Smoky Hot Sauce

Note: You'll need a batch of Smoky Hot Sauce (page 167), which you can make days ahead of time.

Preheat the oven to 375°F. Oil or oil-spray a 9 x 13-inch baking pan.

Combine the Smoky Hot Sauce, milk, salt, and garlic in a medium-sized bowl, and stir until well combined. In a second bowl, toss together the two types of potatoes.

Layer the potatoes and sauce directly in the pan, as described in the first variation on the preceding page.

Cover the pan tightly with foil, and bake at 375°F for 30 minutes. Turn the heat down to 350°F, uncover, and bake for another 45 minutes. Remove from the oven, and let it sit for 10 minutes before serving.

Yield: 6 to 8 servings
Preparation time: 1½ hours (15 minutes of work)

Scalloped Potatoes with Roasted Garlic and Thyme

Oil or oil spray for the pan

2½ cups milk (any kind)

1 teaspoon salt

⅛ teaspoon black pepper

Cayenne to taste

3 to 4 tablespoons Roasted Garlic Paste (page xiv)

2 tablespoons minced fresh thyme (or 2 teaspoons dried thyme)

2 pounds Yellow Finn or Yukon Gold potatoes, very thinly sliced (peeling optional)

½ cup grated hard cheese (gruyère, emmenthaler, parmesan, etc.), optional

Balsamic Drizzle (page 172), optional

"Killer" Scalloped Sweet and White Potatoes with Smoky Hot Sauce

Oil or oil spray for the pan

1½ cups Smoky Hot Sauce (page 167)

1 cup milk (any kind)

1 teaspoon salt

1 tablespoon minced garlic

1 pound Yellow Finn or Yukon Gold potatoes, very thinly sliced (peeling optional)

1 pound sweet potatoes or yams, peeled and very thinly sliced

PIZZETTAS

Homemade pizza is more accessible than you think, especially if you keep a supply of dough in the freezer, and a few topping ingredients on hand. If you make small pizzas ("pizzettas"), you can individualize the toppings, and satisfy the various tastes of everyone in your household without a whole lot of extra work.

1 cup wrist-temperature water

1 package (2 teaspoons) active dry yeast

A pinch of sugar

1 teaspoon salt

1 tablespoon olive oil (plus extra for the bowl)

3 cups unbleached white flour (¼ cup may be whole wheat or rye)

Extra flour for kneading

Cornmeal for the baking tray

Various toppings (see below)

⋯⋯⋯⋯⋯⋯⋯⋯⋯⋯⋯⋯⋯⋯

★ *Prepare the topping ingredients while the dough rises.*

★ *To freeze the dough, divide it in half to fit into two 1-pound ricotta cheese containers or one 1-quart yogurt container.*

★ *Take the container out of the freezer before you go to work, and it will be ready to roll, so to speak, when you get home.*

★ *To make the dough in a food processor, combine 3 cups flour and the salt in the bowl with the steel blade in place. Add the bubbly yeast mixture and the oil. Long-pulse several times until the dough comes together. Turn out onto a floured surface, and proceed.*

★ *For a menu suggestion, see page 211.*

Place the water in a medium-large bowl. Sprinkle in the yeast and sugar, and stir to dissolve. Let it stand 5 minutes, or until the mixture begins to bubble.

Stir in 1 cup of flour, the salt, and 1 tablespoon olive oil. Beat for several minutes with a wooden spoon.

Add the remaining flour ½ cup at a time, mixing after each addition. The dough will be soft, but should not be sticky.

Turn out onto a floured surface, and knead for several minutes. Place in an oiled bowl, cover with plastic wrap, and let the dough rise until doubled in bulk. This will take about 1 hour.

Punch down the dough, and return it to the floured surface. (This is the point at which you can freeze the dough for future use.) Divide it into six equal parts, knead each piece for a few minutes, then let the balls of dough rest for about 10 minutes. (This allows the gluten to relax, so the dough will easily stretch into shape.)

Preheat the oven to 500°F. Patiently stretch each ball of dough into a 6-inch circle. Sprinkle two thin, noninsulated baking trays with cornmeal, and place two circles on each. (Meanwhile, preheat the oven to 500°F.) Sparingly top each pizzetta with whatever your heart desires (numerous topping suggestions follow).

Bake one tray at time in the lower half of the oven for 10 to 12 minutes, or until the edges are crispy and brown. (If you're not sure whether or not it's baked through, you can take one pizzetta out of the oven and cut it in half. If it is still a little doughy on the inside, return it to the baking pan and bake a few minutes longer.) Serve hot, warm, or at room temperature.

Yield: Six 6-inch pizzettas
Preparation time: 1½ hours (about 20 minutes of work)

Mollie Katzen's VEGETABLE HEAVEN

VARIATIONS ON PIZZETTA DOUGH

Focaccia or Fougasse

Prepare the dough as for pizzettas, but let it relax for at least 30 minutes. Form the dough into 2 rectangles, approximately 10 x 15 inches each—or into large ovals. Score it here and there with a sharp knife, or, in the more authentic Italian style, poke it firmly all over with thumbprints. Brush the top surface with olive oil, and sprinkle with crumbled rosemary. Bake on a floured (or cornmeal-sprinkled) noninsulated tray in a preheated 400°F oven for 12 to 15 minutes, or until it gives off a hollow sound when thumped. Cool for 15 minutes before serving.

Cracker Bread

Prepare the dough as for pizzettas, but let it relax for at least 30 minutes. Stretch the dough into 2 large ovals so thin they begin to tear. Sprinkle the tops with coarse salt and cracked pepper, and bake the same as above, but turn off the oven after 25 minutes, and leave the bread in there for about 30 minutes, or until very crisp. Serve topped with olive oil and crumbled goat cheese if desired.

Bread Sticks

Prepare the dough as for pizzettas. Divide the dough into 16 equal sections, knead briefly, and let them rest for 30 minutes. Gently stretch the relaxed dough into long, thin strips, and roll in sesame or poppy seeds, if desired. Bake in a preheated 425°F oven for 10 minutes on a cornmeal-sprinkled non-insulated tray. Serve warm or at room temperature.

NUMEROUS PIZZETTA TOPPINGS

For a traditional pizzetta, just spread on a little Roasted Tomato-Garlic Sauce (page 164), and add a few basil leaves and a light sprinkling of grated mozzarella. For a more unusual experience, try some of the following combinations or improvise on your own. With a good crust and a light hand, it's hard to go wrong.

Caramelized Onion Sauce (page 163)

Crumbled goat cheese

Balsamic Drizzle (page 172)

Spread the onion sauce on the pizzettas, sprinkle with goat cheese, and bake. Top with swirls of Balsamic Drizzle after it comes out of the oven.

Dried Tomato Pesto (page 160)

Kalamata olives, pitted and sliced

Ripe tomato slices

Minced fresh (or crumbled dried) rosemary

Grated parmesan or pecorino cheese

Put everything on the pizzetta before baking. Spread a little more pesto over the top when it comes out of the oven.

Canned artichoke hearts, drained, and sliced

Olives (any kind), pitted and sliced

Ripe tomato slices

Crumbled feta cheese

Arrange everything on the pizzetta; bake and serve.

Tapenade (page 161)

Grated parmesan or pecorino cheese

Spread Tapenade onto the unbaked pizzetta, sprinkle with cheese, and bake. Optional: spread a little extra Tapenade over the top when it comes out of the oven.

Minced fresh (or crumbled dried) rosemary

Grated gruyère cheese

Freshly ground black pepper

Roasted Garlic Paste (page xiv)

Balsamic Drizzle (page 172)

Sprinkle the rosemary, cheese, and black pepper onto the pizzetta, and bake. When it comes out of the oven, spread it with Roasted Garlic Paste and swirl on some Balsamic Drizzle.

Chimichurri (page 165)

Grated sharp cheese (your choice)

Spread a thin layer of Chimichurri onto the pizzetta, sprinkle with cheese, and bake. Spread on a little more Chimichurri when it comes out of the oven.

Grated gruyère cheese (optional)

Red Onion and Shallot Marmalade (page 162)

Bake the pizzetta plain or with just a little gruyère cheese melted on top. Spread with a thick layer of Red Onion and Shallot Marmalade after it is baked.

SANDWICHES TO WRITE HOME ABOUT

Here are some unusual sandwiches that can be made with fairly common ingredients. I especially love the ones that pair fruit with cheese—they're very romantic, somehow (if sandwiches can be considered romantic). Try these and/or experiment with your own brilliant ideas. Use your favorite bread, and follow your instincts as to the amounts and proportions. Sandwiches tend to be very personal things.

Pitted dark cherries with watercress and cream cheese on toasted dill bread

Grilled papaya slices (perfectly—but not too—ripe), with slices of roasted red pepper, eggplant, and onion (pages 96 and 98), a few fresh basil leaves, and grated mozzarella cheese on toasted sourdough

Horseradish Aioli (page 168) with slices of green apple and Pickled Red Onions (page 63) on toasted pumpernickel with thin slices of gruyère melted over the top, and radish sprouts for a garnish

Chimichurri (page 165) on rye bread—with slices of Fuji apple, and cheddar cheese melted over the top

Arugula and thinly sliced pears on toasted walnut bread with crumbled blue cheese

Mini-recipe

Marinate slices of firm tofu in soy sauce, ginger, and garlic, then sauté them in butter or oil on both sides for about 5 minutes. Spread the bread of your choice with mustard and Summer Fruit Salsa (page 157), and place the tofu slices on top. Serve open-faced or closed.

Other Ideas:

★ *All different kinds of Roasted Vegetables (pages 96 to 99) on toasted baguettes, with Horseradish Aioli (page 168), with or without melted cheese*

★ *Chimichurri (page 165) with plain egg salad*

★ *Red Onion and Shallot Marmalade (page 162) with cheese or savory baked tofu*

★ *Tapenade (page 161) with sliced egg, mayonnaise, tomato, and fresh spinach*

★ *Frittata (page 124)*

★ *Gremolata-Ricotta Egg Salad (page 10) with tomatoes, olives, and julienned cooked beets*

★ *GuacaMollie (page 158) in pita bread, with chips on the side*

★ *Chickpea and Sweet Potato Koftas (page 79) and Mediterranean Yogurt (page 169) with diced tomatoes in pita bread*

Mollie Katzen's VEGETABLE HEAVEN

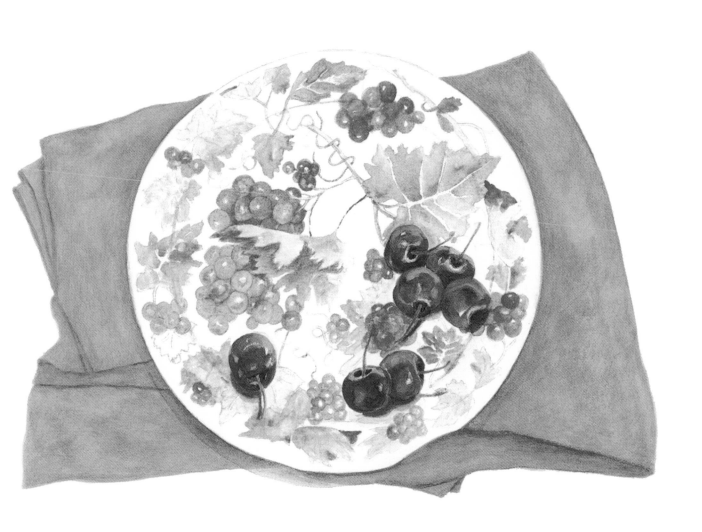

TIDY LITTLE MAIN DISHES

ON TOP OF SPAGHETTI

Pastas for Real Life

I would like to think that some passionate eater of long ago, who loved pasta as much as I do, gave it the name it has today, which has stuck to it as naturally as sauce to a noodle. For the word *maccheroni* is thought to have derived from *ma, che carini!* which literally means, "My! What little dears!"

—Julia della Croce, *Pasta Classica*

What is a great one-dish meal for a person who lives alone and cooks for one, but is also perfect for a family of diverse tastes and needs? And how can this same idea be a wonderful "meal solution" for everybody in between as well? Have you guessed pasta? Do you basically love it, but are a little burnt out, so to speak, on your old recipes? Here are some new ones.

Most of the following pasta recipes call for only a small amount of oil, then make good use of broth and wine to extend the sauce, keeping the fat content down. They are all very flexible, so use these ideas as a springboard to create your own signature dishes. It's hard to go wrong.

ON TOP OF SPAGHETTI
Pastas for Real Life

LINGUINE
WITH WOK-FRIED BROCCOLI, CHERRY TOMATOES, AND CRUMBLY CHEESE

You can make this colorful, family-pleasing dish on a weekday after work, especially if you take a few minutes to cut the broccoli and garlic the night before. Just put up the pasta water first, and cook the vegetables while the water is heating.

Put up a kettle of water to boil for the pasta. Meanwhile, heat a medium-large wok. When it is hot, add about 2 teaspoons of the oil and the broccoli florets. Salt them lightly, and stir-fry over high heat for about 5 minutes, or until they are bright green and just tender. Remove to a small bowl and set aside. Return the wok to the heat.

Pour 2 tablespoons of the olive oil into the wok. When it is very hot, add the tomatoes and 1 teaspoon salt, and stir-fry over high heat for about 5 minutes, or until the tomatoes are wilted. Stir in the wine or bouillon and the garlic, and cook for about 3 minutes. (During this time, put the pasta into the boiling water to cook.)

Add the broccoli stems to the tomatoes, salt lightly, and stir-fry over high heat until they are just tender (5 minutes or so). Spoon in a little of the pasta-cooking water if you'd like the sauce to have more liquid.

Drain the pasta and drizzle it with a little olive oil. Transfer to a serving platter or a large shallow bowl, and spoon the tomato-broccoli mixture over the top. Add the cheese and some black pepper, and gently toss everything together, bringing the pasta up from the bottom as you mix. Taste to correct salt.

Serve hot, garnished with the reserved broccoli florets around the edges and a few dollops of Dried Tomato Pesto on top, if desired.

Yield: 4 to 6 servings
Preparation time: 30 minutes

About 3 tablespoons olive oil

1½ pounds broccoli—tops cut into florets, stems peeled and cut into thin strips

1 to 1½ teaspoons salt

4 cups small cherry tomatoes

1 cup dry white wine or vegetable bouillon (page xiv)

3 tablespoons minced garlic

¾ to 1 pound linguine

1 cup crumbled ricotta salata or feta cheese

Freshly ground black pepper to taste

Dried Tomato Pesto (page 160), optional

⋆ *When cutting the broccoli, use as much of the stems as possible. Shave off the tough outer skin, and cut the sweet, tender inner stem into thin strips.*

⋆ *You can choose between white wine and vegetable bouillon for the sauce. You also have a choice between ricotta salata (a firm, crumbly form of ricotta) and the saltier feta cheese. If you use the bouillon and/or the feta, add less salt at first, and adjust it to taste later.*

⋆ *For a menu suggestion, see page 211.*

RIGATONI AL FORNO
WITH ROASTED ASPARAGUS AND ONIONS

3 to 4 tablespoons olive oil

3 cups chopped onion
  (in large chunks)

¾ pound rigatoni (or a similar
  tube-shaped pasta)

1 pound asparagus, cut into
  2-inch pieces

½ teaspoon salt (plus more, to taste)

3 to 4 tablespoons balsamic vinegar

Freshly ground black pepper

⅓ cup grated parmesan cheese
  (plus extra for the top)

½ cup bread crumbs

Extra balsamic vinegar or Balsamic
  Drizzle (page 172), optional

- -

★ To make this for a crowd, bake two pans simultaneously. (It takes very little extra work to double the yield.)

★ The rigatoni can be cooked a day or two in advance, lightly oiled, and stored in an airtight container in the refrigerator—or you can boil it while you roast the vegetables, as indicated in the recipe.

★ For a menu suggestion, see page 213.

Al forno means "oven-baked," and that's one of the wonderful features of this dish. The vegetables are cooked in a roasting pan right in the oven, and cooked pasta gets added directly to the same pan. Cover, return the pan to the oven, and then bring it directly to the table when it's done. This is a great make-after-work dish, and the cleanup is minimal.

Preheat the oven to 375°F. Put up a large potful of water to boil.

Pour the oil into a 9 x 13-inch baking pan (preferably glass). Break up the onion chunks with your hands, add them to the oil, and stir them around a little so they get coated. Place the uncovered pan in the oven and roast for 5 minutes.

When the water reaches a rapid boil, add the pasta and let it begin cooking while you continue roasting the vegetables.

After the onions have been in the oven for about 5 minutes, stir in the asparagus and sprinkle with ½ teaspoon salt. Spread everything into a single layer, return the pan to the oven, and roast for 5 minutes longer.

Drain the pasta as soon as it is al dente, and stir it into the panful of onions and asparagus. Add the 3 to 4 tablespoons vinegar, black pepper, and parmesan, and mix well. Sprinkle the bread crumbs over the top, and return the pan to the oven.

Bake uncovered for 10 to 15 minutes, or until the bread crumbs are brown and crisp. Serve hot, and pass around the pepper mill, extra parmesan, and a cruet of additional balsamic vinegar—or a bowlful of Balsamic Drizzle—if desired.

Yield: 4 to 5 servings
Preparation time: 30 minutes (10 minutes of work)

TORTELLINI
IN HERBED EGGDROP BROTH

In Italy, tortellini is usually served either in a rich cream sauce or in a very light broth. Preferring the latter, I put together an "American supermarket version" of this soothing dish, using a good vegetable bouillon, a few touches of herbs, and beaten eggs. You can get excellent commercially prepared tortellini—fresh, dried, or frozen—in most supermarkets, so this filled pasta treat can be made with only 5 minutes of work. Maybe it will become a staple in your household on busy winter evenings.

Cook the tortellini in boiling water until tender (about 12 minutes for dried; 5 to 8 minutes for fresh or frozen). Drain and distribute among the serving bowls.

In a medium-sized saucepan heat the bouillon to a boil. Place the eggs in a small bowl, and beat well. Drizzle the beaten eggs into the simmering broth, stirring slowly.

Ladle the hot broth onto the tortellini in the bowls, and serve right away, with small amounts of minced herbs and some ground black pepper sprinkled over the top.

Yield: 4 to 5 servings
Preparation time: 15 minutes (5 minutes of work)

2 cups uncooked cheese tortellini, dried, fresh, or frozen

6 cups vegetable bouillon (page xiv)

2 eggs

Marjoram or oregano, minced fresh or dried

Thyme, minced fresh or dried

Minced fresh parsley

Black pepper to taste

BUCKWHEAT SOBA
WITH SQUASH, SMOKED TOFU, AND BASIL

I rounded tablespoon white or yellow miso

1½ cups hot water

2 teaspoons vegetable or peanut oil

2 cups sliced onion

½ teaspoon salt

2 to 3 cups peeled, diced butternut squash or fresh pumpkin (about 1 pound)

½ pound uncooked buckwheat soba

1 cup smoked tofu, cut into strips (about ¼ pound)

½ cup (packed) fresh basil leaves, coarsely chopped

Red pepper flakes

Lightly toasted pumpkin seeds (aka pepitas)

★ *Squash and pumpkin are interchangeable in this dish.*

★ *For a menu suggestion, see page 213.*

One trip to the natural foods store should cover the entire shopping list for this unusual recipe, which combines the strong, fermented flavor of miso with pungent basil, smoked tofu, sweet squash, and earthy buckwheat soba (Japanese noodles). Sprinkle the top with some lightly toasted pumpkin seeds for the perfect final touch.

Combine the miso and hot water in a small bowl, and mash with a spoon until the miso is mostly dissolved. (It doesn't have to be perfectly smooth.) Set aside.

Heat the oil in a large deep skillet or a sauté pan over medium-high heat. When it is very hot, add the onion, and sauté for about 5 minutes. Sprinkle in the salt, cover, and cook for about 10 more minutes over medium heat. Stir in the squash, cover again, and cook for 10 minutes longer, or until the squash is just tender. Meanwhile, put up a potful of water to boil for the soba.

Stir the miso solution and tofu into the sautéed onion and squash. Turn the heat way down, cover, and let it simmer very quietly while you cook the soba according to the directions on the package.

When the noodles are done to your liking, drain them thoroughly, transfer to a serving bowl, and pour the vegetable-miso mixture over the top. Toss with chopsticks or a large fork, adding the basil and red pepper flakes to taste as you go. Sprinkle the top with pumpkin seeds, and serve hot, warm, or at room temperature.

Yield: 4 to 5 servings
Preparation time: 45 minutes (20 minutes of work)

Mollie Katzen's VEGETABLE HEAVEN

PENNE
WITH MUSHROOMS, LEEKS, AND DRIED TOMATOES

Penne, a tube-shaped pasta, is especially fun to eat when combined with finely chopped ingredients, because little bits of this and that (in this case, chopped vegetables, herbs, and pine nuts) will find their way into the pasta tunnel. Each bite is jam-packed with flavor and texture.

Combine the dried tomatoes, garlic, and water in a small saucepan and bring to a boil. Turn the heat way down, cover, and simmer for 5 minutes. Set aside.

Heat 2 tablespoons olive oil in a deep skillet or sauté pan over medium-high heat. When the oil is very hot, add the leeks and sauté for about 1 minute. Sprinkle with ½ teaspoon salt, turn the heat to medium, and sauté for 5 minutes longer.

Stir in all the mushrooms and the remaining ½ teaspoon salt, cover, and cook for about 10 more minutes over medium heat, stirring occasionally. Meanwhile, put up a large potful of water to boil for the pasta.

Pour the tomato-garlic "soup" into the leek and mushroom mixture, cover, and turn the heat down to a simmer while the pasta cooks.

Cook the pasta in plenty of boiling water until it is just tender. Drain, transfer to a serving bowl, and drizzle with a little extra olive oil. Immediately sprinkle in ¼ cup grated cheese, and give it a good stir, so the cheese can melt evenly into the hot pasta.

Pour the sauce over the pasta, and mix well from the bottom of the bowl. Top with freshly ground black pepper, a handful or two of parsley and pine nuts, and a few dollops of Dried Tomato Pesto, if desired. Serve hot, warm, or at room temperature.

Yield: 4 to 6 servings
Preparation time: 45 minutes (20 to 30 minutes of work)

---

1 cup dried tomatoes (about 2 ounces), cut into small pieces with scissors

3 large cloves garlic, peeled and coarsely chopped

1½ cups water

2 tablespoons olive oil (plus extra for the pasta)

3 cups cleaned, minced leeks (about 2 large leeks)

1 teaspoon salt

¾ pound fresh domestic mushrooms, chopped

¼ pound fresh shiitake mushrooms, stemmed and chopped

¾ to 1 pound penne

¼ cup grated parmesan or pecorino cheese

FOR THE TOP:

Freshly ground black pepper

Chopped flat-leaf parsley

Lightly toasted pine nuts

Dried Tomato Pesto (page 160), optional

★ *This flavorful dish keeps well for several days, and reheats beautifully.*

★ *Use plain dried tomatoes, not the kind that comes packed in oil.*

FUSILLI
WITH SWEET AND HOT PEPPERS, WHITE BEANS, LEMON, AND OLIVES

2 tablespoons olive oil

4 cups thinly sliced bell peppers (about 2 medium peppers)

¼ cup minced garlic

1 to 2 jalapeño chiles, minced (seeding optional)

¾ teaspoon salt (or to taste)

1 15-ounce can cannellini beans, rinsed and drained

1½ cups vegetable bouillon (page xiv)

1 teaspoon minced lemon zest

1 tablespoon fresh lemon juice

About 15 oil-cured olives, pitted and halved

¾ pound fusilli

OPTIONAL GARNISHES:

Twists of lemon peel

Lemon wedges

Chopped flat-leaf parsley

The seeds are the hottest part of jalapeño chiles, so discard them if you prefer a milder result. Wash your hands thoroughly after handling the chiles.

You can make this lively, festive dish even brighter and more beautiful by using a combination of yellow and red bell peppers. Serve it in bowls with cooked greens on the side, and fresh crusty bread to mop up the juices.

Heat the olive oil in a large, very deep skillet or Dutch oven over medium heat. Add the bell peppers and sauté for 5 minutes. Add the garlic, jalapeños, and salt, and sauté for about 10 minutes longer. Meanwhile, put up a large potful of water to boil for the pasta.

Add the beans, bouillon, lemon zest, lemon juice, and olives to the peppers, and stir. Cover, turn the heat down, and let the sauce simmer while the pasta cooks.

Cook the fusilli in rapidly boiling water until it is just tender. Drain, and add it directly to the panful of pepper sauce. Stir well, and cook over low heat for about 3 or 4 minutes. Transfer to a serving dish, and serve hot, adorned with any, all, or none of the optional garnishes.

Yield: 4 to 6 servings
Preparation time: About 30 minutes

Mollie Katzen's VEGETABLE HEAVEN

RICE NOODLES
WITH CASHEW-COCONUT SAUCE

It looks like a long list of ingredients, but most of them just get dumped into the sauce with very little work. And the results are to die for!

NOTE: This recipe will work with transparent Chinese or Thai rice noodles (thick or thin), or with a more opaque Japanese variety. If you can't find any of the above, just substitute plain vermicelli.

Combine the coconut milk and water in a medium-sized saucepan. Add the ginger, lime juice, chiles, garlic, coriander, cilantro, mint, and salt, and bring to a boil. Lower the heat to a simmer, and cook uncovered for 10 minutes. It will curdle slightly, but don't worry. Remove from the heat and stir in the sugar or honey. (At this point, the sauce can steep for several hours—or even overnight—or you can proceed with the rest of the recipe right away.)

Strain the mixture through a fine sieve into a measuring cup with a spout, for easy pouring. Press all the liquid from the garlic, ginger, cilantro, etc., then discard the solids that remain in the sieve.

Place the cashews in a blender, and carefully pour in the coconut milk mixture. Purée until smooth.

Heat a potful of water to a rapid boil. Add the noodles, and cook them according to the directions on the package. Drain the noodles, rinse, and drain again, then transfer to a large, shallow serving bowl. Immediately add the minced scallions and all the sauce. Toss well, using chopsticks or two forks.

Serve hot or warm with wedges of lime, and some or all of the optional toppings sprinkled lavishly on top.

Yield: 4 to 6 servings, depending on what else is served
Preparation time: 30 minutes or less

---

1 14-ounce can lowfat coconut milk

½ cup water

6 slices fresh ginger (¼ inch thick)

2 tablespoons fresh lime juice

2 serrano chiles (red or green), cut in half

6 large cloves garlic, peeled

1 teaspoon ground coriander seeds

½ cup (packed) fresh cilantro leaves

2 tablespoons fresh mint leaves

1 teaspoon salt

1 tablespoon sugar or honey

1 cup toasted cashew pieces

12 ounces uncooked rice noodles

3 scallions, finely minced

Wedges of lime

OPTIONAL TOPPINGS:

Finely minced red serrano chiles or red pepper flakes

Torn cilantro leaves

Finely minced scallions

Minced cashews, lightly toasted

Shredded coconut, lightly toasted

Minced cucumber (peeled and seeded, if necessary)

★ *Make the sauce a day or two ahead, so final preparations can be very quick.*

★ *For a menu suggestion, see page 213.*

FARFALLE

WITH ARTICHOKES, MUSTARD GREENS, AND SLOW-COOKED ONIONS

2 tablespoons olive oil

4 cups thinly sliced onion

¾ teaspoon salt

½ pound mustard greens, chopped

1 13¾-ounce can artichoke hearts, rinsed, drained, and quartered

1 cup vegetable bouillon (page xiv)

¾ pound farfalle

Freshly ground black pepper

Lightly toasted chopped walnuts (optional)

★ *The onions can be cooked in advance.*

★ *For a menu suggestion, see page 211.*

My mother calls them bow-ties and my daughter calls them butterflies, and all three of us concur that this is our favorite pasta shape. Combined with the sensuously bitter combination of artichoke hearts and mustard greens—and the sweetness of slow-cooked onions—the farfalle takes on a distinct character beyond its inspiring shape.

Heat the olive oil in a very large, deep skillet or a Dutch oven over medium heat. When the oil is very hot, add the onion and sauté for 1 minute. Sprinkle in the salt, and sauté for 5 minutes longer. Turn the heat to low, cover, and continue to cook the onions for 20 more minutes. Meanwhile, put up a large potful of water to boil for the pasta.

Stir the mustard greens, artichoke hearts, and bouillon into the onions, and bring to a boil. Turn the heat way down, cover, and simmer gently for 5 to 8 minutes, uncovering a few times to stir from the bottom with tongs.

Cook the pasta until it is just tender. Drain well, and transfer to the panful of sauce. Stir well, and cook over low heat for about 5 minutes. Serve hot or warm, topped with freshly ground black pepper and some chopped walnuts, if desired.

Yield: 4 to 5 servings
Preparation time: 45 minutes (15 minutes of work)

PASTA SHELLS
WITH MARINATED CHICKPEAS
AND AN UNEXPECTED INGREDIENT

How did hominy, an American native, find its way into this otherwise tradi-
tional Italian-style dish? I can explain. Originally I had planned to use two
cans of chickpeas, but I only had one and didn't feel like running to the store.
So I substituted a can of hominy, and it mingled so well with the other ingre-
dients, I rewrote the recipe. The combination of subtle textures in this dish is
just wonderful.

In the mode of the After-Work Special:

Before Work: Combine the chickpeas, hominy, olive oil, garlic,
vinegar, salt, herbs, and mozzarella in a large bowl. Stir, cover tightly, and let stand at room temperature.

After Work: Cook the pasta in plenty of boiling water until it is tender. Drain thoroughly, and add it to the chickpea mixture in the
bowl. Toss well from the bottom, sprinkling in the grated cheese
and chopped parsley as you go. Grind in a generous amount of
black pepper, and serve hot, warm, or at room temperature. Swirl
some Balsamic Drizzle over the top, if desired.

Yield: 5 or 6 servings
Preparation time: 20 minutes, total

---

1 15-ounce can chickpeas, rinsed and drained

1 15-ounce can white or yellow hominy, rinsed and drained

3 tablespoons extra virgin olive oil

1 tablespoon minced garlic

4 tablespoons balsamic vinegar

1 teaspoon salt

½ teaspoon dried thyme

½ teaspoon dried oregano

½ pound fresh mozzarella cheese, cut into small cubes

¾ pound medium-sized (1-inch) pasta shells

¼ cup grated parmesan or pecorino cheese

Coarsely chopped flat-leaf parsley

Freshly ground black pepper

Balsamic Drizzle (page 172), optional

★ *A few minutes of preparation before you go to work in the morning and about 15 minutes more when you get home are all it takes to put together this delicious pasta dish.*

★ *Fresh mozzarella is sublime, but if you can't get it, substitute commercial mozzarella, or a good, mild, soft white cheese.*

COZY ORZO

When I was a child, one of my favorite comfort foods was a dish my mother called noodles and cheese. Although it was just some plain pasta mixed with cottage cheese and a little sour cream, it had a magical calming effect on me. I make a slightly more adult version now, which is a little fancier, but equally comforting.

- 1 pound room-temperature cottage cheese
- 1 teaspoon salt
- ¼ cup minced chives or scallions
- 1 teaspoon grated lemon zest
- Black pepper to taste
- ½ pound orzo (rice-shaped pasta)
- 1 cup frozen peas
- Grated pecorino or parmesan cheese for the top

Combine the cottage cheese, salt, chives or scallions, lemon zest, and black pepper in a medium-sized bowl, and mix well.

Cook the orzo in plenty of rapidly boiling water until it is tender. Place the peas in a colander in the sink, and drain the pasta right into the peas. (This will defrost the peas and cook them slightly.) Shake off the excess water, transfer the orzo and peas to the cottage cheese mixture, and stir gently. Sprinkle with grated pecorino or parmesan, and serve warm or at room temperature, in bowls.

Yield: 4 to 5 servings
Preparation time: 10 minutes

Mollie Katzen's VEGETABLE HEAVEN

TINY PASTA STEW

Use alphabets or little stars, orzo or tiny circles. Or use a combination of them all. The child in your life will love this, and so will the child in you.

Bring the bouillon to a boil in a medium-small saucepan. Add the carrots, and lower the heat to a simmer. Cook for 5 minutes, or until the carrots are just tender, then add the zucchini, optional summer squash, and corn. Simmer for another 5 minutes, or until all the vegetables are perfectly tender.

Stir in the peas, tofu, and cooked pasta, and simmer for just a couple of minutes longer. Serve hot or very warm in small bowls with small spoons.

Yield: 5 cups
Preparation time: 30 minutes (10 minutes of work)

4 cups vegetable bouillon
(page xiv)

½ cup carrots in tiny cubes
(the size of small peas)

½ cup diced zucchini

½ cup diced yellow summer squash
(optional)

½ cup baby corn, in ¼-inch slices

½ cup small peas

½ cup diced firm tofu

I cup cooked tiny pasta
(about 4 ounces uncooked)

★ *Cook the pasta in advance, and store it in an airtight container in the refrigerator. Then you can make this dish on short notice when the need arises. (And it will arise.)*

THE TEN-MINUTE PASTA DINNER

No introductory remarks are needed here. Besides, you don't have time.

Put up the water to boil. When it boils rapidly, add the pasta.

Drain the pasta, transfer it to a bowl, and drizzle with olive oil. Toss with a long-handled fork or with tongs, adding the garlic and greens, and sprinkling in the parmesan and red pepper flakes as you toss.

Serve hot, possibly accompanied by leftover cooked vegetables, straight from the refrigerator or heated up in the microwave.

Yield: 3 to 4 servings (easily multiplied)
Preparation time: 10 minutes

¾ pound pasta, any shape

1 to 2 tablespoons extra virgin olive oil (to taste)

1 tablespoon minced garlic

Chopped fresh spinach or arugula (a few handfuls, if available)

⅓ cup grated pecorino or parmesan cheese (or more, to taste)

Red pepper flakes

★ *Prepare the garlic and greens (if you have them) while the pasta boils.*

PERMISSION TO BE CREATIVE WITH SPAGHETTI

When you say "spaghetti sauce," most people think first of something red and tomato-based. It's good to remember that cooked spaghetti also combines beautifully with many other sauces, dressings, and pastes, the most well-known being that ubiquitous emerald green celebrity, basil-flavored pesto. But perhaps you're a little tired of even the most exquisite pesto, and would like something exotic and new. For a change of pace, try combining freshly cooked spaghetti with some of the sauces and pastes from the "Never A Bland Moment" chapter—or with your favorite salsa, eggplant dip, or vinaigrette. This is a great opportunity to experiment with your improvisational talents. Loose guideline: Use about 2 to 4 tablespoons of sauce per cup of cooked pasta—or just prepare your creation to taste. Cheese is always optional.

The following are my personal favorites. You can use these ideas as a jumping-off place:

Dried Tomato Pesto (page 160)

Roasted Tomato-Garlic Sauce (page 164)

Red Pepper-Walnut Paste (page 159)

Tapenade (page 161)

Chimichurri (page 165)

Vinaigrette (page 173)

NEVER A BLAND MOMENT

Condiments and Sauces

. . . the usual should be made unusual;
extraordinariness should cloak the ordinary.

—M.F.K. Fisher, *An Alphabet for Gourmets*

Asplash, dab, or drizzle of intensely saturated flavor is sometimes all you need to liven up a simple grain, vegetable, or bean dish, or salad. The following recipes range from an unconventional salsa to an unexpected marmalade (where traditional uses of fruits and vegetables are reversed) from potent, colorful pastes (some made without oil), to a traditional yet lowfat gravy, light-but-bold sauces, and a pair of classic vinaigrettes.

Many of these will hold for a long time if stored in tightly covered containers in the refrigerator, so keep several on hand always. Just remember to pull them out when you are in a hurry, or just generally lacking for inspiration. Then you can make a bona fide event out of that baked potato, slice of toast, broiled fish, plain cooked rice—you name it. The uses are practically infinite.

NEVER A BLAND MOMENT
Condiments and Sauces

SUMMER FRUIT SALSA

According to recent surveys, salsas are so popular, they actually outsell ketchup in many supermarkets across the United States. Common though salsas are becoming, you're unlikely to find this one in any store—but if you did, it would likely put ketchup out of the running altogether. It's a refreshing all-fruit version, easy to make and freezable for your year-round pleasure.

Mince the mango, strawberries, and nectarines, and place them in a medium-sized bowl.

Add the remaining ingredients (including the liquid from defrosted raspberries, if applicable), and mix well.

Transfer to a container with a tight-fitting lid, and refrigerate. Use as desired.

Yield: 4 cups
Preparation time: 10 minutes

1 ripe mango, peeled and pitted

10 good strawberries

2 perfectly ripe nectarines, pitted

1 cup fresh raspberries (or frozen unsweetened raspberries, defrosted, but not drained)

¼ teaspoon salt

1 tablespoon minced fresh ginger

3 tablespoons fresh lime juice

1 tablespoon cider vinegar or unseasoned rice vinegar

1 tablespoon sugar

½ teaspoon red pepper flakes

....

Serve this as you would any chutney or fruit sauce. You can spread it on toast and melt some cheese on top, or even spoon it over yogurt or ice cream.

You can freeze this salsa in an airtight container for up to several months.

GUACAMOLLIE

If you crave guacamole, but you don't happen to have any perfectly ripe avocados sitting in your fruit bowl (or anywhere else in your kitchen)—and you'd just as soon not ingest a lot of calories and fat anyway—look inside your freezer. If you have a bag of green peas, you're in luck. This delicious, bright green imitation really hits the spot.

2 cups frozen peas

1 tablespoon plus 1 teaspoon fresh lemon juice

½ teaspoon minced garlic

2 to 3 tablespoons torn cilantro leaves

¼ cup minced red onion

½ cup minced ripe tomato

6 tablespoons yogurt (optional)

Salt to taste

Red pepper flakes to taste

Place the peas in a colander and run warm tap water over them until they are defrosted, but still cold. Drain well, then dump them into a food processor. Add the lemon juice, garlic, and cilantro, and purée until very smooth. Transfer to a medium-sized bowl.

Stir in the onion, tomato, and yogurt, if desired. Add salt and red pepper flakes to taste. Let sit for about 10 minutes, then serve within an hour or two. (Cover tightly and refrigerate in the meantime.)

Yield: 2 cups
Preparation time: 10 minutes

Serve this with chips and steamed or grilled vegetables, with beans and rice, or with any egg dish, cornmeal preparation, soup, or casserole. It also makes a superb sandwich filling.

GuacaMollie doesn't keep well, so make it within an hour or two of serving time. If it sits around much longer than that, it will still taste good, but will lose its cheerful color.

For a menu suggestion, see page 212.

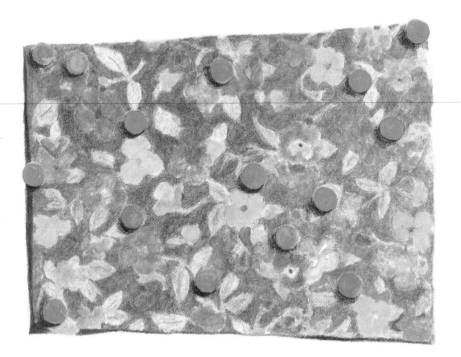

RED PEPPER-WALNUT PASTE

Based on the Middle Eastern sauce called muhammara *(an Arabic word meaning "the color of red bricks"), this delicious paste is simultaneously pungent, slightly hot, and sweet. I make it often and keep it around for many uses: as a topping for pilafs and other cooked grains, for spreading on pizzettas, crostini, crackers, and sandwiches, and as a dip for cooked or raw vegetables. Try spreading Red Pepper-Walnut Paste on grilled tofu, fish, or chicken breasts for a fantastic barbecue experience.*

Place the walnuts and garlic cloves in a food processor and pulse until they are finely ground, but not yet a paste.

Seed the peppers, cut them into chunks, and add them to the walnuts, along with the vinegar, lemon juice, cumin, and honey. Process to a fairly smooth paste, then transfer to a bowl, and season to taste with salt, pepper, and cayenne.

Cover tightly and store in the refrigerator. Use as desired.

Yield: 3 to 4 cups
Preparation time: 10 minutes, after the peppers are roasted

2 heaping cups lightly toasted walnuts

2 to 3 medium cloves garlic

4 medium-sized red bell peppers (about 2 pounds), roasted and peeled—see page 96

1 tablespoon plus 2 teaspoons cider vinegar

3 tablespoons fresh lemon juice

1/4 teaspoon ground cumin

1 teaspoon honey

1 1/4 teaspoons salt (or to taste)

Black pepper and cayenne to taste

....

This keeps well for at least a week if stored in an airtight container in the refrigerator. In fact, the flavors deepen over time.

For a California twist, you can use almonds in place of the walnuts.

For a menu suggestion, see page 212.

DRIED TOMATO PESTO

Deeply flavored and a great shade of dark, adult red, this oil-free, vegan pesto has become my favorite version. Use it solo with hot pasta or dab it on top of more complicated pasta dishes. It adds richness without adding fat.

1 cup (2 ounces) dried tomatoes

1 cup boiling water

½ cup (packed) basil leaves

⅓ cup (packed) parsley

3 medium cloves garlic, peeled and halved

¼ teaspoon salt (or to taste)

Red pepper flakes to taste (optional)

Place the tomatoes and boiling water in a small bowl, cover with a plate, and let stand for 1 hour.

Put the basil and parsley in a blender and process until feathery. Add the garlic and the tomatoes with all their water, and purée until it becomes a smooth paste.

Return it to the same small bowl, and stir in salt and optional red pepper flakes to taste. Cover tightly and refrigerate until use. Bring to room temperature before serving.

Use plain dried tomatoes, not the kind that comes packed in oil. Soak them well ahead of time.

Some other uses for Dried Tomato Pesto: spoon it onto Olive Waffles, (page 119), dab it on Fried Green Tomato Pillows (page 121), or spread it over cream cheese on crackers, crostini, or sandwiches. Also try it on pizzettas, grilled vegetables, grains, beans, and/or baked potatoes.

Amazingly, this keeps for weeks if stored in an airtight container in the refrigerator.

Yield: 1¼ cups
Preparation time: 5 minutes after the tomatoes soak

Mollie Katzen's VEGETABLE HEAVEN

TAPENADE

A little bit of this assertive olive-caper paste goes a long way.

Accordingly, Tapenade (sometimes referred to as Provençal caviar) can transform such simple things as plain boiled potatoes, pasta, or cooked beans into a taste event. You can also use it in small amounts to enhance a variety of more complicated dishes, such as Zuppa di Verdure (page 44), pizzettas, sandwiches, or crostini.

Place the olives, garlic, lemon zest, capers, parsley, and 1 table-spoon of the lemon juice in a blender or food processor, and work until it is almost smooth, but still retains a little bit of texture.

Drizzle in the olive oil, one tablespoon at a time, pulsing between additions. Add only enough oil to bind the paste. Taste to see if it needs more lemon juice.

Scrape the mixture into a small jar with a tight-fitting lid, and store in the refrigerator.

Yield: 1 cup
Preparation time: 10 minutes with pre-pitted olives; 30 minutes if you pit them yourself

1 1/2 cups pitted Kalamata olives

1 medium clove garlic

1/2 teaspoon grated lemon zest

1 tablespoon capers, rinsed and drained

A handful of fresh parsley

1 to 2 tablespoons fresh lemon juice

Up to 3 tablespoons extra virgin olive oil, as needed

Tapenade keeps well for up to a month, if stored in a tightly lidded jar in the refrigerator.

RED ONION AND SHALLOT MARMALADE

Cooking onions and shallots for a good long time over moderate or low heat causes them to caramelize, bringing out and enhancing their natural sweetness. Accents of mustard and lemon or lime give this condiment just the right balance. Although I've listed several uses, you might find yourself eating up the whole batch with a spoon, as I did the first time I made it.

1 tablespoon butter or oil

1 large red onion (about ¾ pound), thinly sliced

5 or 6 medium-sized shallots, peeled and thinly sliced

¾ teaspoon salt

1 teaspoon dry mustard

1 teaspoon lemon or lime zest, grated or minced

2 tablespoons fresh lemon or lime juice (or more, to taste)

··

It's easier to peel the shallots if you blanch them first in boiling water for about 5 minutes.

This makes a wonderful relish, spread on crackers, and served alongside vegetables, casseroles, or soups. It's also a great garnish (divine as a topping for mashed potatoes or rice), and a spectacular spread for sandwiches, crostini, or pizzettas.

Red Onion and Shallot Marmalade holds for weeks if kept in a tightly covered container in the refrigerator or freezer.

For a menu suggestion, see page 211.

Melt the butter or heat the oil in a medium-sized skillet. Add the onion and shallots, and sauté over medium heat for about 10 minutes.

Sprinkle in the salt and mustard, lower the heat slightly, and sauté for another 20 minutes. Cover, turn the heat way down, and cook for another 45 minutes. The onions and shallots will become very soft.

Turn up the heat to medium, cover again, and cook for a final 5 minutes or so. Remove from the heat, and stir in the lemon or lime zest and juice.

Serve at room temperature or cold.

Yield: A generous ½ cup (easily multiplied)
Preparation time: 1½ hours of mostly slow cooking (30 minutes of work)

CARAMELIZED ONION SAUCE

When I read The Wind in the Willows *as a child, I wondered why Mr. Toad would exclaim, "Onion sauce, onion sauce!" when he was perturbed. (Mostly, though, I wondered what onion sauce actually was, since nothing remotely resembling it existed in my mother's repertoire.) Now that I make Caramelized Onion Sauce on a regular basis, I know how deeply sweet and mellow an onion sauce can be. I think someone should advise Mr. Toad to use another expression when he is angry.*

Heat the oil in a large skillet. Add the onions to the hot oil, and cook over high heat for a minute or two, stirring a couple of times. Sprinkle in the salt, lower the heat to medium, and cook, stirring occasionally, for 10 minutes.

Turn the heat to low, cover, and cook anywhere from 30 to 45 minutes longer. (Just stir it once or twice during this time.) Check the onions to see if they're done to your liking. The longer they cook, the sweeter and softer they become. At a certain point, the onions will virtually disintegrate and become a fluffy sauce.

Yield: About 1½ cups (easily multiplied)
Preparation time: Up to an hour (5 to 10 minutes of work)

---

1 tablespoon olive or vegetable oil

4 medium-sized onions, very thinly sliced (about 5 cups)

½ teaspoon salt

....

This sauce is very easy. Once you've sliced the onions, you've done 99% of the work. You can slice the onions well in advance, and store them in a sealed plastic bag in the refrigerator or even the freezer.

You can make the onions more or less well done, depending on whether you want them to retain some texture or to become fluffy. (Each form has its uses.)

Serve Caramelized Onion Sauce on pasta or pizzettas—or in omelettes, with crumbled goat cheese and an elaborate swirling of Balsamic Drizzle (page 172). Or heap it on top of grains, beans, cooked vegetables, or mashed potatoes. You can also serve it cold or at room temperature, on crostini or in sandwiches.

Store the finished sauce in an airtight container in the refrigerator. It will keep for a week or longer.

ROASTED TOMATO-GARLIC SAUCE

2 tablespoons olive oil

3½ pounds fresh tomatoes
(not too ripe)

1 or 2 garlic bulbs

1 teaspoon salt (or to taste)

2 teaspoons red wine vinegar
(or to taste)

Black pepper to taste

....

Use this sauce as you would any tomato sauce—on freshly cooked pasta, in lasagnas or other casseroles, on pizzettas, or wherever else it seems appropriate.

Put in the full two heads of garlic if you plan to serve this within a day of making it. Otherwise, use only one head, as the garlic flavor intensifies over time.

This keeps for up to two weeks if tightly covered and refrigerated.

Here is my current favorite homemade tomato sauce, which is long-roasted instead of long-simmered. The flavors get deeper with this cooking method, and there is very little work required. Basically, you just put the tomatoes and garlic in the oven, and go about your business while they slowly roast on their own. After they cool, peel and purée them, season to taste, and you're done.

Preheat the oven to 375°F. Line a baking tray with foil, and brush it with 1 tablespoon of olive oil.

Cut the tomatoes in half; squeeze out and discard the seeds. Place the tomatoes cut side up on the baking sheet. Slice and discard the tips from the garlic bulbs, and stand the bulbs on their bases on the tray. Drizzle the open tomatoes with the remaining tablespoon of olive oil, and place the tray in the oven.

After 30 minutes, remove the tray from the oven. Turn the tomatoes over, and carefully pour off and save their juices. This will prevent them from stewing in their own liquid, and enables them to acquire a deeper roasted flavor. Return the tray to the oven, and bake for 30 minutes longer.

Cool to room temperature, pull off and discard the tomato skins, and place the tomatoes in a food processor. Break the garlic bulb up into cloves, and squeeze the pulp from each clove directly into the food processor as well. Add the reserved tomato juices, and purée everything together until smooth. You can also leave the sauce a little textured if you prefer.

Transfer to a bowl, and season to taste with salt, vinegar, and pepper. Cover and refrigerate until use.

Yield: About 3 cups
Preparation time: 1¼ hours (10 minutes of work)

CHIMICHURRI

Chimichurri is the national sauce of Argentina, and is also popular in Honduras and other Latin American countries. It is a complex green mixture, similar to a pesto, but containing a greater variety of herbs, and a tartness, due to the presence of vinegar.

This sauce is normally served with roasted or grilled meat or seafood, but it's also delicious on cooked potatoes and other vegetables, pasta, grains, pizzettas, crostini, and sandwiches.

Place the cilantro, parsley, scallions, and oregano in a food processor, and mince very fine. Add the Roasted Garlic Paste, cayenne, vinegar, salt, and pepper, and process to a paste. Drizzle in the oil at the very end, with the food processor still running.

Transfer to a tightly lidded container, and refrigerate until use.

Yield: ½ cup (easily doubled)
Preparation time: 10 minutes, after the Roasted Garlic Paste is made

I cup (packed) cilantro leaves

¼ cup (packed) parsley

6 scallions, in 1-inch pieces

I tablespoon minced fresh oregano
(or I teaspoon dried oregano)

2 tablespoons Roasted Garlic Paste
(page xiv)

A pinch of cayenne

2 tablespoons red wine vinegar

⅛ teaspoon salt

⅛ teaspoon black pepper

¼ cup extra virgin olive oil

....

Make the Roasted Garlic Paste ahead of time.

This keeps for a week or two if stored in a tightly lidded container in the refrigerator. Just use as you would any condiment.

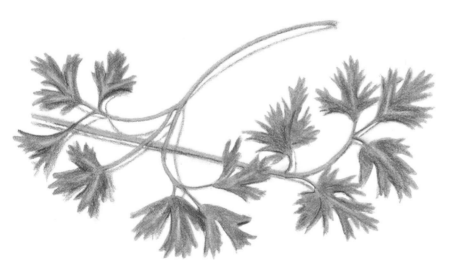

CHIPOTLE CREAM

Chipotle chiles are smoked dried jalapeños. They most commonly come in cans, packed in a tomato-vinegar preparation called adobo sauce. A little bit of canned chipotles-in-adobo goes a very long way, both in terms of heat and powerful smoky essence. In this sauce, sour cream and/or yogurt create a soothing, luxurious vehicle for the wild chipotle flavor.

Place the sour cream and/or yogurt in a small bowl and whisk until smooth.

Whisk in ½ teaspoon minced chipotle chiles, and let it sit for about 10 minutes, so the flavor can develop. Taste to see if it needs more chipotles, and adjust, as desired.

Store in a tightly covered container in the refrigerator. Bring to room temperature before serving.

Yield: 1 cup
Preparation time: 5 minutes

1 cup sour cream or yogurt
(or a combination)

½ to 1 teaspoon canned chipotle
chiles, finely minced

Serve this wherever it seems appropriate—on any egg dish, with beans, rice, or cornmeal preparations, or drizzled onto soups. It's especially divine on Sante Fe Stew (75), Savory Corn Cakes (120), or Fried Green Tomato Pillows (121).

After you open the can of chiles and take out what you need, store the remainder in a tightly lidded jar. They will last indefinitely.

For a menu suggestion, see page 211.

SMOKY HOT SAUCE

WITH SCORCHED TOMATOES AND CHIPOTLE CHILES

"Where there's smoke, there's fire." Here's an edible case in point.

Preheat the broiler. Line a baking tray with foil, and oil it lightly. Core the tomatoes, cut them in half around the middle, and squeeze out and discard the seeds. Place the tomatoes cut side down on the tray, and put the tray under the broiler for 15 to 20 minutes, or until the skins turn black. Remove from the broiler, and allow to cool until comfortable to handle, then remove and discard the skins.

Transfer the tomatoes plus all their cooking juices to a blender, add the salt and minced chipotles, and purée until smooth.

Transfer to a tightly lidded container, and refrigerate until use.

Yield: About 3 cups
Preparation time: 25 minutes (5 minutes of work)

A little oil for the tray

3 pounds ripe tomatoes

1 teaspoon salt

1 teaspoon canned chipotle chiles, finely minced

....

Spoon generous amounts of this potent sauce on top of—or next to—cooked grains, beans, potatoes, sweet potatoes, any cornmeal preparation (Spoonbread, Savory Corn Cakes, Fried Green Tomato Pillows), grilled eggplant, etc., etc., etc. It's especially good with eggs cooked any way.

This keeps for weeks if stored in an airtight container in the refrigerator.

For a menu suggestion, see page 213.

NEVER A BLAND MOMENT

HORSERADISH AIOLI

Aioli, the classic Mediterranean garlic mayonnaise, gets a makeover. Whipped silken tofu, the ultrasmooth kind that comes in little vacuum-packed boxes, does the best mayonnaise impersonation this side of Provence, bringing the fat and cholesterol content way down and the protein component way up in the process. Horseradish, garlic, and lemon spike the tofu with a perfect zip.

NOTE: Adding some real mayonnaise to this sauce gives it some extra richness. But it's not necessary—the Aioli tastes great either way.

1 10-ounce package silken tofu (soft variety)

1 medium clove garlic

2 teaspoons prepared horseradish

½ teaspoon salt (rounded measure)

2 tablespoons fresh lemon juice

1 tablespoon olive oil

Up to ½ cup commercial mayonnaise, regular or lowfat (optional)

Place everything except the optional mayonnaise in a blender and whip until smooth. Transfer to a bowl, and whisk in the mayonnaise, if desired. Cover tightly and refrigerate until use.

Yield: 1½ to 2 cups
Preparation time: 10 minutes or less

Serve Horseradish Aioli with raw or steamed vegetables, as a garnish for soups, on top of cooked beans, steamed greens, pasta, or rice, spread onto crackers or sandwiches, with cooked fish . . . many etceteras. It is especially good with Vegetarian Salade Niçoise (page 15).

This sauce keeps for several weeks if stored in a tightly covered container in the refrigerator.

MEDITERRANEAN YOGURT

I first envisioned this recipe as a kind of multiherb Mediterranean pesto with a touch of fruit. It tasted okay that way, but was dark and somewhat drab, both in looks and in taste. So I stirred in some yogurt to lighten it up, and what a success! It popped! It sparkled! It became Mediterranean Yogurt, now one of my favorite condiments.

Place the garlic, all the herbs, the dried fruit, and the walnuts in a food processor, and pulse until it forms a paste.

Transfer to a bowl and stir in the lemon juice and yogurt. Add salt and cayenne to taste.

Cover tightly and refrigerate until use. For a finished look, you can sprinkle a little extra cayenne on top, and decorate with small sprigs of parsley and a few walnut halves just before serving.

Yield: 3 cups
Preparation time: 10 minutes

1 medium clove garlic

⅓ cup parsley

⅓ cup cilantro leaves

⅓ cup fresh dill sprigs

⅓ cup fresh basil leaves

⅓ cup fresh mint leaves

2 tablespoons fresh thyme

3 or 4 dried apricots
 (a soft, tart variety)

⅓ cup golden raisins

⅓ cup lightly toasted walnuts

1 tablespoon fresh lemon juice

2 cups firm yogurt

Salt to taste

Cayenne to taste

OPTIONAL GARNISHES:

A light dusting of cayenne

Small sprigs of parsley

Walnut halves, lightly toasted

This sauce can be served alone, as an appetizer or a light lunch entrée. It is also amazingly compatible with a number of foods. You can serve it as a dip for raw or steamed vegetables, in pita bread with anything and everything, as a sauce for vegetables or grains, on baked fish . . . The list is endless.

Mediterranean Yogurt keeps for about a week in a tightly covered container in the refrigerator. However, the color won't hold past the first day.

For a menu suggestion, see page 212.

SWEET AND SOUR DIPPING SAUCE

½ cup unseasoned rice vinegar

½ cup honey

½ teaspoon salt (possibly more, to taste)

½ teaspoon red pepper flakes

OPTIONAL ADDITIONS:

Minced cilantro

Minced cucumber

Minced red onion

Minced red bell pepper

Chopped, toasted peanuts
(up to 1 cup)

....

Sweet and Sour Dipping Sauce is good spooned onto Vietnamese Salad Rolls (page 11), or for dunking steamed or roasted vegetables. Also try drizzling it onto plain cooked rice or noodles.

The optional peanuts can be chopped coarsely or minced. (The easiest way is to buzz them for a few seconds in a blender.)

For a menu suggestion, see page 213.

Throw together this Southeast Asian-inspired sauce in minutes flat, then relax and enjoy it at your leisure. You can choose to make just the basic, uncluttered version, or spruce it up with some or all of the optional additions.

Heat the vinegar until it is warm enough to dissolve the honey. Place the honey in a medium-small bowl, pour in the warm vinegar, and stir until the honey completely disappears.

Stir in the remaining ingredients, including as many of the optional additions as you choose. Serve warm or at room temperature.

NOTE: If you will be storing this sauce for any length of time, leave out the optional peanuts until shortly before serving time, or else they will get rubbery.

Yield: About ¾ cup, without the optional additions; up to 1¼ cups with the additions. Very easily doubled.

Preparation time: 10 minutes

MOLLIE'S SPECIAL LOWFAT MUSHROOM GRAVY

Here's good news for all you vegetarians (vegans included) who still long for some old-fashioned, down-home gravy on your mashed potatoes (or on anything else, for that matter). This yummy rendition looks and tastes like the traditional stuff, but contains no meat or dairy products, and only a minuscule amount of fat.

Heat the oil in a large saucepan or deep skillet. Add the onion and sauté over medium heat for about 5 minutes.

Stir in the garlic, mushrooms, and salt. Sauté for 5 more minutes, then cover and cook for 10 minutes over medium heat. Add the sherry, stir, and cover again. Cook for another 10 minutes.

Place the flour in a sifter or strainer, and gradually shake it into the pan as you stir constantly with the other hand. Keep stirring for a minute or two after all the flour is in, to keep the mixture from clumping.

Pour in 1½ cups of the bouillon, stirring vigorously. Cook over low heat for about 5 minutes longer, then remove from heat and taste to adjust salt, if necessary. If it seems too thick, stir in a little extra bouillon. Serve hot, on—or next to—just about anything.

Yield: 3 to 3½ cups
Preparation time: 45 minutes (about 20 minutes of work)

2 tablespoons vegetable oil

I cup minced onion

I tablespoon minced garlic

I pound mushrooms, sliced or chopped

½ teaspoon salt (possibly more, to taste)

3 tablespoons dry sherry

¼ cup unbleached white flour

1½ to 2 cups warm vegetable bouillon (page xiv)

• • • • • • • • • • • • • • • • • • •

This tastes great on cooked grains, potatoes, vegetables, warm open-face sandwiches, pasta, omelettes—you name it.

Store the gravy in a covered container in the refrigerator or even the freezer. It keeps and reheats very well.

BALSAMIC DRIZZLE

Balsamic vinegar, that musty, dark, aged-in-wood variety many of us have fallen in love with, makes a wonderful syrup when cooked down to about half its volume. You can drizzle this amazing stuff over more foods than you'd ever imagine—everything from roasted vegetables and bean soups to potato dishes and pizzettas. It's even great on pancakes, fruit, and frozen desserts. This might just be the most versatile one-ingredient sauce ever. Added bonus: it's fat-free.

1 cup balsamic vinegar

Place the vinegar in a small saucepan and heat to boiling. (You might want to open your kitchen windows. This gives off strong fumes!)

Turn the heat way down, and simmer uncovered for 30 or so minutes, or until the vinegar is reduced in volume by about half. Transfer to a bowl, cover tightly, and store indefinitely at room temperature.

NOTE: If it becomes too thick as it sits around, you can loosen it up by zapping it briefly in a microwave.

Yield: 1/2 cup (easily multiplied)
Preparation time: 30 minutes (1 minute of work)

You don't need to use an expensive brand of balsamic vinegar for this recipe. In fact, the ordinary, more moderately priced supermarket varieties work the best.

Store Balsamic Drizzle in a covered container in the refrigerator or at room temperature. Theoretically it will keep forever, but undoubtedly you will use it up sooner than that.

For a menu suggestion, see page 212.

TWO VINAIGRETTES

I will now share with you my highly unevolved, low-tech method for making salad dressing: Put everything in a jar with a tight-fitting lid, screw the lid on securely, and shake. That's it. Perfect every time.

The following recipes are two of my favorites. Make plenty of each, keep them in the refrigerator, and use as needed for salads and for cooked vegetables as well. These dressings keep for months.

Orange Vinaigrette

Combine everything in a jar with a lid, cover, and shake well. Shake again before each use.

Yield: 1½ cups
Preparation time: 10 minutes

Mustard Vinaigrette

Same procedure as above.

Yield: 1½ cups
Preparation time: 10 minutes

Orange Vinaigrette

2 teaspoons grated orange zest

½ cup orange juice

4 tablespoons red wine vinegar or sherry vinegar

2 medium cloves garlic, finely minced

2 tablespoons finely minced fresh parsley

1 teaspoon salt

½ cup extra virgin olive oil

Mustard Vinaigrette

2 medium cloves garlic, finely minced

2 tablespoons prepared mustard (the grainy kind)

3 tablespoons minced fresh parsley

3 tablespoons minced fresh dill (or 1 tablespoon dried dill)

3 tablespoons balsamic vinegar

1 tablespoon fresh lemon or lime juice

½ cup apple juice

1 teaspoon salt

½ cup extra virgin olive oil

PEANUT-CHILE DRESSING

½ cup good peanut butter

1 tablespoon honey

1 cup boiling water

6 tablespoons cider or unseasoned rice vinegar

2 teaspoons minced garlic

1 tablespoon Chinese sesame oil

1 tablespoon soy sauce

1 teaspoon dry sherry or Chinese rice wine (optional)

1 teaspoon salt (or to taste, if peanut butter is salted)

1 small (2-inch) serrano chile, minced (seeding optional)

· ·

Seed the chile if you prefer a milder dressing. Wash your hands after handling it.

This will keep well for weeks if stored in an airtight container in the refrigerator.

Drizzle Peanut-Chile Dressing onto an ordinary green salad, and suddenly you'll feel as though you are dining in a superb Thai restaurant. You can also use this to dress the filling for Vietnamese Salad Rolls (page 11), or as a dipping sauce for raw, steamed, or grilled vegetables.

Place the peanut butter and honey in a medium-sized bowl. Add about ½ cup of the boiling water and mash with a spoon until uniform.

Add the remaining water and all the other ingredients, and stir until well blended.

Store in a tightly covered container in the refrigerator. Whisk vigorously from the bottom before using.

Yield: 1½ cups (more than enough for one batch of Vietnamese Salad Rolls)
Preparation time: 10 minutes

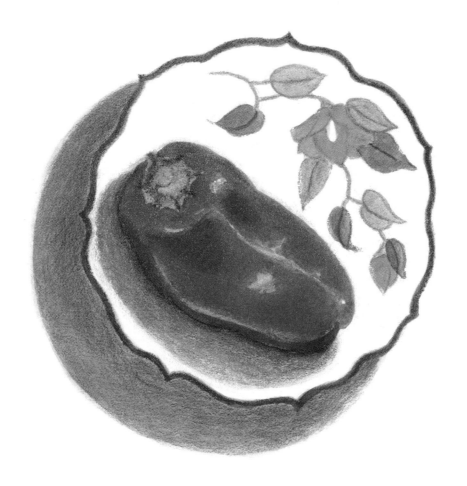

NEVER A BLAND MOMENT

TOO MANY DESSERTS

"Ice cream!" Sun. Light airy cakes.
A clear glass tumbler of water, icy cold.
Our dreams take flight, into a chocolate world
Of rosy dawns on milky Alpine peaks.

—**Osip Mandelstam** (translated by Robert Tracy)

Usually we eat to satisfy plain old hunger, but almost as often we eat in response to some vague sense of yearning as well. One kind of yearning that isn't vague at all is the very clear need from time to time for a fabulous ending, a grand finale granting us a moment of luxury. Then we get up from the table, and return to our routines, but we do so in a lingering heightened state, having danced with the divine. Ah, the hidden, elusive benefits of Eating Dessert!

There's quite a range to choose from here: excellent cookies and some very special cakes, light fruit preparations, and a few explosively good tarts and pies. Puddings, mousses, sorbets—and even a Cloud—are all waiting for you in the pages that follow.

TOO MANY DESSERTS

BLACKBERRY BUCKLE
WITH WARM VANILLA-LEMON SAUCE

A buckle is a yellow cake with a generous amount of berries mixed directly into the batter. This one, made with blackberries, tastes best served warm, surrounded by a lovely puddle of freshly made Vanilla-Lemon Sauce. Try making it for afternoon tea or Sunday brunch.

NOTE: This is a wonderful way to make use of tart or underripe berries— just increase the amount of sugar slightly.

Preheat the oven to 350°F. Butter an 8-inch-square pan. Place the blackberries in a bowl and toss gently with 1 tablespoon sugar (or more, if they are very tart or underripe). Set aside.

In a medium-sized mixing bowl, cream the butter with ⅔ cup sugar until light and fluffy. Add the vanilla, then the eggs, one at a time, beating well after each addition.

In a separate bowl, stir together the flour, baking powder, salt, and lemon zest. Stir this into the butter mixture until well combined, and fold in the berries at the end.

Turn the batter into the prepared pan, and bake for 45 minutes to an hour, or until the top is uniformly golden and springy to the touch. Cool on a rack for at least 15 minutes before serving.

If you decide to use the sauce, prepare it while the buckle cools. To serve, spoon a little onto the plate, and place a square of cake on top.

Vanilla-Lemon Sauce

Heat the milk and vanilla together in a small saucepan. Meanwhile, combine the sugar, cornstarch, salt, and lemon zest in a small bowl. When the milk is warm but not yet hot, pour about half of it into the cornstarch mixture, whisking until all the dry ingredients are completely dissolved. Pour this mixture back into the saucepan, and whisk vigorously.

Keep it cooking over medium heat, whisking steadily, until it is glossy and thickened (about 3 to 5 minutes). Serve hot or warm.

Yield: 6 or more servings
Preparation time: 1¼ hours (20 minutes of work)

A little butter for the pan

3 cups blackberries, picked over

1 tablespoon sugar (or to taste)

¾ cup (1½ sticks) butter, softened

⅔ cup sugar

1½ teaspoons vanilla extract

3 large eggs

1 cup unbleached white flour

½ teaspoon baking powder

A scant ½ teaspoon salt

1½ teaspoons minced or grated lemon zest

Vanilla-Lemon Sauce (recipe follows), optional

Vanilla-Lemon Sauce

1½ cups milk (lowfat okay)

1½ teaspoons vanilla extract

3 tablespoons sugar

2 tablespoons cornstarch

A pinch of salt

1 teaspoon grated lemon zest

....

☆ *You can also use frozen, unsweetened berries. Don't bother to defrost them—just break them up so that they are separate, and proceed.*

☆ *Raspberries make a good substitute, if you can't get blackberries.*

☆ *For a menu suggestion, see page 213.*

CHERRY UPSIDE-DOWN GINGERBREAD

Even if you don't particularly like gingerbread, you will be captivated by this bold, spicy version, which is baked on a bed of sour cherries and almonds, and then inverted to become a spectacular dessert event.

¼ cup (½ stick) butter, melted

¼ cup brown sugar

½ cup slivered or sliced almonds

I can sour cherries, drained (or 2 cups fresh sour cherries, pitted)

2 tablespoons unbleached white flour

6 tablespoons butter

3 tablespoons grated fresh ginger

½ cup light-colored honey

⅓ cup light molasses

¾ cup yogurt

I large egg

I teaspoon grated lemon zest

2 cups unbleached white flour

1½ teaspoons baking soda

½ teaspoon salt

½ teaspoon ground cloves or allspice

½ teaspoon cinnamon

¼ teaspoon nutmeg

⅓ cup minced candied ginger

∙∙∙∙∙∙∙∙∙∙∙∙∙∙∙∙∙∙∙∙∙∙∙∙∙∙∙∙∙∙∙∙∙∙∙∙∙∙∙

☆ *You can use canned sour cherries (packed in water) or fresh ones. Don't use sweet cherries, or this dessert will become cloying and lose its distinctive edge.*

☆ *Use scissors to mince the candied ginger.*

☆ *For a menu suggestion, see page 211.*

Preheat the oven to 350°F. Brush a 9 x 13-inch baking pan with ¼ cup melted butter, and sprinkle with brown sugar and almonds. Place the cherries in a small bowl, and toss with 2 tablespoons flour, then distribute them in the pan.

Melt 6 tablespoons of butter in a small skillet. Add the fresh ginger and sauté over medium heat for about 3 minutes, or until fragrant. Remove from heat.

Combine the honey and molasses in a medium-sized mixing bowl and beat at high speed with an electric mixer for a minute or two. Add the sautéed ginger, scraping in all the butter, and beat for a minute longer. Beat in the yogurt, egg, and lemon zest, and set aside.

Sift together the flour, baking soda, salt, and spices into a medium-large bowl. Make a well in the center and pour in the honey mixture and the candied ginger. Mix by hand briefly but thoroughly, until everything is incorporated.

Gently spread the batter over the cherries in the pan. Bake for 30 to 35 minutes, or until the surface is springy to the touch. Cool for at least 15 minutes, then invert onto a tray for a dramatic presentation. Serve hot, warm, or at room temperature. NOTE: If you are insecure about inverting the whole panful of gingerbread, and you don't particularly care about making a show of it, just cut the gingerbread in the pan, and turn each piece over as you serve it.

Yield: A lot (enough to serve 8 or more)
Preparation time: 1 hour (25 minutes of work)

AMARETTO-PEACH CRUNCH

Peach crisp goes to Italy.

Preheat the oven to 350°F. Arrange the peach slices in an 8 x 8-inch pan or a gratin dish. (If you are using frozen peaches, defrost them first.) Sprinkle with lemon zest, lemon juice, and Amaretto, if desired.

Place the amaretti in a food processor and grind into crumbs with a few short bursts. Add the almonds during the last burst or two, so they get broken up but not finely ground. Stir in the optional sugar, if desired. (If you are in need of a little exercise, you can bypass the food processor. Put the cookies in a plastic bag and whack them mercilessly with a rolling pin. Add the almonds and optional sugar, and shake well.)

Transfer the cookie mixture to a bowl, pour in the melted butter, and mix with a fork until well combined. Sprinkle this topping over the peaches, patting it into place. Bake for 25 minutes, or until golden. Serve warm, at room temperature, or cold—plain or à la mode.

Yield: About 6 servings

Preparation time: 45 minutes (20 minutes of work—less, if the peaches are presliced)

2 pounds sliced peaches, fresh or frozen

2 teaspoons grated lemon zest

2 tablespoons fresh lemon juice

2 tablespoons Amaretto liqueur (optional)

36 amaretti cookies (crunchy Italian almond macaroons)

1 cup sliced almonds

¼ cup brown sugar crystals (optional)

½ cup (1 stick) butter, melted

Vanilla ice cream (optional)

⋆ Frozen peaches work well here, so remember this in the dead of winter, when you need to be reminded of summer.

⋆ For a lovely variation, try using pitted sweet cherries (fresh or frozen), in combination with the peaches, or by themselves.

⋆ For a menu suggestion, see page 211.

RASPBERRY-RHUBARB BUNDLES

Warm fruit makes a lovely dessert, especially when wrapped in crispy filo dough. In this recipe, raspberries and rhubarb make a tart, stunning-colored filling for flaky little pastry "purses." Because the filo is sprayed lightly with oil rather than brushed all over with butter, the delicious result is practically fat-free.

Oil spray

3 cups raspberries

3 cups rhubarb, cut into ½-inch slices

½ cup sugar plus 4 to 5 teaspoons more, for the top

2 tablespoons water

2 tablespoons instant tapioca

10 sheets of filo dough

....

★ *You can use frozen unsweetened fruit. To freeze rhubarb, cut it into small pieces, then freeze in a sealed plastic bag. Defrost before using.*

★ *The filling must be made far enough in advance to have time to chill. You can make it up to several days ahead.*

★ *These bundles reheat surprisingly well in a toaster oven.*

★ *For a menu suggestion, see page 211.*

Preheat the oven to 400°F. Spray 10 muffin cups with oil spray.

Place the raspberries, rhubarb, sugar, and water in a medium-sized saucepan, and bring to a boil, Reduce the heat to low, cover, and simmer for 10 minutes. Liquid will accumulate in the pan.

Sprinkle the tapioca into the fruit, stir well, and cover. Simmer for 10 to 15 minutes longer, or until the mixture is soft and thick, and the tapioca has become transparent. Transfer to a small bowl, and cool to room temperature, then cover and chill thoroughly.

Lay the filo sheets on a flat surface, and cut the whole pile into quarters with a sharp knife. Take 4 pieces of filo, stack them neatly (no oil or butter in between), then gently push them into a muffin cup, causing the sides of the filo to come up. Fill the indentation with about 3 to 4 tablespoons of chilled filling, then gather the dough just below the edges and gently squeeze closed like a purse. (You can ruffle the edges slightly to make it pretty.) Spray with oil spray, and sprinkle with about ½ teaspoon sugar. Repeat with another stack of 4 filo pieces, and so on, until you have a muffin pan brimming with 10 filled bundles.

Bake for 10 to 12 minutes, or until the edges of the pastries are golden. Don't bake for too long, or the steam from the filling will soften the pastry bottoms and the bundles will leak. Remove from the pan and serve immediately, reminding your guests that the fruit filling is hot.

Yield: 10 bundles
Preparation time: 40 minutes, plus time for the filling to chill (15 minutes of work)

LEMON CLOUD

The next time you make a special dinner, surprise your family and friends with this tart, lowfat dessert soufflé. If you put it in the oven as you sit down to dinner, it will be ready in all its puffy splendor just at the right time. (As with all soufflés, Lemon Cloud collapses soon after it is baked, so if you want puffy splendor, serve it immediately. On the other hand, if you don't care about puffy splendor, serve this within an hour or two of baking, and it will taste just as wonderful.)

Separate the eggs, placing the yolks and whites in two separate medium-sized bowls. Cover both bowls and let the eggs come to room temperature.

Preheat the oven to 350°F. Lightly butter the bottom and sides of a 9-inch (8-cup) soufflé dish and dust it with sugar.

Add ½ to ⅓ cup sugar, the flour, lemon zest, and salt to the yolks, and whisk for about 2 minutes until creamy and smooth. Pour in the yogurt and lemon juice, and whisk for a minute longer, or until uniform. Set aside.

Beat the egg whites at high speed with an electric mixer until they form soft peaks. Sprinkle in the remaining ⅓ cup sugar, and continue to beat the egg whites until they form stiff peaks.

Fold about half the egg whites into the lemon mixture, using a rubber spatula and a gentle turning motion to bring the lemon mixture up from the bottom of the bowl. (It doesn't need to be uniform.) Fold in the remaining egg whites. Pour the batter into the prepared baking dish, and bake on the center rack of the oven for 30 to 35 minutes, or until puffy on top, and just a little bit wobbly in the middle.

Remove from the oven, and serve immediately.

Yield: 4 to 6 servings
Preparation time: 45 to 50 minutes (15 minutes of work)

4 whole large eggs, plus 1 extra egg white

A little butter and sugar for the baking dish

½ to ⅔ cup sugar

⅓ cup unbleached white flour

1 tablespoon grated lemon zest

¼ teaspoon salt

1 cup yogurt (lowfat okay)

⅓ cup fresh lemon juice

....

Add the smaller amount of sugar if you like your desserts really tart.

Separate the eggs ahead of time, so they can come to room temperature.

For a menu suggestion, see page 213.

TINA'S TRIFLE

Here's a new-fangled approach to the classic English dessert, created by my classic English friend, Tina Salter. Layers of spiked pound cake and fruit are topped with lowfat vanilla yogurt instead of the traditional rich custard, making this an easy, throw-together dish that is lower in fat than the original.

6 cups pound cake in 1-inch cubes
   (about ¾ pound)

½ cup cream sherry

¼ cup fruit juice or nectar (guava,
   strawberry, apricot, etc.)

2 to 3 cups raspberries, fresh (or
   frozen/defrosted and drained)

4 cups vanilla yogurt
   (a 32-ounce tub)—lowfat okay

OPTIONAL TOPPINGS:

Extra raspberries

Sliced fresh fruit (kiwifruit, starfruit,
   mango, banana, peach, etc.)

Sliced almonds

Pomegranate seeds

Arrange the cake cubes in your favorite medium-large glass bowl, and drizzle with sherry and fruit juice or nectar. Sprinkle on the raspberries. Cover the bowl tightly and chill for at least 4 hours.

Shortly before serving, pour the yogurt over the top, and spread it into place. Decorate lavishly with fresh fruit, sliced almonds, and pomegranate seeds, if desired, and bring the whole serving bowl to the table to impress your guests. To serve, scoop it out with a spoon, digging down to the bottom to get lots of soaked cake for each portion.

Yield: 8 to 10 servings
Preparation time: 10 minutes, plus at least 4 hours to chill

★ *Since you are unlikely to have extra pound cake sitting around your house with nothing to do, go ahead and buy a commercially prepared cake. Sara Lee brand works best.*

★ *The recipe calls for raspberries, but you can substitute any kind of ripe, juicy fruit. I once made this with the filling from Raspberry-Rhubarb Bundles (made without the tapioca), and it came out great.*

★ *For a menu suggestion, see page 213.*

YOGURT-BERRY SWIRL

It doesn't get much simpler than this. There are no rules—you just create a beautiful swirling pattern of yogurt and puréed berries on a plate. No two will ever be alike.

Pick over the berries, if you are using fresh ones. Combine them with the sugar and lemon juice in a blender or food processor, and purée.

Strain the purée into a bowl to separate out the seeds. Taste to adjust the sugar and lemon juice, and set aside.

In a separate bowl, beat the yogurt with a small whisk until it is the consistency of a sauce. For each serving, spoon about ⅓ cup yogurt onto the center of a dessert plate, spreading it into a wide strip down the middle.

Place a spoonful or two of puréed berries on both sides of the yogurt, and spread it into place.

Draw a toothpick or a dinner knife through the purée and the yogurt from side to side, creating a beautiful swirling pattern. Garnish with a few mint leaves and whole berries, if desired, and serve.

Yield: 6 servings
Preparation time: 10 minutes

3 cups fresh raspberries or blackberries (or frozen, unsweetened berries, defrosted)

6 tablespoons sugar (or to taste)

1 tablespoon fresh lemon juice (or to taste)

2 cups vanilla yogurt (lowfat okay)

OPTIONAL:

Mint leaves

A few whole berries

⁎ You can make the berry purée up to a week in advance. Store it in a tightly lidded container in the refrigerator. Assemble the final product just before serving.

⁎ For an elegant touch, serve this on chilled plates.

⁎ For a menu suggestion, see page 211.

CHOCOLATE-TOPPED ALMOND CAKE

After baking and assembling this classic Italian-style cake, wrap it tightly and refrigerate for 24 hours before serving. The almond flavor will ripen, and the chocolate topping will become delightfully crunchy.

A little butter and flour for the pan

¾ cup blanched almonds, lightly toasted

2 tablespoons plus ½ cup sugar

⅓ cup unbleached white flour

6 tablespoons butter, softened

1 teaspoon vanilla extract

¼ teaspoon almond extract

¼ teaspoon salt

3 large eggs

FOR THE TOP:

⅓ cup semisweet chocolate chips

Confectioners' sugar

A few extra almonds, sliced or slivered, blanched, and lightly toasted (optional)

For a menu suggestion, see page 213.

Preheat the oven to 350°F. Lightly butter and flour a 9-inch round cake pan.

Place the almonds and 2 tablespoons sugar in a food processor or a blender, and grind to a powder with a few short bursts. Stir in the flour and set aside.

Combine ½ cup butter and ½ cup sugar with the extracts and salt in a medium-sized mixing bowl, and beat with an electric mixer until creamy. Add the eggs one at a time, beating well after each.

Using a light hand and a rubber spatula, quickly fold in the flour-almond mixture. Spread the batter into the prepared pan and bake for 35 to 40 minutes, or until it is golden and the top springs back when lightly touched. Remove from the oven, and let it sit for 30 minutes. Then remove the cake from the pan, transfer to a plate, and cool completely.

Melt the chocolate chips gently in a double boiler or in a microwave at a low power. Sift some confectioners' sugar onto the cake, and sprinkle with slivered almonds, if desired. Use a small spoon to drizzle the melted chocolate over the top in a lacy pattern or an abstract expression. Let the chocolate harden before serving.

Yield: A 9-inch round (about 6 servings)
Preparation time: 1 hour, 10 minutes (20 minutes of work)

MINIATURE CHOCOLATE SOUFFLÉ CAKES

There's something about having your own individual chocolate cake—and getting to devour it all in one sitting—especially this one, which I dare say verges on perfection. Everyone deserves to feel like royalty once in a while, even if the experience is fleeting. (But then you can always make these again.)

Preheat the oven to 350°F. Lightly butter the bottoms of six 4-ounce ramekins, and place them on a baking tray.

Separate the eggs, placing the yolks in a small bowl and the whites in a medium-large one. Cover tightly and let come to room temperature.

Gently melt the butter and chocolate together in a double boiler or a microwave at low power. Transfer to a medium-large mixing bowl, and allow to cool for 20 minutes or so. Meanwhile, beat the egg whites until they form soft peaks, gradually sprinkling in the sugar. (You don't need to clean the beaters before proceeding to the next step.)

When the chocolate has cooled down beat in the egg yolks. Continue to beat for a few minutes, gradually adding the extracts.

Spoon ⅓ of the beaten egg whites into the chocolate, and fold briefly. Then slide in the remaining egg whites, and fold together deftly and gracefully with a rubber spatula, bringing the chocolate up from the bottom, until the batter is well blended. (It doesn't have to be perfect.)

Spoon the batter into the prepared ramekins, and place the whole tray on the center rack of the oven. Bake for 10 to 15 minutes, or until puffed up nicely. The centers of the cakes should still be a little soft.

Remove the tray from the oven, and let the ramekins rest for about 10 minutes. You may serve the soufflés in the ramekins, or loosen the sides with a dinner knife, and transfer the cakes to individual serving plates. Spoon some whipped cream on the side, and decorate with fruit and small sprigs of mint, if desired. Serve soon, as this tastes best fresh and warm.

Yield: 6 small cakes
Preparation time: 50 minutes (15 minutes of work)

A little butter for the ramekins

4 large eggs

⅓ cup butter

6 ounces semisweet chocolate
 (1¼ cups chocolate chips)

¼ cup sugar

1 tablespoon vanilla extract

1 drop almond extract

OPTIONAL GARNISHES:

Whipped cream

Raspberries, or slices of kiwifruit
 or mango

Sprigs of fresh mint

· ·

Separate the eggs well ahead of time, while they're still cold; cover, and let come to room temperature.

Melt the chocolate and butter about 20 minutes ahead of time, so they have time to cool, but won't harden.

If you don't have ramekins, you can use custard cups.

For a menu suggestion, see page 212.

MEXICAN CHOCOLATE CAKE
WITH MOCHA BUTTERCREAM

A little butter or oil for the pan

3 ounces Ibarra or semisweet chocolate

3 ounces unsweetened chocolate

2 cups cake flour

2 teaspoons baking powder

½ teaspoon salt

¾ teaspoon cinnamon (if using the semisweet chocolate)

I cup (2 sticks) butter, softened

I cup plus 2 tablespoons granulated sugar

I teaspoon vanilla extract

4 large eggs

I cup milk

Mocha Buttercream (recipe follows)

OPTIONAL TOPPINGS:

Cinnamon

Unsweetened cocoa

Confectioners' sugar

* Melt the chocolate about 20 to 30 minutes ahead of time, so it can cool to room temperature.

* Wrap any leftover cake tightly so it won't dry out, and store at room temperature. The flavors deepen as it sits around.

* For a menu suggestion, see page 211.

Chocolate and cinnamon make a terrific combination. Mexican cooks have known this for centuries, but chefs in the United States are just beginning to catch on. In this dense, not-too-sweet layer cake, a delicious mocha filling adds a touch of coffee flavoring to the chocolate and cinnamon, sending it over the top.

NOTE: Ibarra chocolate is a sweet variety that is laced with cinnamon. You can find it in the imported foods section of quality supermarkets. If you don't have Ibarra chocolate, use semisweet chocolate and a little cinnamon instead.

Preheat the oven to 350°F. Lightly grease the bottom and sides of a deep 9-inch springform pan with oil or butter.

Melt the two types of chocolate together in a double boiler or in a microwave at a low power. Set aside to cool to room temperature.

Sift together the flour, baking powder, and salt into a medium-sized bowl. (Add the cinnamon, as well, if you are not using the Ibarra chocolate.)

Place the butter, sugar, and vanilla in a large mixing bowl and cream at high speed with an electric mixer. Add the eggs, one at a time, beating well after each. Pour in the cooled chocolate mixture, and beat well until everything is incorporated.

Add ⅓ of the flour mixture, stirring until it is just barely incorporated, then pour in half the milk. Stir briefly, then repeat with another ⅓ of the flour and the remaining milk. Add the rest of the flour mixture, and stir just enough to blend. (Don't overmix, or the cake will toughen.)

Spread into the prepared pan, and bake for 55 minutes, or until a toothpick inserted all the way into the center comes out clean. Cool completely before assembling and frosting.

To Assemble

Cut the cake into 3 equal layers, using a long serrated knife and a gentle sawing motion. (You can also use dental floss—just wrap it around the cake at the desired spot, and pull.)

Spread Mocha Buttercream between the layers, and stack them evenly.

Spread the sides and top with buttercream. Artfully sprinkle the top with extra cinnamon, cocoa, and confectioners' sugar, if desired. (For a really fancy touch, sift the toppings onto the cake through a stencil.)

Yield: 1 dense 9-inch layer cake, about 5 inches high (enough to serve 10 or more)
Preparation time: 1½ hours, plus time to cool (30 minutes of work)

Mocha Buttercream

You can make this while the cake bakes.

Combine all ingredients in a medium-large bowl, and mix slowly (without breathing) until everything is moistened.

Beat at high speed with an electric mixer until the frosting is uniform and fluffy. If it seems a little too wet to spread, you can beat in up to ½ cup additional confectioners' sugar.

Mocha Buttercream

1 cup (2 sticks) butter, softened

3½ cups confectioners' sugar (possibly a little more)

½ cup unsweetened cocoa powder

1 teaspoon vanilla extract

½ cup very strong black coffee

APRICOT-ALMOND TART

The next time fresh apricots are at their peak, buy extra and freeze them. (Cut them in half and remove the pits first.) Then you can enjoy this elegant dessert any time of year. Once you've made the crust, assembling the rest of the tart is a breeze.

1 unbaked "Perfect Ten" Tart Crust (recipe opposite)

4 cups halved, pitted apricots (fresh or frozen/defrosted)

2 large eggs

1/2 cup sugar

3 tablespoons unbleached white flour

1/4 teaspoon salt

3/4 cup ground almonds

1/4 cup milk or cream

1 teaspoon vanilla extract

1/2 teaspoon almond extract

1 cup thinly sliced almonds

OPTIONAL ACCOMPANIMENTS:

Confectioners' sugar

Whipped cream

Vanilla yogurt (lowfat okay)

Prepare the "Perfect Ten" crust, and fit it into a 9- or 10-inch tart pan. Place the tart pan on a baking tray for easy handling.

Preheat the oven to 375°F. Arrange the apricot halves facedown in the unbaked crust.

Place the eggs and sugar in a medium-sized bowl, and whisk them together until light and fluffy. Gradually sprinkle in the flour, salt, ground almonds, milk or cream, and extracts. Keep whisking for a minute or two, or until everything is incorporated. Pour this mixture over the apricots, and sprinkle the top with sliced almonds.

Bake in the center of the oven for 45 to 55 minutes, or until golden brown. (For a crispier crust, transfer the tray to the bottom rack of the oven for the last 10 minutes of baking.) Serve warm or at room temperature—plain, or with confectioner's sugar sprinkled on top and whipped cream or vanilla yogurt on the side.

Yield: 4 to 6 servings

Preparation time: 1 1/4 hours (20 minutes of work, including crust)

The crust can be made way ahead and stored in the freezer in a sealed plastic bag. No need to defrost before assembling the tart.

If you are using frozen apricots, defrost them first.

You can use canned apricots (packed in juice) if you're in a pinch. Drain them before using.

For a menu suggestion, see page 213.

"PERFECT TEN" TART CRUST

A great 10-inch crust in 10 minutes flat. This is good for sweet and savory tarts alike.

1 ½ cups unbleached white flour

a pinch of salt

½ cup (1 stick) cold butter

1 to 3 tablespoons cold water

Place the flour and salt in the bowl of a food processor fitted with the steel blade. Cut in the butter in slices, and buzz several times until the mixture is uniform and resembles coarse meal.

Continue to process in quick spurts as you add the water, 1 tablespoon at a time. As soon as the dough adheres to itself when pinched together, stop adding water, turn it out onto a floured surface, and push it together into a ball.

Roll the dough into an 11-inch or so circle (slightly bigger than a 10-inch round). Lift the dough into the tart pan, nudging it gently into the corners, and use your hands to form an even edge all the way around. Wrap tightly, and store in the refrigerator or freezer until use.

Yield: 1 10-inch crust
Preparation time: 10 minutes

TART TART

Attention grapefruit lovers! This just might be the dessert you've been waiting for.

This recipe is dedicated to Christine Swett, who diligently and cheerfully tested this recipe at least a dozen times, until it came out perfect.

½ recipe Walnut-Pecan Shortbread dough (page 208)

4 egg yolks

½ cup sugar

3 tablespoons flour

2 teaspoons finely minced lime zest

2 teaspoons finely minced grapefruit zest

⅔ cup fresh grapefruit juice

½ cup fresh lime juice

1 teaspoon butter

1 cup pink grapefruit sections

Bake and cool the crust first, then cook the filling and let it come to room temperature. (All of this can be done well ahead of time.) Assemble the tart shortly before serving.

For a menu suggestion, see page 211.

Preheat the oven to 375°F. Make the shortbread dough and roll it out between two sheets of plastic wrap into an 11- to 12-inch circle about ¼ inch thick. Remove the top sheet of plastic, and use the other as a helper to flip the crust into a 9-inch tart pan. Press the dough down, ease it into the corners, and sculpt a strong edge with your fingers. Prick the dough all over with a fork. (*Really* all over, as in every quarter inch.)

Bake in the middle of the oven for 20 to 25 minutes, or until it is deeply golden all over (darker than cookies). Cool completely before filling. NOTE: Don't worry if the dough puffs up during baking. It will eventually settle down.

Combine the egg yolks, sugar, flour, and citrus zests in a heavy saucepan. Pour in the fruit juices, whisk thoroughly, and bring to a boil over medium heat. Boil gently for 2 minutes, whisking frequently. Remove from heat, and pour into the cooled shell. Immediately dot the top with butter to prevent a skin from forming, and set aside to cool to room temperature. It will thicken as it cools.

Arrange the grapefruit sections over the top of the filling in a lovely pattern. To serve, remove the rim from the tart pan, place the tart on an elegant plate, and bring it to the table to receive admiration. Then cut into wedges and dig in. NOTE: This can also be chilled and served cold.

Yield: 5 to 6 servings
Preparation time: 1 hour, plus time to chill (35 minutes of work)

BLUEBERRY-LEMON MOUSSE PIE

Lighter than light, this pie will make your spirits float.

Use only the freshest, firmest blueberries you can find. (Frozen berries won't do the trick.)

Crust

Preheat the oven to 350°F. Break the graham crackers into a food processor, then use the machine to grind them into fine crumbs. Transfer to a medium-small bowl. You should have about 1½ cups of crumbs.

Stir in the melted butter and mix until uniformly combined. Press into the bottom and sides of a 9-inch pie pan, forming a ¼-inch edge with your fingers. Bake for 10 minutes, then cool completely.

Filling

Combine the cornstarch and sugar in a small saucepan. Whisk in the lemon juice and water and keep whisking until smooth.

Place the saucepan over medium heat and whisk as you heat the mixture to the boiling point. Immediately reduce the heat to medium, and whisk fairly constantly as it cooks for 5 to 8 minutes, or until thick. Remove from heat, stir in the lemon zest, and let the mixture come to room temperature.

Place the egg whites in a medium-sized mixing bowl and beat at high speed with an electric mixer until stiff but not dry. Place the cream in a second medium-sized bowl, and without cleaning the beaters, beat until softly whipped.

Gently fold the egg whites into the lemon mixture, followed by the whipped cream and the blueberries. Spread the mousse into the cooled crust, and chill for an hour or longer. Decorate the top of the pie with extra blueberries and a few very thin strands of lemon peel, if desired. Serve very cold.

Yield: 5 or 6 exquisite portions
Preparation time: 45 minutes, plus time to chill (20 minutes of work)

Crust

12 cinnamon graham crackers (full rectangles)

6 tablespoons melted butter

Filling

¼ cup cornstarch

½ cup sugar

½ cup fresh lemon juice

½ cup water

1 teaspoon grated lemon zest

2 egg whites, at room temperature

½ pint cold heavy cream

2 cups perfect blueberries, plus a few extra for the top, if desired

Thin strands of lemon peel (optional)

⁕ The crust can be made well ahead.

⁕ Grate the zest and carve the optional peel for the topping before squeezing the lemons.

⁕ Separate the eggs for the filling ahead of time, so the whites can come to room temperature. Use the yolks for spreading on unbaked bread (it makes a great crust).

⁕ Prepare the lemon filling (short of beating and adding the egg whites and cream) well ahead of time, so the mixture can cool to room temperature.

⁕ Don't forget to allow time for the assembled pie to chill.

⁕ For a menu suggestion, see page 212.

HOMEMADE BUTTERSCOTCH PUDDING

2 cups milk (lowfat or soy okay)

1 tablespoon butter (optional)

4 tablespoons light brown sugar

¾ teaspoon vanilla extract

¼ teaspoon salt

3 to 4 tablespoons cornstarch

As a child, I believed that butterscotch was a special kind of plant that gave off golden candies wrapped in exquisite papers. Just the thought of this made me feel downright religious. I now understand that butterscotch is not a plant, but a combination of some very ordinary flavors (brown sugar, vanilla, and sometimes butter). However, the religious experience persists.

Combine the milk, optional butter, 3 tablespoons of the brown sugar, vanilla, and salt in a medium-small saucepan, and place it over medium heat until the mixture is hot to the touch. Don't let it boil.

Place the cornstarch in a medium-small bowl. Pour in about half the milk mixture and whisk vigorously until all the cornstarch is dissolved, then pour the solution back into the saucepan and return it to the heat.

Let the mixture come almost to a boil, whisking it frequently. Lower the heat to a simmer, and cook, whisking often, until it becomes thick and shiny. This will take about 5 minutes.

Pour the pudding into a lovely serving bowl and sprinkle the remaining brown sugar over the top. Let it cool to room temperature, then cover the bowl tightly with plastic wrap and refrigerate until cold.

Yield: 4 servings
Preparation time: 15 minutes, plus time to chill

CLASSIC TAPIOCA PUDDING

Straight to you from the "A" list of comfort foods.

Place the tapioca in a strainer, rinse it for a minute or two under cold running water, then dump it into a medium-sized saucepan. Add the water, place the saucepan over medium heat, and bring to a boil, whisking a little to separate the pearls.

Pour in the milk, and crumble in the sugar. Add a dash of salt, and heat it to the boiling point one more time.

Lower the heat to a slow simmer, partially cover, and cook gently for 30 minutes, or until it is quite thick. Transfer to individual bowls while still hot, then let it cool to room temperature. You can serve the pudding right away, or if you'd like it cold, cover the bowls with plastic wrap and chill. Serve topped with a few raspberries or a dab of raspberry jam, if desired, for a nice little hit of color.

Yield: About 4 servings
Preparation time: 45 minutes (5 minutes of work)

⅓ cup noninstant tapioca pearls

2½ cups water

1 12-ounce can evaporated milk (skim or regular)

½ cup brown sugar

A pinch of salt

A few raspberries, or a touch of raspberry jam (optional)

....

This keeps well for up to 5 days if tightly covered and refrigerated.

For a menu suggestion, see page 213.

PUMPKIN MOUSSE
WITH GINGERSNAP CRUMBS

Mostly pure pumpkin, and highly seasoned with lemon, maple syrup, and sweet spices, this terrific dessert is lightened by the presence of whipped silken tofu, one of the smoothest substances on earth. The tofu is utterly neutral in flavor, but adds a wonderful creamy texture, as well as a nice hit of protein.

Place everything except the pumpkin and the gingersnaps in a blender, and purée until smooth.

Add half the pumpkin, and purée again. Transfer to a medium-sized bowl and beat in the remaining pumpkin with a whisk until the mixture becomes uniformly creamy. Taste to see if it needs more lemon juice.

Cover tightly and chill for several hours or overnight, so the flavors combine and deepen. To serve, spoon the mousse into decorative bowls and sprinkle with gingersnap crumbs. Serve immediately, so the crumbs won't turn soggy.

Yield: About 6 servings
Preparation time: 10 minutes, plus time to chill

---

1 10-ounce box silken tofu (soft variety)

½ cup real maple syrup

1 teaspoon grated lemon zest

2 tablespoons fresh lemon juice (possibly more)

1½ teaspoons vanilla extract

½ teaspoon cinnamon

¼ teaspoon ground ginger

A pinch of ground cloves

A pinch of salt

3 cups (a 29-ounce can) solid-pack pumpkin or fresh, cooked pumpkin, if you have some on hand

8 gingersnaps (2-inch-diameter), crushed with a rolling pin

You can substitute cooked squash or sweet potato for the pumpkin.

This keeps well for up to a week, if stored in an airtight container in the refrigerator.

Don't add the gingersnap crumbs until the very last minute. They don't stay crisp for long.

For a menu suggestion, see page 212.

BITTERSWEET CHOCOLATE-BANANA MOUSSE

It's hard to believe this rich-tasting, velvety-smooth dessert contains no dairy products. Silken tofu makes it all possible. If you are serving this to tofu-phobes don't reveal the ingredients until after they've had a taste. They'll never believe what they're eating.

Melt the chocolate chips in a double boiler (or very carefully in a microwave at a low power).

Meanwhile, place the tofu and a handful of banana chunks in a blender and begin to purée. Gradually add the remaining banana, processing between additions to make sure it all whips up smoothly. Add the vanilla, sugar, salt, and vinegar as you go.

Pour in the melted chocolate (okay if still hot), scraping in every last bit. Purée one more time until very smooth and uniform, and taste to adjust the sugar. Transfer the mousse to a container or to individual serving dishes, cover tightly with plastic wrap, and chill for at least 2 hours before serving.

Yield: 4 to 6 intense servings
Preparation time: 10 minutes, plus 2 hours to chill

¾ to 1 cup semisweet chocolate chips

1 10-ounce box silken tofu (soft variety)

2 large ripe bananas

1 teaspoon vanilla extract

2 to 3 tablespoons light brown sugar

¼ teaspoon salt

1 teaspoon raspberry vinegar

⋆ *The chocolate flavor is very deep when you make this with ¾ cup chocolate chips, and downright intense if you add the full cup. You can vary the amount according to your taste.*

⋆ *This keeps very well for several days in an airtight container in the refrigerator.*

⋆ *For a menu suggestion, see page 211.*

FILLED FIGS
WITH MASCARPONE, GORGONZOLA, AND PINE NUTS

Brace yourself for a peak sensual experience.

Place the mascarpone in a small bowl and stir to soften. (Be patient—it's a bit sticky.) Slowly stir in the crumbled gorgonzola and 3 tablespoons of the toasted, cooled pine nuts, and gently mash until it is well blended. Add a dash of salt to taste, if desired.

Cut the figs in half lengthwise, so they can retain their lovely shape. Use your finger or the back of a teaspoon to slightly depress the open center of each fig, then sprinkle the figs with a little lemon juice.

Mound a small amount of the cheese mixture in the middle of each open fig, pressing down lightly. Drizzle a little honey over the filling, and place a few extra pine nuts decoratively on top.

Arrange the stuffed figs on your favorite fancy plate, and scatter some lavender blossoms and/or leaves over and among them. Cover the plate tightly with plastic wrap, and refrigerate until serving time.

Yield: 12 filled fig halves
Preparation time: 10 minutes

⅓ cup mascarpone cheese

3 tablespoons crumbled gorgonzola cheese

¼ cup pine nuts, lightly toasted and cooled

A dash of salt (optional)

6 medium-sized ripe figs, about 2 inches long

Fresh lemon juice

A little honey

Lavender flowers and/or leaves (optional)

....

⭐ Use only the ripest, most flavorful figs. If they're out of season, you could substitute another soft-fleshed ripe fruit, like nectarines, apricots, or cherries.

⭐ Mascarpone is a sublimely smooth, slightly sweet Italian cream cheese. If you don't have mascarpone, substitute a high-quality cream cheese. Also, if you can't get authentic gorgonzola, use a good brand of domestic blue cheese instead.

⭐ Filled Figs are good at room temperature or cold. They'll keep for several days; carefully seal up the whole plate of figs and refrigerate.

⭐ For a menu suggestion, see page 212.

APPLE PIZZA

Children love this cross between a dessert and a snack, partly because it's "silly," but also because it tastes so good. (When you serve it to adults, call it a galette, and they'll love it, too.)

Preheat the oven to 400°F. Set the pizza shell on a baking tray, and sprinkle it with cheese.

Arrange the apple slices on top of the cheese in a spiral pattern. Sprinkle with sugar to taste.

Bake for 15 minutes, or until the apples are beginning to brown around the edges. Remove the pizza from the oven, and let it sit for about 10 minutes.

If you intend to glaze it, melt the apricot jam, and brush the top surface with the melted jam. Serve hot, warm, or at room temperature.

Yield: 4 to 5 servings
Preparation time: 30 minutes (10 minutes of work)

1 12-inch Boboli pizza shell (thin variety)

1 cup cheddar cheese, grated

3 to 4 medium-sized tart apples, peeled and thinly sliced

1 to 2 tablespoons sugar (depends on the apples)

¼ cup apricot jam (optional glaze)

* *You can use mild, medium, or sharp cheddar, depending on your inclination.*

* *For a menu suggestion, see page 211.*

PINEAPPLE POMEGRANITA

Blissfully refreshing, this sophisticated frozen dessert doubles as a palate cleanser.

1 large ripe pineapple, peeled and cored

1 to 2 cups pomegranate seeds

OPTIONAL:

2 tablespoons candied ginger, minced

2 tablespoons minced fresh mint

Sugar to taste

Sprigs of mint for garnish

∙∙∙∙∙∙∙∙∙∙∙∙∙∙∙∙∙∙∙∙∙∙∙∙∙∙∙∙∙∙∙∙∙∙∙∙∙∙

✷ *You can make this with just pineapple, if you can't get your hands on some pomegranates. On the other hand, you can make it entirely with pomegranate seeds too, for a truly exotic dessert. (Use 4 cups pomegranate seeds if using them solo.)*

✷ *For a menu suggestion, see page 213.*

Chop the pineapple into small pieces, saving as much of the juice as possible. Put the pineapple and the pomegranate seeds in a food processor, and pulse several times to mince the fruit almost—but not quite—to a pulp.

Transfer the mixture to a shallow glass bowl or pan, and add the ginger and/or minced mint, if desired. Taste for sweetness, and add sugar if needed.

Place the bowl or pan in the freezer for 3 hours, interrupting it every 30 minutes or so to poke it assertively with a fork. Then cover the bowl or pan, and freeze overnight, or for a minimum of 6 hours longer.

About 15 minutes before serving time, take the granita out of the freezer and let it sit at room temperature. Just before serving, drag a fork through the granita to break it into tiny ice crystals. Serve right away in stemmed glassware, for a particularly elegant presentation. Garnish with sprigs of mint, if desired.

Yield: 6 servings
Preparation time: 20 minutes of work, plus a minimum of 9 hours to freeze

CARIBBEAN SUNDAES

Think of this as a virtual reality trip to a Caribbean island.

The following is more a description than an actual recipe. It is very similar to a spectacular dessert my family and I enjoyed on the island of Guadeloupe one winter.

For each sundae, arrange the various accoutrements (as many or as few as you like) on a plate, then place two or three small scoops of Tropical Ice Cream alongside or on top. Decorate with additional accoutrements, if desired, to make this really fancy.

Yield: 1 pint per recipe
Preparation time: 5 minutes each

TROPICAL ICE CREAMS

We're going to cheat a little here. But once you taste these, will you care?

Guava Ice Cream

Mash everything together until uniform. Transfer to a container with a tight-fitting lid, and freeze until use.

Passionfruit Ice Cream

Same instructions as above.

Banana Ice Cream

Purée everything together in a food processor. Transfer to a container with a tight-fitting lid, and freeze until use.

VARIOUS ACCOUTREMENTS:

Puréed raspberries, strained and sweetened

Slices of mango, kiwifruit, and/or banana

Nutella or semisweet chocolate, melted or grated

Shredded unsweetened coconut, lightly toasted

Thinly sliced almonds

Guava Ice Cream

2 cups softened vanilla ice cream

1 cup frozen guava juice concentrate, defrosted

¼ cup fresh lime juice (include pulp)

Passionfruit Ice Cream

2 cups vanilla ice cream, softened

¾ cup frozen passionfruit juice concentrate, defrosted

¼ cup fresh lime juice (include pulp)

Banana Ice Cream

2 cups vanilla ice cream, softened

1 medium-sized banana (perfectly ripe)

2 to 3 tablespoons fresh lemon or lime juice

For a menu suggestion, see page 212.

RAINBOW SORBET TORTE
WITH CHOCOLATE CRUST

2 cups crumbled chocolate wafer
   cookies (about 30 cookies, or
   most of a 9-ounce package)

6 tablespoons melted butter

3 to 5 pints assorted fruit sorbets

. . . .

*Use any sorbet combination that
appeals to you. (My own favorite
sorbet team consists of raspberry,
mango, and lemon.)*

*If you have a freezer full of frozen
summer fruit, try making this with
homemade sorbets (recipe opposite).*

*You can make this cake taller or
smaller, depending on the capacity of
your springform pan and the desired
yield.*

*The crust can be made days—or
even weeks—ahead and refrigerated
or frozen. Just wrap the base of the
springform pan tightly and store the
crust without the rim, so it won't
take up too much room. Replace the
rim before filling.*

For a menu suggestion, see page 212.

*Once the crust is made, the rest of the work consists of opening up a few
pints of assorted sorbets and spreading them on top. Do you think you can
handle it?*

Preheat the oven to 350°F. Combine crumbs and butter in a medium-sized bowl, and press the mixture firmly into the bottom of a
9 x 3-inch springform pan. Bake for 10 minutes, then cool.

Let the sorbets soften in the refrigerator for 30 minutes, or at room
temperature for 10 to 15 minutes (depending on the weather).
Spoon one pint of sorbet into the crust, and spread it evenly to the
edges. Repeat with the remaining sorbets, creating layers. Press
down firmly to eliminate any air pockets, then cover the top with
plastic wrap.

Freeze for at least 4 hours, or until firm. Let the torte stand at room
temperature for about 10 minutes (or in the refrigerator for about
30 minutes) before removing the rim of the pan. To serve, dip a
sharp knife into hot water, and slice the torte into wedges.

Yield: 12 to 20 servings (depending on how many pints of sorbet you use)
Preparation time: 15 minutes, plus time to freeze

INSTANT FRUIT SORBETS

When your favorite fruit is in season, buy extra, cut it into chunks, and freeze it in sealed plastic bags. This way you'll have the makings for the best (and least expensive) fruit sorbets ever. All you need to do is partially defrost the fruit, then purée it in the food processor with a little sugar syrup and lemon juice to taste. You don't need an ice cream machine at all! If you have a stash of frozen fruit and a food processor, you're in business.

These are the fruits that work the best for sorbets: peaches, apricots, strawberries (wiped clean, rather than washed), cantaloupes, honeydews, mangoes, watermelon (seeds removed), papayas, pears. Choose only the ripest specimens in season. NOTE: Don't use raspberries or blackberries— the seeds are too crunchy.

Freeze the fruit in airtight plastic bags until solid.

About 20 minutes before serving time, remove the fruit from the freezer and let it stand at room temperature, or remove it from the freezer an hour ahead, and put it in the refrigerator. (You want it to thaw only slightly.)

Place the fruit in a food processor and pulse until it is finely chopped. Add simple syrup, and lemon juice, if desired, to taste (the amounts will depend on the ripeness of the fruit—and on you), and long-pulse until very creamy. Serve immediately.

Simple Syrup

The formula for simple syrup is easy to remember: equal parts water and sugar, e.g., 1 cup sugar and 1 cup water. Place the sugar in a saucepan, add the water, and stir to dissolve. Bring to a boil, and cook for 2 minutes. Cool, then store in a jar in the refrigerator and use as needed. It keeps indefinitely.

Yield: 2 cups (1 pint)
Preparation time: 5 minutes, once the fruit is frozen

Per Recipe

2 cups peeled, cubed fruit
(1-inch cubes)

2 to 4 tablespoons simple syrup
(recipe below)

1 to 2 tablespoons lemon juice
(optional, to taste)

....

★ *You can store the sorbet in the freezer, but it will become very solid, and will need to partially thaw for up to 30 minutes—and then be reprocessed—before serving.*

★ *For a menu suggestion, see page 213.*

PEANUT BUTTER-FUDGE BROWNIES

When I was ten years old, I thought that chocolate-covered peanut butter cups were the pinnacle of pleasure. And now, no matter how mature and sophisticated my palate has become, I still love the combination of chocolate and peanut butter. What's interesting about these brownies is that the peanut butter flavor is subtle—you can't really detect it until the second or third bite. Try this on people who think they won't like it. They (and you) will be surprised.

A little oil or butter for the pan, if it's not nonstick

½ cup (1 stick) butter, softened

1 cup peanut butter

1 cup (packed) light brown sugar

½ cup granulated sugar

4 large eggs

1 teaspoon vanilla

1 cup unsweetened cocoa powder

1 cup unbleached white flour

¼ teaspoon salt (omit if using salted peanut butter)

1¼ cups semisweet chocolate chips

½ cup minced peanuts (optional)

....

✴ *Use a good unprocessed peanut butter, chunky or smooth.*

✴ *For a menu suggestion, see page 212.*

Preheat the oven to 350°F. Lightly grease a 9 x 13-inch pan (unless it's nonstick).

Cream together the butter, peanut butter, and sugars in a medium-large mixing bowl with an electric mixer at high speed. Turn the speed down to medium, and add the eggs one at a time, and the vanilla, beating well after each. Stir in the remaining ingredients, and mix by hand until everything is uniformly blended.

Spread the batter into the prepared pan, and bake on the center rack of the oven for 15 to 20 minutes, or until the top feels firm, and a toothpick inserted all the way into the center comes out clean. Cut into squares while still hot, but let them cool in the pan for at least 30 minutes before serving. Serve warm, at room temperature, or cold.

Yield: About 1½ dozen medium-sized brownies
Preparation time: 1 hour (10 minutes of work)

Mollie Katzen's VEGETABLE HEAVEN

ORANGE CHOCOLATE CHIP COOKIES

Even the most devoted chocolate chip cookie sort of person needs a new twist on this favorite treat every now and then. Here it is.

Preheat the oven to 350°F. Lightly grease a baking tray, or line it with parchment paper.

Place the butter and sugars in a medium-sized mixing bowl. Cream together at high speed with an electric mixer for about 2 minutes. Add the eggs one at a time, beating well after each. Stir in the vanilla and orange zest.

In a separate bowl, sift together the flour, salt, and baking soda. Add this to the butter mixture, along with the chocolate chips and walnuts, if desired, and stir until thoroughly combined.

Drop by rounded teaspoons onto the prepared baking tray. Bake for about 12 minutes, or until lightly browned on the bottom. Cool completely on a rack before serving.

Yield: About 40 cookies
Preparation time: 45 minutes to 1 hour (15 minutes of work)

A little oil or butter for the baking tray (optional)

1 cup (2 sticks) butter, softened

⅓ cup (packed) light brown sugar

⅓ cup granulated sugar

2 large eggs

2 teaspoons vanilla extract

3 tablespoons grated orange zest

1¾ cups unbleached white flour

¼ teaspoon salt

½ teaspoon baking soda

2 cups semisweet chocolate chips

1 cup minced walnuts (optional)

For a menu suggestion, see page 212.

TOO MANY DESSERTS

SESAME STARS

If you love both halvah and shortbread, these cookies are for you.

Preheat the oven to 375°F. Lightly sprinkle a baking tray with sesame seeds.

Cream together the butter, sesame butter or tahini, and sugars in a medium-large mixing bowl. Add the eggs one at a time, beating well after each. Beat in the vanilla.

Sift the flour, baking powder, and salt directly into the butter mixture, and stir until thoroughly combined. Turn the dough out onto a lightly floured surface, and roll it out ¼ inch thick. Cut into 2½-inch shapes with a knife or a cookie cutter and place the cookies on the prepared baking tray.

Sprinkle the cookies with a few sesame seeds and some extra granulated sugar. Bake for 12 to 15 minutes, or until lightly browned around the edges, then cool on a rack for at least 10 minutes before serving.

Yield: 4 dozen 2½-inch cookies
Preparation time: 30 to 40 minutes (15 minutes of work)

A few sesame seeds for the pan, plus more to sprinkle on top

1 cup (2 sticks) butter, softened

1 cup sesame butter or tahini

1 cup (packed) light brown sugar

¼ cup granulated sugar

2 large eggs

2 teaspoons vanilla extract

4 cups unbleached white flour (plus extra for rolling the dough)

1 teaspoon baking powder

½ teaspoon salt

Granulated sugar for the top

* *You can use either sesame butter (made from toasted, unhulled seeds) or tahini (made from raw, hulled seeds) with equally good results. Just be sure whichever you use is soft and fluid enough to drip down in a steady stream from a spoon.*

* *I love to cut these cookies in the shape of stars. But you can make them any shape you like—they will still have the same flavor.*

* *You can chill or freeze the dough practically indefinitely if you wrap it well and seal it in a plastic bag. Let it warm up almost to room temperature before rolling it out.*

* *For a menu suggestion, see page 212.*

Mollie Katzen's VEGETABLE HEAVEN

GINGER THINS

Don't let their mild-mannered appearance fool you. These modest-looking little cookies are pure dynamite.

Cream together the butter, cream cheese, and sugar in a medium-sized mixing bowl. Add the ginger(s), egg, and vanilla, and beat at high speed for a minute or two.

In a separate bowl, stir together the flour, salt, and spices. Add this to the butter mixture, and mix thoroughly.

Turn the dough out onto a lightly floured surface. Flour your hands, then gently shape the dough into a log about 2 inches in diameter. Roll the log tightly in wax paper or plastic wrap, seal it in a plastic bag, and freeze until solid (several hours, overnight, or indefinitely).

Preheat the oven to 375°F. Without defrosting the dough, use a very sharp knife to slice it into thin (⅛-inch-thick) wafers. Place the cookies close together on a lightly greased baking tray, and sprinkle them with some brown sugar crystals or a little extra granulated sugar. Bake for 12 to 15 minutes, or until lightly browned around the edges. Cool on a rack for at least 10 minutes before eating.

Yield: About 4 dozen cookies
Preparation time: 15 minutes of work; 30 minutes to bake them all (plus freezing time in between)

½ cup (1 stick) butter, softened

½ cup (4 ounces) cream cheese, softened

1 cup sugar

⅓ cup finely minced fresh ginger

¼ cup finely minced candied ginger (optional)

1 large egg

1 teaspoon vanilla extract

2 cups unbleached white flour

¼ teaspoon salt

½ teaspoon cinnamon

½ teaspoon ground cloves

A little butter for the baking tray

Brown sugar crystals, or extra granulated sugar

....

✦ *Freezing the dough in a little log shape, then slicing it while still frozen enables you to make wafer-thin cookies.*

✦ *Ginger Thins keep extremely well if stored in an airtight cookie tin.*

✦ *For a menu suggestion, see page 212.*

WALNUT-PECAN SHORTBREAD

Once I started adding ground nuts to shortbread dough, I was instantly hooked, and haven't made plain shortbread since. The nuts get thoroughly coated with butter and toasted to perfection during the baking, and the cookies get infused with a flavor that is out of this world.

Preheat the oven to 375° F.

Place the butter and sugar in a large mixing bowl. Beat at high speed for about 3 minutes, then stir in the nuts.

Add the flour and salt directly to the batter. Mix the dough with a spoon (and/or your hands, if necessary), working as quickly and efficiently as possible, just until the dough holds together.

Flour a clean, dry surface and roll the dough to about ½ inch thick. Cut it into simple shapes with a knife or a cookie cutter, and place the cookies on ungreased baking trays.

Bake for 10 to 12 minutes or until lightly browned on the bottom. Cool for at least 10 minutes before eating.

Yield: About 5 dozen 2-inch cookies
Preparation time: 30 to 40 minutes (20 minutes of work)

---

1 cup (2 sticks) butter, softened

⅔ cup sugar

½ cup ground pecans

½ cup ground walnuts

2 cups unbleached white flour
  (plus extra for rolling the dough)

¼ teaspoon (rounded measure) salt

....

Grind the nuts in a food processor or blender with a series of short pulses, so they turn into a fine powder, rather than nut butter.

This recipe also makes a great pie or tart crust (see page 192). It's enough for two 9-inch pans.

You can make the dough in advance and refrigerate or freeze it indefinitely in a sealed plastic bag.

Store the cookies in an airtight tin. They keep for a long time.

COCONUT MACAROONS

Easy to make, and delectable beyond compare, these chewy little puffs will keep for weeks if refrigerated in an airtight tin.

Preheat the oven to 350° F. Lightly brush a baking tray with a little oil or melted butter. (You can also just line the tray with parchment paper, making the greasing unnecessary.)

Combine the coconut, sugar, and salt in a medium-sized bowl, and mix until well combined.

Place the eggs and vanilla in another medium-sized bowl, and beat at high speed with an electric mixer or a whisk for about 3 minutes, or until the eggs become a pale, creamy foam. Add the eggs and the optional melted butter, if desired, to the coconut mixture, and combine thoroughly.

Drop by rounded teaspoons onto the prepared baking tray and bake on the center rack of the oven for 15 minutes, or until golden on the tops and edges. Carefully remove the macaroons from the tray and transfer to a wire rack. Allow to cool for at least 15 minutes before serving.

If you choose to dip the macaroons in chocolate, let them cool completely before proceeding. To make the optional Chocolate Glaze, gently melt the butter and the chocolate together in a double boiler or in the microwave at a low power. Be careful not to overheat the chocolate, so it will retain its shine. (Overheating chocolate gives it a matte surface.) Meanwhile, line a couple of dinner plates with wax paper.

Remove the chocolate from the heat. Carefully dip the top and/or side of each macaroon into the hot mixture, then place the dipped cookies on the paper-lined plates until the chocolate hardens. (Work quickly enough so that the chocolate stays supple.) When the chocolate solidifies, store the macaroons in a cookie tin in the refrigerator.

Yield: 1½ dozen small cookies (easily multiplied)
Preparation time: About 45 minutes (15 minutes of work)—less, if you omit the glaze.

A little oil or melted butter for the baking tray (optional)

3 cups shredded unsweetened coconut

⅓ to ½ cup sugar (depending on your taste)

¼ teaspoon salt

3 large eggs

1 teaspoon vanilla extract

3 tablespoons melted butter (optional)

Chocolate Glaze (optional)

2 tablespoons butter

½ cup semisweet chocolate chips

∗ *For a richer taste, add the optional melted butter.*

∗ *You will get slightly more volume if you use extra-large eggs.*

∗ *The chocolate coating is optional, but sublime. (However, the macaroons also taste great plain.)*

∗ *For a menu suggestion, see page 212.*

Mollie Katzen's VEGETABLE HEAVEN

26 MENUS

as shown on public television's

MOLLIE KATZEN'S COOKING SHOW: VEGETABLE HEAVEN

SUNSET DINNER

Chickpea Soup with Golden Spices / *34*

Linguine with Wok-Fried Broccoli, Cherry Tomatoes,
and Crumbly Cheese / *141*

Arugula Salad with Orange Vinaigrette / *22*

Cherry Upside-Down Gingerbread / *180*

CARIBBEAN SURPRISE

Caribbean Composed Salad / *14*

Coconut Rice with Ginger, Chiles, and Lime / *83*

Soft Lentils with Roasted Tomatoes
and Caramelized Onions / *70*

Bittersweet Chocolate-Banana Mousse / *197*

ITALIAN HARVEST

Zuppa di Verdure / *44*

Parmesan Crisps / *56*

Panzanella / *16*

Amaretto-Peach Crunch / *181*

CRAZY QUILT

Black-Eyed Pea and Squash Soup
with Shiitake Mushrooms / *41*

Miniature Potato Dumplings
with Sage and Chives / *52*

Kale Crunch / *58*

Cherry Tomato Chewies / *60*

Green Salad

Apple Pizza / *199*

SOUTH OF THE BORDER

Savory Corn Cakes / *120*

Chipotle Cream / *166*

Black Beans in Mango Sauce / *73*

Onion-Wilted Spinach Salad
with Cumin, Avocado, and Apple / *21*

Mexican Chocolate Cake with Mocha Buttercream / *188*

FIRESIDE MEAL

Broccoli-Stuffed Mushrooms / *114*

Sesame Bread Sticks / *133*

Farfalle with Artichokes, Mustard Greens,
and Slow-Cooked Onions / *148*

Tart Tart / *192*

LATE WINTER BOUNTY

Root Vegetable Soup / *40*

Toasts

Red Onion and Shallot Marmalade / *162*

Giant Mushroom Popover / *128*

Asparagus in Warm Tarragon-Pecan Vinaigrette / *112*

Yogurt-Berry Swirl / *185*

CALIFORNIA SPRING

Avocado-Pear Sorbet / *3*

Vegetarian Salade Niçoise / *15*

Pizzettas / *132*

Raspberry-Rhubarb Bundles / *182*

CALYPSO CARNAVAL

Jamaican Salsa Salad / 12

Chips

Firecracker Red Beans / 72

Rice

Bitter Greens with Sweet Onions
and Tart Cheese / 105

Caribbean Sundaes / 201

ASIAN ALLURE

Big, Bold Noodle Soup / 37

Kung Pao Lettuce Cups / 13

Green Onion Wonton Strips / 54

Sesame Stars / 206

Assorted Asian Fruit

TEX-MEX LUNCH

Tortilla Soup with Roasted Red Peppers / 38

Olive Waffles / 119

GuacaMollie / 158

Reversed Salad in One Bowl / 20

Rainbow Sorbet Torte with Chocolate Crust / 202

SUPPER IN THE PARK

Chilled Honeydew Soup with Mint and Lime / 29

Sandwiches To Write Home About / 136

Pickled Red Onions / 63

Peanut Butter-Fudge Brownies / 204

LE PIQUE-NIQUE

Roasted Eggplant Salad with Mustard Vinaigrette / 8

Frizzled Leeks / 59

French Picnic Tart / 125

Wild Rice Pilaf with Oranges and Cherries / 82

Miniature Chocolate Soufflé Cakes / 187

CARAVANSARY

Tunisian Tomato Soup with Chickpeas and Lentils / 46

Fantastic Bulgur Dish / 93

Red Pepper-Walnut Paste / 159

Green Salad with Blue Cheese, Walnuts, and Figs / 19

Blueberry-Lemon Mousse Pie / 193

FAMILY FEAST

Focaccia or Fougasse / 133

Green and White Beans
under Garlic Mashed Potatoes / 69

Simplest Tomato Salad / 7

Fresh Fruit

Balsamic Drizzle / 172

Orange Chocolate Chip Cookies / 205

MOLLIE'S FAVORITE LUNCH

Tomato-Fennel Consommé / 31

Chickpea and Sweet Potato Koftas / 79

Mediterranean Yogurt / 169

Roasted Vegetables (a big platter) / 96

Filled Figs with Mascarpone, Gorgonzola,
and Pine Nuts / 198

SWEET, SOUR, AND SAVORY

Sliced Oranges and Grapefruit

Cauliflower Kukus / 123

Bitter Greens with Sweet Onions and Sour Cherries / 104

Ginger Thins / 207

Pumpkin Mousse / 196

AUTUMN COLORS

Lentil Soup with a Hint of Fruit / 35

Golden Rice Pie with Spinach Filling / 126

Orange, Beet, and Fennel Salad / 24

Coconut Macaroons / 209

MIDDLE EASTERN DELIGHT

Breaded Sautéed Yogurt Cheese on Salad Greens / 17

Couscous-Quinoa Tabouli / 6

Hummus

Roasted Beans with Garlic and Olives / 68

Pita Bread

Apricot-Almond Tart / 190

MARRAKESH EXPRESS

Almond-Stuffed Olives and Dates / 51

Moroccan Roasted Vegetable Stew / 100

Couscous with Touches of Orange, Dill,
and Pistachio / 90

Pineapple Pomegranita / 200

SOUTHWEST SUMMER

Savory Granita Duet / 5

Santa Fe Stew / 75

Warmed Corn Tortillas

Green Salad

Blackberry Buckle with
Warm Vanilla-Lemon Sauce / 179

PERSIAN BANQUET

Persian Eggplant Appetizer / 9

Persian Layered Pilafs / 84

Sweet Potatoes and Spinach
in Spiced Orange Sauce / 110

Instant Fruit Sorbets / 203

PACIFIC RIM

Vietnamese Salad Rolls / 11

Sweet and Sour Dipping Sauce / 170

Sizzling Long Beans with Garlic and Chiles / 102

Rice Noodles with Cashew-Coconut Sauce / 147

Classic Tapioca Pudding / 195

RAINY DAY SPECIAL

Tomatillo-Chile Soup / 36

Frisée and Mushroom Salad
with Warm Garlic Vinaigrette / 18

Buckwheat Soba with Squash, Smoked Tofu,
and Basil / 144

Chocolate-Topped Almond Cake / 186

MIDSUMMER MEDLEY

Watermelon Sparkler / 4

Pea Shoots with Garlic / 109

Sugar Snap Peas with a Single Herb / 108

Whipped Sweet Potatoes with Lime / 113

Fried Green Tomato Pillows / 121

Smoky Hot Sauce / 167

Tina's Trifle / 184

ELEGANT COMFORT FOOD

Potato Soup with Rosemary
and Roasted Garlic / 33

Yuppie Platter:
A Warm Salad of Radicchio, Belgian Endive,
and Goat Cheese / 23

Rigatoni al Forno with Roasted Asparagus
and Onions / 142

Lemon Cloud / 183

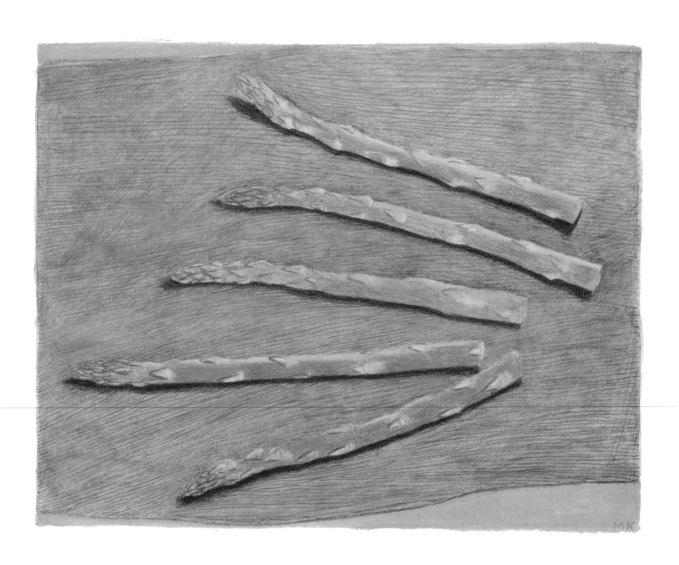

Mollie Katzen's VEGETABLE HEAVEN

INDEX